# PUBLIC CONTROL OF PRIVATELY RENTED HOUSING

STUDIES IN URBAN AND REGIONAL POLICY

Series Editor: Andrew Thomas

This book is one of a series on Urban and Regional Policy
published by Gower in association with the Centre for Urban
and Regional Studies.  The series is intended to provide a
vehicle for findings in the broad field of urban and regional
studies with a particular emphasis on the dissemination of
empirical and theoretical research.

Studies in Urban and Regional Policy complements the existing
range of Centre publications.  These are designed to find a
wide audience for the results of continuing research in the
fields of housing, regional and local economic development,
planning and leisure and tourism.  These areas of interest
have been developed through funding from central and local
government, research councils and charitable trusts since the
Centre was established in 1966 as a Department of the Faculty
of Commerce and Social Science at the University of
Birmingham.

# Public Control of Privately Rented Housing

JOHN DOLING
*Centre for Urban and Regional Studies,*
*University of Birmingham*

MARY DAVIES
*Institute of Local Government Studies,*
*University of Birmingham*

Gower

Published by
Gower Publishing Company Limited,
Gower House, Croft Road, Aldershot, Hampshire GU11 3HR,
England

and

Gower Publishing Company,
Old Post Road, Brookfield, Vermont 05036, U.S.A.




British Library Cataloguing in Publication Data

Doling, J.F.
    Public control of privately rented housing.——(Studies
    in urban and regional policy)
    1. Rental housing——England   2. Rent control——England
    I. Title      II. Davies, E.M.
    333.33'8      HD7288.85.G7


ISBN 0-566-00732-0

# Contents

# Preface

This book began its life in 1980 as a modest research project funded by the Social Science Research Council which was intended to examine some particular aspects of the fair rents system introduced by the 1965 Rent Act. The description of the proposed study given in the application to the SSRC outlined the general objectives.

'The proposed research follows on from earlier studies of the determinants of house prices to examine the determinants of fair rents. It will be an indirect examination both of the interpretation which rent officers have made of fair rents legislation and the consistency with which these interpretations are applied. Information for 1500 properties from the list of comparables will be collected from 3 rent offices in the West Midlands, and together with relevant census data describing the social environment of each dwelling, will be used as the basis of a statistical study. The correlations and regression coefficients produced will be used to determine the strength of the factors underlying the assessment of the fair rents. They will also enable consideration of whether there is any consistency between districts, and between previous and fair rents.'

Grant HR 7072 enabled the employment of a research assistant for three months to collect the data necessary to carry out the statistical exercises intended. Information was extracted from the Register of Fair Rents, held as public records in a central store in the West Midlands County, about rents determined for individual dwellings. To this was added information about the location or neighbourhood of each dwelling. Regression analysis then provided a tool whereby the relationship, between fair rents on the one hand and dwelling and locational variables on the other hand, could be examined in order to seek the rules which were implicit in the rent determinations made. Methodologically this was a parallel to the numerous hedonic price studies of owner occupied dwellings which had been conducted by urban economists.

In the process of carrying out this essentially statistical task two particular limitations of the study soon became apparent. First there was a detailed methodological concern that fair rent levels could in part be explained by variables which were not contained in the Register and which had not otherwise been obtained. The research was extended for example by visual inspection of some of the dwellings to provide additional information about the physical condition of the dwelling fabric. Second, and more fundamentally, attempts to understand and explain the results led the authors increasingly into the wider context in which the fair rent determinations are made. This wider context included the nature of the legislation; the meaning or meanings which have been given to the adjective 'fair'; the administrative character of the rent officer service; the effect of the courts in maintaining the interpretation of the legislation; the interests of landlords and tenants and their relationship with the fair rent system; and the consequences of the system on the future of the privately rented housing sector.

The results of the gradual widening of the horizens of the research have been that it has gone beyond the limited statistical analysis originally proposed to become a study of a particular example of the way in which the state has intervened in market processes and the results of that intervention. Specifically, the work came to centre on two main areas concerned with the interpretation of the concept of equity in the context of the fair rent system. Firstly an empirical study of the administrative discretion of rent officers: the methods and rules which they have adopted, the consistency with which they operate and what this has meant for the parties involved. In this there is much speculation, for example about the internal workings of the rent officer profession and the ways in which this might relate to fair rent levels, which as a result of the particular methodological approach adopted remains unsubstantiated. Secondly, an examination of the implications of the way in which that discretion has been practised for the desire of landlords to leave the sector. Thus both areas are concerned with the effect, in practice, of state intervention, the objective of which was, at least nominally, to create fairness where the market had created unfairness.

In writing, one particular concern has been to describe the nature and interpretation of the statistical techniques used in Chapters 4 and 5 in a way which could be comprehensible to those without a statistical background. Even so many will wish to avoid these sections and rely on the conclusions to these chapters.

Whether or not the outcome of these endeavours has been worthwhile is for the reader to decide, and certainly the authors would not deny responsibility for any errors. Nevertheless they would like to record their gratitude to a number of people who helped on the research. Bruce Stafford and Andy Thomas who collected much of the original data; Mr John Hayes, the Chief Rent Officer in the West Midlands Metropolitan County who both facilitated access to the rent registers and has been willing to discuss aspects of the operation of the system; Mr Frank Allaun, M.P.; Mr Ken Drinkwater, the Rent Officer in Lambeth; a number of other, anonymous, rent officers; and Mr Moyle of Avon Estates.

# 1 Housing markets and social policy

## ECONOMIC GOOD OR SOCIAL SERVICE?

Britain, over the last century or so in particular, has experienced the combined growth of public sector activities and public expenditure. Between 1890 and 1955, and in a series of plateaus connected by expenditure peaks at times of war or preparation for war, public expenditure increased tenfold in real terms (Peacock and Wiseman 1961). The reasons for this growth have been widely discussed from a number of perspectives, including welfare economics (e.g. Musgrave and Musgrave 1982), policy studies (e.g. Walker 1982) and political economy (e.g. Gough 1979). Although it may be the case that the apparent objectives or rationales for social policy have little to do with why the policy was implemented in the first place (see George and Wilding 1976), nevertheless the decisions to expand the arms of the public sector have represented society's choices about how goods and services should be produced and allocated.

In the case of housing, as with other goods and services, this means that there are fundamental questions about how it should be treated. At one end of the scale housing can be treated as an economic commodity which like cars, clothes and video machines is subject to the laws of the market place. That is, houses are supplied if and when entrepreneurs see the opportunity for a reasonable return. They are then purchased, if the entrepreneur has correctly assessed the market, by those willing and able to pay the price which would attain that return. This treatment of housing accords it no special position which distinguishes it from any other economic good. Consequently the amount and quality of housing which both the country as a whole and the individual gets is a function of the willingness and ability of consumers to pay for housing services.

At the other end of the scale housing can be treated as a social service. That is, as an integral part of the welfare activities of the state perhaps because it is deemed either that the market on its own will not produce enough decent housing and/or that it is in some sense undesirably distributed. As a social service it is the state which decides how much housing to supply and then allocates it using some criteria which are different from those of the market place, for example on the basis of need.

There are of course numerous intermediate positions between these two poles. The market may be left largely to its own devices but with some controls on the actions of individuals. Thus suppliers may be prohibited by law from producing goods below a certain quality. Or the state may introduce subsidies which leave market mechanisms free to operate but encourage greater consumption, by all or by some. Or the provision of a service may tend towards the social service model but without total insulation from market forces. For example, a private sector may be retained, as with private education and private health care, or fees and charges maintained, as with prescription charges.

In western industrialised countries governments have intervened widely in the provision and distribution of housing in these various ways, although the extent to which this has been effected by adopting a social service approach has been limited (Fuerst 1974; Pugh 1980). In Britain, for example, from a predominantly public health focus in the last century, the nature and extent of housing policy has developed to the point where virtually no aspect of the provision and distribution of housing is unaffected by government intervention. New houses are required to meet certain standards of construction and layout. Existing houses are subject to statutory controls over unfitness. Rights of possession are legally defined. In all tenures the price mechanism has been altered and in some cases obscured by the actions of government. The result has been that decisions about the use of resources and the types of houses produced in Britain have taken directions structured by the thrust of central government policy.

Although in general terms this situation is not uncommon, Britain is unusual in having such a large public or social service sector. In most western countries the direct provision of housing by the state is uncommon. As Donnison and Ungerson (1982, p.63) have indicated:

'Only in this country do public authorities acquire the land, build the dwellings, receive the subsidies, allocate the completed accommodation and collect the rents. No other market economy has so much publicly owned housing'.

Thus in the USA, for example, the public sector accounts for a mere 1 per cent of the total housing stock, and in Australia 6 per cent (Kemeny 1981).

The extent to which the state in Britain has placed housing in a position outside the market might be seen as a measure of its social progress. But what is often not realised is that the public housing sector is only public in a particular and narrow way. Council housing is not publicly financed out of taxation, for example, but from 'loans raised directly or indirectly from the money market' (Merrett 1979, p.160). Thus in Britain public housing more accurately means housing which is publicly managed. The source of finance for its development and for long periods after until loans are fully repaid, its ownership is, analytically if not legally, to be found in private money markets where it has to compete for funds with private economic units.

'Thus whilst the Local Authority _develops_ sites for the housing of the working population, _owns_ the stock of council dwellings and _manages_ this accommodation, in actually bringing the stock into existence it has always relied on private individuals, institutions and companies for the supply of land, for dwelling production and for the raising of loan finance' (Merrett 1979, p.167).

In addition to this and as with other areas of the welfare state, recent years have seen a resurgence of the market orientated approach, 'reverting somewhat to the view of housing as a market commodity, with public intervention concerned more with helping people to compete in that market than with offering them public provision instead' (Klein et al. 1974, p.51). This trend has been apparent throughout much of the 1970s under both Labour and Conservative administrations (Doling 1983b). Thus in 1976 the action which Denis Healey as Chancellor of the Exchequer took in response to economic trends was to enforce public expenditure cuts (Pliatzky 1982). But by far the greatest move in this direction has come since the 1979 election with the Conservative government successively drawing back the limits of the public sector. In a series of moves public subsidies, which had previously helped to reduce public sector rent levels, have effectively been withdrawn whilst the 1980 Housing Act has given tenants the right to transfer their tenure status. The result has been that for the first time this century the size of the public sector, in both absolute and relative terms, has been reduced. In December 1978 it accounted for 32.0 per cent of all dwellings in Great Britain, but three years later had fallen by one percentage point to 31.0 per cent.

The situation in Britain, as elsewhere then, is that policies stop short of providing all housing using the social service model but instead address inadequacies of the market without totally replacing the market. The norm is that market processes and the resulting provision and allocation are deemed acceptable, provided that these can be modified to a greater or lesser extent.

This reliance on the modified private sector solution to the housing problem has been part of an approach to housing which has been distinctly different from some other areas of social policy such as health care and education (although these too have been subject to recent public expenditure cuts). In these areas much of the debate and legislation has revolved around the principle of equality of life chances. But in housing 'the idea of a basic minimum of house-room and amenities rather than equality seems to have been the

3

objective' (Mishra 1981, p.122). This reliance on a large private sector has, as Malpass and Murie (1982) note, given housing policy a number of distinguishing characteristics.

Firstly, governments have to recognise the inter-connections between different parts of the housing system. In particular developments in one tenure can affect the situation in other tenures. Thus if favourable subsidy treatment is meted out to one tenure this may in the long run lead to the decline of other sectors.

Secondly, because the private market is large, and because without regulation its outcomes are unacceptable, governments 'do not permit a free market' (Malpass and Murie 1982, p.6). Rather they implement policies intended to regulate and control in order to manage both supply and demand.

Thirdly, housing policy has been rigidly tenure specific. Households in each tenure have different legal status, subsidies provided in different ways and in different amounts. New dwellings in the public sector have in the past been subject to Parker Morris standards whereas the private builder has been directed by the market, for example.

Fourthly, the existence of a large private sector has resulted in a public housing sector which is 'qualitatively different' from the public sector in some other social services. Thus whereas the National Health Service and state schools are first resorts for most people, state housing, by contrast, is generally a last resort.

Fifthly, in the public housing sector the principle of direct charges to consumers in the form of rent has been retained. This puts the payment for consumption in both the public and private sectors in direct competition and means that consumers are not faced with a public sector which is 'free' and a private sector which is at a price.

Finally, British governments have 'accepted the continuation of a large private sector, and repeatedly they have assumed that state subsidies and the expansion of public housing were temporary expedients brought about by unusual circumstances' (Malpass and Murie 1982, p.7).

## POLICY IN THE PRIVATE RENTED SECTOR

Many of these characteristics of the mixed economy in housing are apparent in the rental policies of most western governments which historically have intervened in the working of their privately rented housing sectors to the extent of modifying market forces. Generally this has consisted of limiting escalating rents by imposing some sort of rent freeze. Thus in Britain in 1915 an act of Parliament restricted the rents which landlords of residential property could charge tenants. The decision to place the act on the statute books was not taken lightly. Direct limitation of the

4

profits to be made from housing was an interference with the operation of the market which many accepted only reluctantly and under pressure. The pressure arose from a real fear that in time of national war the large rent increases which had occurred in certain parts of the country would lead to extensive civil strife. In these circumstances the restrictions placed on rent levels were accepted by many but only as a temporary expedient.

Notwithstanding early intentions, the privately rented housing sector has not, in its entirety, subsequently returned to unrestricted market processes. In at least some parts of the sector rent control continued until recently in the form of rent freezes at levels which they had reached at a point in the past plus periodic, across the board, increases to allow for inflation or repairs and maintenance costs. In addition, since 1965 the 'fair rents' system has been extended to embrace different parts of the sector. Rather than apply national standards this system allows assessment of the rents of individual residential dwellings and of individual increases over time. Despite such differences the two systems have in common the restriction of rents to levels below free market rents, combined with security of tenure for tenants. They thus constitute a particular model of state intervention in which market processes are modified but not entirely replaced. They also follow from a general reluctance to use the private landlord as an instrument of housing policy, but rather to discard his role by creating a fossilised backwater (Donnison 1967). The general problem is that with a market based housing policy the state has 'to manage the market by a strategy that on the one hand guarantees standards but on the other hand retains profitability' (Malpass and Murie 1982, p.10). At the same time the cost to consumers must fall within limits which they can reasonably be expected to pay.

In other countries governments have frequently pursued rent policies which in part and in apparent intention were consistent with these constraints. Thus in West Germany, Holland, France, Denmark and the US absolute freezes on rents have been relaxed and at the same time private landlords have been given some encouragement to add to the stock of rental housing. The motives for this encouragement were 'a mixture of ideology and necessity' (Harloe 1980, p.32 ) which prevented the replacement of private by public investment. Thus in America, for example, 'interests which favoured large scale public housing were never able to obtain sufficient political support for their cause, while in other countries, such as Holland and West Germany, lack of available public finance in the face of severe housing shortages persuaded even those who were opposed in principle to private landlordism to accept that it had a role to play' (Harloe 1980, p.32). In Sweden encouragement to private landlords to add to the housing stock was given in the form of subsidies, but these were tied to a form of rent control which whilst guaranteeing landlords a profit also guaranteed that the subsidies were passed on to tenants in the form of lower rents (Kemeny 1981).

In Britain the problem of supplying new rental housing was placed in the hands not of the private landlord but of local authorities. As a consequence during the period in which rent restriction has been a dimension of British housing policy, the privately rented sector has been allowed to, and at times perhaps encouraged to, decline in both quantitative and qualitative terms. At the turn of the century around 90 per cent of the nation's housing stock was let by private landlords; at the present time the proportion is about 14 per cent. Privately rented housing is also frequently in a poorer state of repair than housing in other tenures.

It is often argued that both these problems are directly and solely consequential on the imposition of rent restriction because this has taken away any incentives to landlords either to stay in the industry or to carry out even essential repairs. Obscuring the price mechanism has thus led to the failure of the market to respond to the housing needs of the nation. In addition, it is argued that not only would the restoration of the price mechanism lead to a reversal of these trends but that it would solve other problems. These include the anomalies in rent levels for similar properties in similar locations which occur largely because of differences in the dates at which they were controlled, decontrolled or brought into the fair rent system; the so called 'overconsumption' problem arising because rents below market levels do not provide sufficient incentive for small households to vacate large properties; and immobility resulting from the unwillingness of tenants in controlled or regulated lettings to give them up without the certainty of finding alternatives.

Close examination of the privately rented sector and relevant legislation reveals only limited support for these conclusions. The sector has declined in importance for reasons which lie in part beyond the rent acts. The financial equation facing landlords was, from their point of view, deteriorating even before 1915, and the introduction of subsidies to other tenures has meant that a return to a free market alone would not go far enough to redress the balance. Overconsumption, according to some criteria, as well as housing in bad repair, exists in all tenures. In particular it is significant that the large scale decontrol arising from the 1933 and 1957 Rent Acts did not lead to a revitalisation of the sector. Some landlords did nothing to raise rents partly because not all landlords are economic men seeking to maximise profits. Some landlords raised rents but only to a small extent. Some raised rents to exorbitant levels, attempted to evict existing tenants and sold their properties into owner occupation as quickly as possible. When landlords did receive increased returns they did not necessarily increase their expenditure on repairs and maintenance. By and large decontrol did not lead to increases in the size of the sector, nor to reductions in the injustices and anomalies in rent levels.

This is by no means a new insight into the effect of the rent acts. There now exists a number of contributions, which will be discussed later, to debates about the decline, function and operation of the privately rented sector and which argue that its problems are not primarily a function of rent restriction. Notwithstanding this, there continue to be strong representations from the property lobby and others to the effect that the removal of rent restriction is the panacea for the ills of the sector. Ideological affinities with this argument, for example, led to the introduction in the 1980 Housing Act of provisions which weakened the protection of the rent acts for certain lettings with respect to both rent levels and security of tenure.

The ambiguity underlying these different interpretations of the effects of the rent acts is perhaps not so much a reflection of any misunderstanding about what the rent acts do but of a failure to appreciate what they do not do. It lies not with the fact that the rent acts restrict rents but with the fact that they have not attacked the underlying processes which have resulted in the particular problems which many see as being consequences of the rent acts. The rent acts in other words have been blamed for things for which they are neither responsible nor for which they were ever intended to be responsible. It might be argued in particular, that the vitality and size of the privately rented sector has been eroded not by rent restriction but by subsidies to owner occupiers attracting those tenants able to afford higher prices into another tenure.

In reality rent act legislators have failed to grasp the significance of such inter tenural relationships. As in other housing legislation each tenure has effectively been treated separately as if each was an independent entity unaffected by and unaffecting events and processes in other tenures. Thus those drawing up the rent acts have often demonstrated a continuing propensity to look no further than the private rented sector for solutions. With both rent control and rent regulation the objectives of legislation have been limited. They have been short term and narrow reflecting a general (though certainly not complete) concensus about the nature of the problem. As far as the 1965 fair rent legislation was concerned this was based upon a belief that there was nothing essentially wrong with the operation of the private rental market. There were, admittedly, examples of harassment by landlords wishing to gain vacant possession and excessive rents in areas of great housing shortages but the general view was that these were exceptional. It was thought that most landlord-tenant relationships were amicable and that market processes generally resulted in satisfactory outcomes. The fair rents legislation thus provides a particular model of state intervention the results of which have been far from unproblematic.

7

## THE IMPLEMENTATION OF RENT POLICY

It is now conventional wisdom that the making of policy is in itself only part of the problem facing governments in their attempts to achieve objectives. That is, if this or other legislation is not having the intended effects, or if it is having unintended effects then this may be occurring, not because the broad policy it embodies is deficient, but because of the way in which it is being implemented. As Hill (1980, p.80) has pointed out:

> 'this concern with the ineffectiveness of policies is now recognized as requiring the asking not only of questions about the character of the policy but also about what is wrong with the implementation process and the organizations responsible for implementation'.

Indeed a number of recent studies have demonstrated the existence of the implementation minefield. Pressman and Wildavsky (1973), for example, demonstrated that even given ordinary circumstances - where a programme faced no great conflicts, no large scale political opposition and no lack of funds - there were nevertheless frequent problems of implementation. Even the most robust policies tend to go awry through under performance, delay and escalating costs, because the 'character and degree of many implementation problems are inherently unpredictable' (Bardach 1977, p.5). The result of such revelations has been that 'into the minds of many has come the realisation that the transition from decision to action in the policy process is neither smooth nor obvious' (Jenkins 1978, p.203).

In Britain such concerns have been fostered as part of a general recognition of the failure of the welfare state to carry out its welfare functions as anticipated. In this context the study of implementation has been encouraged as an alternative focus to that of policy analysis at the central government level:

> 'the impact of policies is affected as much by the mediation of other key actors - the "implementers" - as by the intrinsic merits or feasibility of the policy itself. To recognise the crucial role of policy mediators is to redefine the policy process as the centre's manipulation of the external world via the manipulation of the actions of the periphery. The problem for central policy-makers becomes one of deploying instruments and influence to achieve desired ends' (Young 1981, p.35).

A category of implementation study, which has long formed an important strand of the social policy literature, has examined certain types of person or profession involved in mediating between policy and the public. Under various labels-'street-level bureaucrats', 'social gatekeepers' and 'urban managers' - study of 'what actually happens in the exchanges between

8

these people and the public' (Hill 1980, p.81) has been widespread. This has been particularly the case in the field of urban studies following the work of Pahl (1970) who identified a large group of professions whose members were responsible for making decisions about scarce resources and facilities which included 'public housing managers, estate agents, local government officers, property developers, representatives of building societies and insurance companies, youth employment officers, social workers, magistrates and councillors' (Pahl 1970, p.220). As the managers of the urban system he argued that they controlled certain aspects of the life chances of individuals in the population so that the explanation for economic and social inequalities could be accomplished through analysis of the values and actions of those who 'manage'. Despite a period in the mid seventies when the approach was widely criticized (Norman 1975; Saunders 1979) it is now experiencing a resurgence of interest (Williams 1982).

Although rent officers do not seem to share all the characteristics of many of the other urban managers studied, the level of discretion enjoyed by rent officers is not unusual. Indeed whereas those employed in the rent officer service have particular job specifications, making their jobs different from the jobs of most other people, they nevertheless share many common job characteristics with Pahl's urban managers. They, like the rent officer, have considerable levels of discretion over decisions which directly affect individual members of the public, in particular over the granting or withholding of certain benefits. For example, legislation allows officers in the Department of Health and Social Security considerable discretion, largely with the intention that the system can respond flexibly to local labour market and other conditions (Ginsburg 1979, p.100). Even with detailed internal guidelines they nevertheless have to use personal judgement about the merits of each case and therefore how much or how little benefit each individual is to receive. Likewise, building society managers are commonly faced with more demands for mortgage funds than they have funds available. Although they operate within the private sector building societies do not set market clearing rates of interest but use non price rules and discretion which lead to personal decisions about who will be granted and who will be denied loans (Ford 1975).

In the case of rent officers they have been given wide ranging discretion. The word 'fair' was based on notions of equity which were undefined in the legislation or elsewhere. The whole concept of what was a 'fair' rent was left unspecified except in the vaguest terms. Whereas this ambiguity may have aided the passage of the 1965 Act onto the statute books, it has not subsequently ensured any particular interpretation of the rent levels. Not only is the statutory formula which defines what a fair rent should be vague, but the legislation has given rent officers considerable personal autonomy such that, except in the few cases of appeal, there

is no other individual or body vested with the powers of
correcting any resulting anomalies. In these circumstances
the way in which rent officers have made their determinations,
the rules they have developed, whether these vary from area to
area, and whether the rules have been implemented consistently
are legitimate questions. Recent authors on discretion have
made the same general observation: 'whether or
not...discretionary powers are greater than can be justified,
the ways in which these powers are exercised are, or at least
ought to be, a matter of considerable importance' (Adler and
Asquith 1981, p.1).

## PLAN AND SCOPE OF THE BOOK

Since the passing of the first rent regulation act in 1965
there has been little published research which has monitored
either the effects or the operation of the rent acts.    The
Labour  government's rent act review of the mid seventies
remains unpublished although some of its background studies
(e.g. Paley 1978) and the more general Housing Policy Review
(DOE 1977a) are available.    The major work has been by the
Francis Committee which in 1971 reported on a wide ranging
examination of the workings of the fair rent system,
concluding that although there were detailed criticisms,
broadly it seemed to be working well (Francis 1971).    However
certain legislative and administrative changes have
subsequently taken place.    The nature of the housing market,
and the place of the privately rented sector within it, as
well as the general policy environment, also have changed.
More recently the all party House of Commons Environment
Committee's investigation into the private rented sector
concentrated particularly on the problems facing the sector
but dealt only summarily with the administrative discretion
and working of the rent officer service (House of Commons
1982).

    The present work extends beyond the largely administrative
and procedural investigations of the Francis Committee, and in
certain respects it looks more deeply into some of the
concerns of the Environment Committee.    It focusses on the way
which, in one area of housing policy, the state's attempts to
modify market processes have worked out in practice.    On one
level this is an attempt to establish how, given the statutory
discretion, the word 'fair' is being interpreted in practice.
This is not achieved through the identification of one or more
verbal definitions of what a fair rent is or should be and
based upon interviews with rent officers, landlords and
tenants.    The identification comes through evidence of rents
actually registered.    This means that rather than rely on
stated objectives with a possible and unknown divergence
between such objectives and their implementation the
consequences of implementation are examined through the
relationship between properties and rents.    This in particular
enables analyses to be made of the extent to which
implementation has been consistent in a way that supports
criticisms of rent anomalies.    Thus the relationship between

properties and rents can be examined for indications of how
the word 'fair' has been translated in practice and also shows
to what extent the in built discretion has resulted in
consistent interpretation.

At another level the significance of the output of the
service is examined in terms of the relationship between rent
levels and the decline of the privately rented housing sector.
Evidence of the financial position of those in the market,
together with the nature of subsidies to,and taxes on, those
in the different housing tenures, are assembled to demonstrate
the extent of the economic rationale for the decline of the
sector and to illuminate the failure of policy in this area to
retain profitability for suppliers.

Chapter two is essentially a chronological account, starting
at the outset of the nineteenth century, of the changing
operation and fortunes of the privately rented housing sector
and, in particular, the nature of rent restricting
legislation. This is not to suggest that legislation directed
at this sector has been a necessary and logical development
arising from historical trends. But neither did the present
system arise out of a vacuum, and an examination of the
changing nature of the sector illustrates some of the
limitations of market provision and allocation of rented
housing.

In Chapter three the principles and operation of the present
fair rent system are discussed in more detail. The
flexibility built into it does not impose conformity on
procedures or on outputs of the system. To what extent this
has resulted in lack of conformity or consistency however, has
in the past not been fully apparent. The sketchy evidence
available is partly substantiated in Chapters four and five.
In the first of these an attempt is made to illuminate the
interpretation given by rent officers of the statutory but
imprecise formula for determining fair rents. It shows to
what extent rent officers in Birmingham have determined fair
rents which reflect market rents and which also reflect an
identifiable set of rules. In the second of these chapters
analysis of fair rent determinations evaluates how consistent
or inconsistent they are, and thus the extent of rent
anomalies between individual dwellings and between
administrative areas. Chapter six returns to the themes of
chapter two and examines barriers to the imposition of greater
consistency.

Chapter seven considers the second of the major themes,
namely the relationship between the setting of rents below
market levels and the decline of the sector. It argues
that rent is only one source of income which landlords derive
from residential property and that when this is added to
capital gains the income from their investment compares
reasonably in percentage terms with many alternative
investments. The apparent economic difficulties of landlords
are shown to be a consequence not of rent restriction but of

the difficulty of realising capital gains, and of the existence of subsidies to other tenures.

Finally, chapter eight examines the significance for housing policy of the findings and arguments presented.

# 2 The development of rent restricting legislation

When it was introduced, the fair rent system arrived not in the context of a privately rented sector which had a history of stability but in the context of turmoil and decline. The private landlord had been the free market solution to housing the swelling urban masses in nineteenth century Britain bringing houses, in their hundreds of thousands, to the market place. Nevertheless, the market did not provide sufficient incentive to meet the needs of many households. Moreover, the economic and political context soon changed. Economically the supply and demand sides of the equation altered, partly as a result of state intervention: later the landlord became politically expendable. Following the first world war state subsidies increased the relative attractiveness of other forms of housing tenure and the landlords' ability to compete was further limited by statutorily imposed rent control. The insecurity of both landlords and tenants, proposals to extend control or decontrol, and the changing tenure balance all meant that by 1965 the privately rented sector had declined to a minor proportion of the market. At the same time control, decontrol and new lettings outside the rent acts had led to widespread anomalies in rents. But the fair rent system which it was argued would bring logic to the rent structure did nothing to revitalise the sector.

## BEFORE THE RENT ACTS

It is a great oversimplification to talk about the Victorian, or the nineteenth century, housing market as a phenomenon which was constant over time and space. Although at the end of the century the owner occupation rate for the country as a whole was about 10 per cent, for example, some communities had owner occupation rates on a par with present day levels: the rates in some South Wales mining towns reputedly being about 60 per cent (Daunton 1976). Nevertheless, there were spatial and temporal similarities, the identification of which lends support to assertions that the removal of restrictions on rents and of security of tenure would not be sufficient either to revive the fortunes of the landlord, or to remove injustices and anomalies which were and are widespread in the sector. The market did not operate smoothly; the profit motive led some landlords to invest in other spheres particularly at times when relative rates of return from housing declined; and generally it did not encourage the supply of decent housing for the poorest members of society. Moreover as the century progressed the incentives to landlords became worse rather than better. The improvement of

housing conditions on a wide scale had to await the arrival of
state encouragement for other tenure forms.

Prior to the nineteenth century and its rapid urbanisation
and industrialisation, peasants under feudalism and agrarian
capitalism frequently either built their own houses or had
them provided by their employer. The social and economic
relationships which developed around the production of
commodities also developed around the supply and allocation of
housing. What began with 'the establishment of the prime wage
contract between capital and labour and the "free" market in
labour power' extended to embrace housing such that 'the
vestiges of individual employer interest in the welfare of
employees, particularly their housing, all but disappeared'
(Ginsburg 1979, p.115). Housing thus became just as much a
commodity to be bought and sold in the market place as those
commodities being produced in the new factories. Moreover
the law governing the relationship between landlords and
tenants and the barriers placed on evicting tenants, which had
been present in earlier years, seem to have weakened in favour
of the landlord (Nevitt 1970).

Housing thus became a market commodity subject to the
largely unfettered forces of demand and supply. Detailed
knowledge of how this market operated is in certain respects
fairly limited (Ginsburg 1979; Dyos 1968), but in essence it
seems to have been similar to many other markets. Suppliers
provided housing when they saw an opportunity to make a profit
which they felt was reasonable. What was a reasonable profit
varied over time and space, but would have been related to
profit levels which could have been achieved from alternative
investments. Once supplied, houses were allocated to those
people who were able and willing to pay the going rents.
People did not necessarily get the housing which was
commensurate with their needs therefore, but the housing which
was commensurate with their financial status. This meant, of
course, that the market gave no incentive to suppliers to
provide housing for those who could not afford to pay for it.

For the most part it was considered neither desirable nor
necessary for the state to intervene in this. There was a
widespread belief that state intervention in general was
undesirable: the philosophy of laissez-faire and the belief in
self help providing the rationale for non-intervention
(Gauldie 1974). This is not to say that individuals or
Parliament itself never considered involvement in the housing
market. Pressure to do so came from a number of directions:
revolution in France deeply impressed those in power in
England who saw the slums as breeding grounds for British
revolutionaries and insanitary conditions generated contagious
diseases which were no respecters of social or economic class
(Wohl 1977).

If the state was not sufficiently concerned to wield
influence in the housing market, then neither did intervention

meet the interests of employers. Dyos, for example, has argued:

> 'One of the most general reasons for the slums of Victorian England simply was that the capital which might have wrought a change was being ploughed heavily back into the commercial machine instead of being distributed in higher wages, and its earnings benefitted particular social classes differentially. If better houses had been built to house the workers during the nineteenth century, the higher wages paid out to make this possible would probably have raised the costs of our exports and reduced the capital being sent abroad, which would in turn have held back the growth of exports. Another way of putting this would be that slums were necessary so as not to dissipate too many resources in housing, and that while labour was abundant, cheap and docile this was economically justifiable. The logic of this, tacitly accepted at the time, is that the slums helped to underpin Victorian prosperity' (Dyos 1967, p.27).

The housing market in nineteenth century Britain was therefore a market which was largely unrestricted by state intervention. Although from the middle of the century onwards the state did become more involved by passing a number of statutes relating to housing supply these were generally voluntary rather than compulsory. For the most part production and consumption followed the economic criteria of the market place. In the light of this it is interesting to ask how well this market operated. Was freedom from interference by the state accompanied by the development of houses sufficient in number to meet the needs of the growing population? Was their standard sufficient to provide families with adequate space? Did the market provide incentives to producers in times of shortage? In what sense was there justice between landlords and tenants? Finally, was there anything about the nature of the nineteenth century housing market which would suggest that if today the state withdrew from the housing market present problems would be quickly overcome?

### The demand for housing

At the outset of the nineteenth century the population of England and Wales numbered 8.9 million but by the middle of the century this had doubled to 17.9 million, and by the start of the present century almost redoubled. This unprecedented increase in population imposed strains on the physical infrastructure which were exacerbated by the fact that much of the increase was concentrated around the expanding numbers of jobs in the rapidly developing urban areas. In the first half of the century, for example, Bradford's population increased eight times, Liverpool's four and a half times and Manchester's four times (Burnett 1978).

The great mass of this growing population was poor.

Although some had made great gains from this period of rapid
economic growth their numbers were limited. For most people
national economic vitality had not improved their personal
economic circumstances although the situation varied from
place to place. In some cities the population experienced
long periods of growing prosperity, but this was frequently
not the case. The problem was not simply that there was such
a high proportion of semi skilled and unskilled workers, nor
was it that their wages were relatively low when compared with
the cost of living. Employment, even for skilled workers, was
volatile. Many people were not employed on a permanent basis
but by the day or even by the hour. Irregularities in wages
thus made any long term financial commitment difficult to
sustain.

In addition to this, large numbers of people in urban areas
were living without any wages at all. Many people lived by
begging or by sifting through others' rubbish to extract
usable or saleable scraps. Because there were so many people
who scrounged for a living or who were employed only casually,
'there were always takers for the most abject living
conditions offered. No form of shelter was too dark, dirty
and cramped for people whose days were spent, for instance,
walking the sewer pipes in search of saleable objects lost
down the drains. Cheapness, and even more important, time to
pay, were the criteria which made a house desirable for too
large a proportion of town-dwellers' (Gauldie 1974, p.153).
In the absence of higher wages and state subsidies the
effective demand for housing was low. Large numbers of the
population simply could not afford the basic necessities of
life.

**The supply of housing**

There were a number of functions in the process of converting
land from open countryside into urban residential streets
undertaken by landowners, developers, financiers and
builders. In practice, distinctions between them were not
always clear cut largely because 'the opportunities were in
fact far too numerous and diverse for a standard response'
(Dyos 1968, p.644). At one extreme each of these functions
might be carried out by one person; at the other there were
numerous gradations. But the production of housing was not a
smooth, well-oiled and perfectly functioning process because
of the characteristics of the process, the commodity and the
people involved.

The amount of development taking place meant that people
engaged in construction activities accounted for a major part
of the workforce (Board of Trade 1908). The residential
construction industry itself however was characterised by a
large number of small firms. In Leicester in 1870, of 105
applications for permision to build in the city 79 were for
four houses or fewer and only one for over twenty houses
(Pritchard 1976). In London from the 1840s to the 1870s 80

16

per cent of firms built no more than six houses per year (Dyos 1968).

One of the reasons for the size structure of the industry was the ease of entry into the sector. The activity required little or no capital and it was not difficult for one man or a small group of men to set up in business. Even technically, getting into the business was not difficult with the technical press supplying what 'amounted to a complete kit of plans, designs, and bills of quantities for almost any beginner in suburban estate development' (Dyos 1968, p.661). The corollary of this was that the industry was frequently insecure and generally inefficient (Burnett 1978).

Landlordism was also characterized by small holdings. The average number of houses owned by each landlord in one district of Cardiff in 1884, for example, was 4.2 (Daunton 1976). For many, landlordism was viewed as a source of a small, but steady income. Thriftier members of the artisan classes who had saved sufficient money to purchase a couple of houses, widows with savings, shopkeepers and small businessmen preferred 'safety in the form of a small yearly income rather than greater possible profits over a longer period of time' (Gauldie 1974, p.182). Generally the builder of a row of houses would live in one and receive an income from letting the others, but sometimes selling them at a later date to a landlord or owner occupier (Green 1980).

Problems of supply arose partly because housing is a capital intensive commodity. Not only is it costly but the length of time involved in the development process means that capital is tied up for a considerable period before any returns can be gained in the form of rents or capital price. This, combined with the generally small scale nature of the organisations involved made residential development particularly dependent upon external sources of finance. Builders themselves were rarely men of capital, many being ex-workmen. Landlords, too, frequently raised two thirds of the value of the property on a mortgage (Cairncross 1953). The finance came from a variety of sources including building societies, insurance companies and solicitors often acting for individuals. The major sources of finance, in particular the banks, were not as prominent in residential development as they might have been however. They were frequently wary of dealing with insecure enterprises run by small operators (Burnett 1978). Moreover many large investors themselves had money tied up in existing housing either as landlords or holders of mortgages and it was thus sometimes in their interest that shortages and the resulting high rents and mortgage security continued (Gauldie 1974).

Reliance on external sources of finance made housing particularly susceptible to external economic conditions. The result was that the building industry responded unevenly to the need for housing. Whereas the population continued to increase steadily there was a great deal of residential

development in some years but not in others.   Building cycles
have been charted and show that in the latter part of the
century low levels of activity were separated by peaks in the
mid 1870s and a double peak around 1900.

There has been a great deal of discussion concerning the
factors determining these building cycles (see Lewis 1965).
Much has been written, for example, about the importance of
the development of the limited liability legislation in mid
century following which public joint stock companies began to
multiply (Sayer 1967).   Their importance was, it has been
argued, that in providing opportunities for people with small
amounts of money to invest in industry they were an
alternative to investments in building societies or housing.
Likewise, explanations centred around investment diversion
from housing into other sectors have received attention from
Cooney (1949) who related the building cycles to the movement
of capital between America and Britain in the search for more
profitable outlets.   When the US economy was booming capital
moved to it from Britain and vice versa.   Others have argued
that domestic influences such as internal migration and
demographic trends were more important (Habakkuk 1962) or that
there was no evidence that booms came to an end because of
investment diversion (Saul 1962).   The search for a single,
simple reason to explain the sequence of building booms and
troughs has been criticized on the grounds that 'the
interaction of... forces is very complex and even so provides
only incomplete answers' (Aldcroft and Richardson 1969, p.46).
Nevertheless some combination of factors, although not
necessarily the same combination on each occasion, brought
about the failure of the residential development process to
consistently and continually respond to the housing needs of
the British people.

The activities of the private landlord were also affected,
from early in the century, by tax arrangements which treated
investors in manufacturing industry and building societies
more favourably.   When income tax was reintroduced in 1803 the
payment of tax on rental income was in accordance with the
general rules applying to other sources of income.   But within
three years the landlord was singled out for special treatment
which denied him the right to deduct the cost of repairs from
rental income apparently because of 'the fraudulent returns
made by landlords claiming tax relief on repairs carried out
by their tenants' (Nevitt 1966,   p.44).   Later in the century,
in 1878, manufacturers were granted a concession, in the form
of a deduction from their gross profits, of an amount which
they would need to set aside to cover the costs of replacing
machinery with a limited life span.   A similar concession was
not extended to landlords to cover items of limited life,
capital equipment such as hot water heaters.   While levels of
taxation were low this unfavourable treatment was not always
of great significance particularly in periods during which
rental returns were high.   Nevertheless at other times it has
provided a strong incentive for the diversion of funds from
residential to industrial investments (Nevitt 1966, p.47).

The economics of supply and demand meant that such housing as was built for the working classes tended to be both small and of low quality. Houses were squeezed into whatever space was left after the development of factories, railways and canals. Sites were overdeveloped, sometimes by building the houses back to back, sometimes by increasing the capacity of the house by building a cellar to accommodate a second (or even third) family. Quality was sacrificed by generally skimping on materials, the digging of inadequate foundations and the frequent failure, until stricter controls were imposed later in the century, to provide sufficient basic services such as water supply, privies and sewers. Contemporary reports and surveys paint vivid pictures of the appalling conditions in which many people lived. Conditions were frequently squalid and insanitary: many lived in misery, suffering high rates of infant mortality and low life expectancy.

Throughout the century the national deficit of houses, that is the difference between the number of families and the number of houses, increased forcing more and more families to share their accommodation (Gauldie 1974). Sharing also occurred for reasons other than housing shortage, however. At times of economic depression, and there were a number of such depressions of varying intensity throughout the century as unemployment and wage cuts increased, the number of houses occupied actually decreased (Cairncross 1953). The poor were obliged by their economic circumstances to move into smaller premises, to share with relatives or friends, or to sublet from other tenants.

Landlords of the housing which was being subdivided (and subdivision also took place because of local shortages) could in many cases obtain higher returns as a result. By crowding more and more people into a building and obtaining from each a small rent, the total rent for the building could be increased. Gauldie (1974,p.159) has presented the equation: 'it was possible to house up to sixty people in houses let originally at £35 per year and producing an income of £70, each flat being sub-let, the individual rooms sub-let again, and beds within the rooms relet again at 3d. a night.'

The relationship between landlord and tenant was not always straightforward. Large landlords frequently handed over the management of their properties to others who would organise the carrying out of repairs and collecting of rents. The results of this were frequently of benefit to neither landlord nor tenant. Between them often 'stretched a whole chain of shadowy intermediaries, held in their contracted order by a series of sub-leases which divided responsibilities for the upkeep of the property and inflated the rents paid for it' (Dyos and Reeder 1973, p.380). Repairs were not always carried out, overcrowding was encouraged and any increase in rents rarely reached the owner in full.

Forced to remain in close proximity to their sources of

employment and credit, because of the nature of transport
technology and the level of fares, the poor were often
trapped in the slums of the inner parts of the Victorian city.
The better off working classes, including those who simply had
regular employment, could escape to the suburbs. Those left
behind in the centrally located properties were at the mercy
of landlords who collectively were in a position to subdivide,
ignore repairs and maintenance and at the same time charge
exorbitant rents. The poor were thus placed in the position
of living in the worst property whilst frequently still paying
high rents.

A further paradox was that housing need, clearly evident in
the amount of overcrowding, existed side by side with empty
housing. The downward stickiness of rents meant that they did
not quickly adapt themselves to falls in building costs
(Singer 1941). Neither were landlords quick to reduce rents
on unoccupied dwellings (Lewis 1965). In this sense the
market was not self regulating. It was not simply a case that
need for housing was not expressed in terms of effective
demand but that even prices failed to reflect real changes in
the market.

It was in the latter half of the century that a number of
philanthropic individuals and institutions attempted to
provide housing for those sectors of the population for which
the market had failed to cater. As experiments to demonstrate
that men of good intention and sound business sense who were
willing to accept a modest return of around 5 per cent on
their investment could produce decent houses for the poor,
they largely failed (Gauldie 1974). Their contribution to the
housing stock was small, their efforts further emphasised the
gap between the high cost of housing and the inability of the
poor to pay an economic rent. Although some, such as the
Peabody Trust, managed to charge rents below market levels,
these rents were in fact subsidised. Most of this voluntary
housing sector could not build down to the wages of the very
poorest (Wohl 1977).

In the last quarter of the century the ability of developers
to provide new housing for the very poorest was further
reduced. From 1875 onwards acts concerned with public health
imposed minimum standards on new residential construction in
relation to water supply, drainage, ventilation, and the space
between buildings. Developers were thus obliged to provide
more facilities for each dwelling and yet were not allowed to
build as many dwellings on any given area of land. The cost
of housing was increased as a result. In addition the fiscal
policies of both the central and local state were eroding
landlords' returns. Although rents facing households were
generally rising over the period from 1875 to the start of
World War I the 'increment was not appropriated by the
landlords. It was largely creamed off by the state, and by
local government in particular' (Offer 1980, p.248). Thus by
the end of the Edwardian period government was taking in the
form of taxation some 23 per cent of rental outlay to be spent

on roads, sewers, parks and other urban improvements (Offer 1980).

Although there was a building boom from 1896 to 1906 the demand came largely from the artisan classes. Following that peak, production fell off rapidly so that by 1914 it was at a very low level: a trend, which for one writer at least 'proves dramatically that the private landlord, far from being killed off by rent control .... had already decided to go out of business long before rent control was ever thought of' (Berry 1974, p.19).

## THE INTRODUCTION OF RENT CONTROL

The housing shortages which existed at the outset of war in 1914 were exacerbated by events at home which resulted in increases in demand in certain places without commensurate increases in supply. There was an influx of workers into the munitions factories many of which were located in the larger urban centres. Real wages in these industries were higher than they had been before the war and the rent levels which their workers could afford were higher than the rest of the population. But there was little opportunity for builders and landlords to respond. Shortages of building materials were aggravated by the new high rates of interest. This had two consequences. Firstly, as had happened throughout the previous century, the existence of alternative and more lucrative investments provided little encouragement to expand the supply of housing: investors could obtain a higher rate of return from the War Loan, for example, than they could from housing mortgages (Beirne 1977). Secondly, existing landlords were facing a combination of higher interest rates on their mortgages and higher demand. In Barrow-in-Furness, for example, where Vickers had an engineering factory the working population increased during the first three years of the war from 16,000 to 35,000. The resultant overcrowding was intense, reaching 'the level of nine or even ten persons to a room' (Orbach 1977, p.11). Landlords saw the need and the consequent opportunity to raise rents.

Many were not able to pay the higher rents however. The budgets of the families of those fighting on the European mainland and those not able to gain access to well paid jobs in the munitions factories were squeezed by the continuing low level of their wages and the new rent levels. Growing unrest and protest from those trapped in this way culminated in a rent strike in Glasgow. Disorder was not confined to this city however with similar strikes in Birkenhead, Birmingham, Coventry, Dudley, London and Northampton (Orbach 1977).

It is by no means certain whether in isolation such events would have led to significant developments in the role of the state in housing. Throughout the previous century response to the housing conditions of the poorest sectors of society had been tardy, and frequently left to the discretion of local authorities. It is true that there had been legislation to

21

improve standards but in practice this affected new rather than existing property. Large numbers continued to be unprotected from the laws of the market place. The new element in the situation was clearly the war although the working classes may have organised their protests more effectively. As Cullingworth (1979,p.62) has pointed out 'The normal reaction had been to do nothing ... but now the political pressure was too strong to resist.'

Without the willing cooperation of the sort of people who were taking part in acts of civil disorder the war could not be fought. Men would not willingly enlist in the army knowing that their wives and families would be left at the mercies of their landlords. In addition unrest in the form of industrial militancy was threatened. There were strikes and walkouts in a number of Clyde shipyards and any extension of this would have had similarly disastrous consequences for the war effort and would have posed a threat to the economic order generally (Beirne 1977).

The Increase of Rent and Mortgage Interest (War Restrictions) Act 1915 established the basic principle of all subsequent British rent restricting legislation: to give tenants fair or reasonable rents coupled with security of tenure. The second objective was a necessary corollary of the first since any protection regarding rent is illusory unless backed by a right to remain in the property (Megarry 1949). As far as rents were concerned these were frozen at the levels which were charged on 3 August 1914. The market was thus fossilised at a particular point in time. Landlords were not allowed to charge rents higher than they had done on that date, neither could they circumvent this restriction by evicting their tenants in order to sell to an owner occupier or to obtain a different tenant.

Although the civil unrest was largely confined to those parts of the country designated as Munitions Areas, rent control was not restricted to them. In part this was because it was evident that even in normal peacetime conditions there were areas where houses could not be built profitably to let at rents which working class tenants could afford (Orbach 1977). Nevertheless, many clung to the belief that the present problems were solely housing problems. And although this was an error of analysis, making the housing shortage a problem of the 'market' was a temptation which it was not easy to withstand. With it, there emerged a belief that a market solution, in terms of supply and demand, would come in due time (Orbach 1977). The act thus established a principle which has been followed in all subsequent rent restricting legislation in this country. The view of the problem was not that wages were too low or that external factors had changed the economics of landlordism, but that there was a temporary failure of the market which would be corrected in due course.

Central to this aspect of the debate, as it was to be on

22

numerous later occasions, was therefore the view that there
was nothing wrong with (and indeed much to be praised about)
the principle of the market allocation of housing.  Indeed the
decision to tie rents to their level at a particular time when
state intervention was still at a minimum was an implicit
recognition that market prices were at least, under certain
circumstances, fair to all concerned.  As Bowley (1945, p.205)
later put it:

'it was considered that the rents actually prevailing
before the scarcity created by the Great War should be
maintained as in some way fair... The ceiling on rents had
originally been fixed as the rents existing on the day
war was declared in 1914; it could be claimed these
included no element of  war profiteering - they were fair
in the special context of those years.... [But] the rents
of 1914 were ordinary market rents.  It is not usually
claimed that these are necessary fair rents in any ethical
sense of the  term.  They are merely the rents resulting
from the interaction of supply  and demand ... They were
it is true, more or less free from the particular  element
of profit stigmatized as due to "war profiteering"; they
were by no  means necessarily free of other elements of
profit stigmatized by moralists  as unfair.'

Despite the pressure for rent legislation, many found its
acceptance easier if it could be viewed as a temporary
expedient.  As soon as the war ended the market would be able
to make good the shortages of housing; thus the market itself
would be sufficient to ensure that landlords could not charge
excessive rents.  Indeed many believed that the legislation
would continue in force for a period of only 6 months after
the end of the war.

Nevitt (1970, p.128), quoting from House of Commons
speeches, draws attention to the fact that at least one
member, Sir Walter Essex, had appreciated that such a return
to a free market would not be easily achieved:

'...I think that those who harbour the comforting thought
that this is a temporary measure, temporary in its
entirety, temporary in its acceptance of a principle, are
hugging a delusion which they are certain to find is a
delusion before they are many years older...'

He went on to say that the same working class pressure which
was in the process of achieving the concessions embodied in
the 1915 Act could be applied in subsequent years:

'The War is not the last emergency which will come upon
this country.  After the War those who are the judges of
the probability of things tell us there will be a long,
acute period of commercial depression set in, and then you
will have the working classes of this country, who are
today not as thrifty as we would like them to be in this
time of prosperity, pressing their leaders and making it a

condition of their support by saying, "You did it before. When our incomes and wages were high you gave us relief and protection against the raising of our rent. You have the power and you have shown yourselves able to use it."'

## THE INTER-WAR YEARS

Essex's remarks proved to be very perceptive. Having committed itself to restricting the price mechanism central government found it difficult to alter course (Cullingworth 1979). The Liberal coalition fought and won the December 1918 general election on Lloyd George's slogan: 'Homes for Heroes'. The returning heroes as well as those who had worked for the war effort at home had been promised and expected decent housing. But by the end of the war there was a severe housing shortage: very few new dwellings had been built since the outbreak of hostilities so that the '1919 shortage was, therefore, the 1914 shortage accentuated' (Burnett 1978, p.217). Prices generally had risen dramatically over their 1914 levels whilst building materials, in particular, were available only at high prices. The index of building costs experienced a dramatic rise in 1915 reaching a peak in 1920 when it was about twice the prevailing average for the previous 70 years. The consequence was that the building of housing for the working classes was unremunerative (Cullingworth 1979). At the same time, though many young men had lost their lives in the trenches, the pace of family formation continued. The shortage of dwellings was estimated as at least 600,000. The result was that any desires or intentions to decontrol the sector had to recognise that the market, if left to itself, would not resolve the problems.

The Hunter Committee, which had reported late in 1918, concluded that rent restrictions could not at that time be removed. Nevertheless expectations remained that conditions would soon return to normality and that decontrol should then be carried out (Beirne 1977). Accepting this, the government passed the Increase of Rent and Mortgage Interest (Restrictions) Act 1919 which prolonged the duration of rent restriction until 25 March 1921. At the same time it extended the scope of control to include dwellings with higher rateable values. Thus, having accepted the burden of restricting the upward movement of prices, the government found it difficult to extricate itself from its new responsibility (Cullingworth 1979).

New housing legislation, however, went far beyond placing direct restrictions on the rents which could be charged. The state came to accept that major intervention, on a scale unprecedented in the housing sector, was necessary if rental housing was to be expanded in numbers. In 1919, as a result of the Housing and Town Planning Act, 'the British system of council housing was born' (Murie et al. 1976, p.94). This removed the major onus for supplying new housing from the landlord and placed it on the shoulders of local authorities by instructing them to survey their areas and, once approval had been given by the Minister of Health, to provide for housing need. Local authorities were provided with generous subsidies: any losses incurred in excess of the amount of money represented by a penny rate were to be borne by the Exchequer. Moreover, rents were not to be related to the costs of provision but to the general level of controlled rents prevailing in the area.

The act fell short of the expectations held of it. By 1921 fewer than half of the 600,000 new dwellings which were considered necessary had been built. Nevertheless the act had fundamental implications for the private rented sector. For the first time the private landlord was facing competition from a supplier backed by huge resources and without the need to show a profit in the normal way. Moreover, because local authorities were required to bear only a small amount of the costs there was little incentive for them to be conservative in numbers or costs and dwellings were thus often built to a very high standard. The private landlord was thus effectively rejected as the principal mechanism for supplying rental housing.

For the next twenty years a succession of committees was set up to investigate the workings of the rent acts, which continued to be the subject of a great deal of discussion (Greve 1965). The Salisbury Committee reporting in 1920 reaffirmed the need for control to continue. Its recommendations embodied in the Increase of Rent and Mortgage Interest (Restrictions) Act 1920, set the basis for legislation for unfurnished dwellings until 1965, although, at the time, it was intended that restrictions would last only until 24 June 1923.

The main provisions of the 1920 Act were that:

a) Restrictions only applied to dwellings under certain rateable values: £105 in London; £90 in Scotland and £78 elsewhere. They did not apply to new houses, council houses, furnished lettings or lettings with board.

b) Rents were set by reference to those charged at the outbreak of war with a 15 per cent increase allowed for inflation and with a further 25 per cent allowable if the landlord was responsible for all repairs.

Further committees followed: Onslow in 1923, Marley in 1931, and Ridley in 1937. They were confronted with the same dilemma which had come to a head in 1915. For the most part there was a continuing belief that rent control, because it restricted the price mechanism, was constraining the provision of private housing to let. At the same time, it was recognised that the abolition of rent control could lead to social and industrial unrest (Murie et al. 1976). Indeed even the increases allowed under the 1920 Act had resulted in rent strikes in West Scotland and Glasgow where it was reported in 1922 that 30,000 tenants were refusing to pay extra rent

(Beirne 1977). The result was that control continued throughout the inter war period.

Following the lead of the Rent and Mortgage Interest Restrictions Act 1923, however, subsequent legislation, until the eve of the Second World War, also attempted to achieve some limited decontrol. Landlords were able to set higher rents when and if properties became vacant. This 'creeping' decontrol was later supplemented by 'block' decontrol which was applied to all dwellings above certain rateable values. The argument used was that there was no shortage of the more expensive housing and thus that the market could be freed without hardship. But room for manoeuvre was limited. Despite increases in the housing stock increases in need had been even greater. 'New families arose more quickly than new houses' with the result that the 'housing shortage had risen from 600,000 to over 800,000' (Lewis 1965, p.227).

When the Marley Committee reported in 1931 it argued that houses with a high rateable value should be decontrolled on the grounds that there was no shortage of this type of property. Indeed the greater part of the housing which had been built since the end of the war for local authority tenants and owner occupiers had been aimed, because of its cost, at the better off working class families. The report also concluded that dwellings with low rateable values were being decontrolled too quickly and that at a time when the need for such housing was still pressing this was causing great hardship (Abbey 1957).

Marley's recommendations on decontrol were embodied in the 1933 Rent and Mortgage Restrictions (Amendment) Act. Dwellings with the lowest rateable values were no longer to be subject to creeping decontrol. It was clear from the debates leading up to the implementation of the act, however, that the Conservative party spokesmen had a clear long term aim of restoring the whole of the privately rented sector to the forces of the market place. If decontrol was not to be applied to low rated dwellings this was merely a temporary expedient until shortages were finally eradicated. Indeed, further than this some argued that the shortage of cheaper housing would only be eradicated if they were decontrolled. Labour spokesmen were equally adamant that decontrol should not be pursued. The tenor of the arguments on both sides was not to be very different a quarter of a century later (Barnett 1969).

**Decline of the sector**

Throughout this period the importance of the privately rented sector declined, at least in numerical terms, from 7.1 million to 6.6 million dwellings. The major element in this decline was the sale of about 1.1 million rented dwellings into owner occupation (Table 2.1). With the building societies expanding their activities the demand for owner occupied houses was buoyant throughout the period. The money value of the total

26

assets of the building society movement, which had increased by a factor of nearly 3 during the fifty years between 1870 and 1920, increased ten fold during the interwar period (Kirkwood 1979). In 1928 the number of borrowers was 554,000; by 1937 this had become 1,392,000 (Berry 1974). The demand for owner occupation was also fuelled by the continuing threat of de-control, not simply because of the fear of increased rental payments but of the loss of security of tenure. Indeed the latter 'became one of the owner-occupiers' principal assets, encouraging people to buy homes of their own and to outbid private landlords who might contemplate building on the same sites' (Donnison 1967, p.229).

Landlords were also faced with new situations which encouraged them to sell to owner occupiers. Under the impact of higher building costs and increased demand the value of housing during the post war period was higher than it had been in 1914. This meant that for the first time a large part of the nation's housing stock had two values: the value of the house with a sitting tenant which was related to the allowed return on its 1914 value, and the higher value of the house with vacant possession (Pawley 1978). Landlords could thus make greater profits by selling their houses at the prices owner occupiers were willing to pay and investing the money elsewhere. As Pawley (1978) has shown, elsewhere was frequently a building society account so that in a sense landlords were helping to fuel the very demand which was undermining landlordism. This was compounded because the growth of owner occupation generally deprived landlords of the more affluent, reliable and stable tenants. The attraction of letting property to tenants as an investment was thus further undermined (Kirkwood 1979).

The secondary cause of decline during this period was the losses due to slum clearance. In the early post war period, when there had been a large deficit of houses, the emphasis of housing policy had been on building as many new houses as possible. However, the 1930 Housing Act (the Greenwood Act) turned attention towards slum clearance by introducing a new subsidy system related to the number of people rehoused as a result of slum clearance. Basing the subsidy on numbers of people and not, as previously, on numbers of houses developed gave local authorities the incentive to rehouse large, poor families. At the same time local authorities were required to prepare slum clearance plans.

Because many of the worst properties had been built in the nineteenth century and let to tenants, most clearance was of privately rented property. Compounding the poor physical standard of these properties even when new, was the fact that it had become increasingly difficult for landlords to carry out regular maintenance. Rent control combined with high costs of labour and materials thus 'added to the slum creation process' (Kirkwood 1979, p.133).

Table 2.1
Components of change of the private rented sector
England and Wales 1914-1975
(millions of dwellings)

| | | |
|---|---|---|
| 1914 Stock | | 7.1 |
| | | |
| Change 1914-38 | | |
| Sales to owner occupation | -1.1 | |
| Demolitions and changes of use | -0.3 | |
| New building and conversion | +0.9 | |
| Net change | -0.5 | |
| | | |
| 1938 Stock | | 6.6 |
| | | |
| Change 1938-60 | | |
| Sales to owner occupation | -1.5 | |
| Sales to local authorities | -0.2 | |
| Demolitions and changes of use | -0.4 | |
| New building and conversion | +0.1 | |
| Net change | -2.0 | |
| | | |
| 1960 Stock | | 4.6 |
| | | |
| Change 1960-75 | | |
| Sales to owner occupation | -1.1 | |
| Sales to local authorities | -0.1 | |
| Demolitions and changes of use | -0.8 | |
| New building and conversion | +0.3 | |
| Net change | -1.7 | |
| | | |
| 1975 Stock | | 2.9 |

Source: DOE (1977b) Table IX.2


Offsetting these losses through sales to owner occupiers and demolition, was the construction of 900,000 new homes to let (Table 2.1). Throughout the two decades of the interwar period the economic conditions for adding to the sector gradually improved. Although building costs had risen dramatically after 1914 they had reached a peak by 1920 and subsequently declined. By the early 1930s they were still half as high again as they had been in 1914, but the earnings of men in full time employment had doubled (DOE 1977b). This meant that some addition to the privately rented stock was financially viable:

'The average rent (excluding rates) of interwar houses built for private owners was an estimated 10s a week in the mid-1930s, compared with 7s 6d for decontrolled pre-war houses and 6s for those houses still in controlled tenancies. At 10s a week a return of about 4 or 5 per cent on the original cost was possible, which compared reasonably well with returns elsewhere. Rents of 10s a week could be obtained because there were still

28

considerably fewer houses than households until the end of the 1930s, and because they were within reach of the better paid wage earner: average earnings were some 60-65 shillings a week' (DOE 1977b, p.64).

In addition to the financial equation the rent acts did not apply to houses built after 1919, 'nor was there any serious suggestion that control should subsequently be extended to new houses and flats' (Kirkwood 1979, p.131). There was thus no immediate reason why landlords should not add to the stock of privately rented housing and indeed it is reported that between 1933 and 1939 over 60,000 houses per year were being built for private letting (DOE 1977b).

Nevertheless the 900,000 new homes to let, which were built in the interwar period, represented less than one quarter of all new construction. The same period saw the development of 1.1 million dwellings by local authorities and 2.9 million by private enterprise for both tenants and owner occupiers. Moreover, it has been suggested that even the figure of 900,000 had only been reached because an appreciable number of the homes built in the late 1930s for sale were later let to tenants because some developers 'had misjudged the vacant possession market' (Kirkwood 1979, p.131).

The net result of the absolute decline in the number of privately rented houses and the expansion of owner occupied and local authority tenures was that, relatively, the privately rented sector became less predominant. The widely reported figure of 90 per cent of the housing stock being privately rented at the outbreak of World War I had been reduced to 58 per cent by 1938 (Table 2.2), a trend which was to accelerate in later years.

Table 2.2
The privately rented sector (England and Wales)

| Date | Number (millions) | Percentage of the total stock |
|------|-------------------|-------------------------------|
| 1914 | 7.1 | 89.8 |
| 1938 | 6.6 | 58.0 |
| 1951 | 6.4 | 52.0 |
| 1960 | 4.6 | 31.0 |
| 1966 | 3.9 | 24.0 |
| 1971 | 3.3 | 19.0 |
| 1976 | 2.8 | 15.0 |
| 1981 | 2.5 | 13.0 |

Sources: DOE (1977b); Housing and Construction Statistics

## THE SECOND WORLD WAR

An act in 1938 was intended to extend block decontrol but any thoughts of a quick return to market determined rents were abruptly terminated with the imminence of the War. The Rent and Mortgage Interest Restrictions Act of 1939 was designed to prevent any repetition of the rent increases and subsequent civil unrest which had occurred in 1915. With a few exceptions all unfurnished privately rented dwellings were controlled and rents fixed at their September 1939 levels. For houses which were already controlled these were for the most part 1914 rent levels plus 40 per cent, and for other houses their actual levels at that date. The act thus fossilised the inconsistencies in the rent structure which had developed as a result of control, decontrol and new housing not subject to control. Even ten years earlier there had been numerous cases of very different rents being charged for very similar houses (Lewis 1965), but now the situation was exacerbated. In addition, whereas rent control may be logical in certain circumstances, the tying of controlled levels to those a quarter of a century earlier was clearly a dubious concept. 'The price of something in 1914, a house or anything else, can be of little practical interest in 1939 or 1943' (Bowley 1945, p.201).

If anything the housing shortage in 1945 was probably even greater than that in 1915. On the one hand there had been considerable reduction of the housing stock. As a result of enemy action about half a million dwellings had either been destroyed or were beyond practical repair. Many more houses had been damaged. The deterioration of the housing stock, aggravated by insufficient maintenance both before and during the war, contributed to the slum clearance problem which was estimated at a further half million dwellings (Berry 1974). On the other hand, considerable new household formation together with increases in the birth rate had taken place: a boom in marriages in 1939 and 1940 being followed by baby booms in 1942 and 1946-1947.

Even before the end of hostilities attention had turned to the problems of reconstruction. Amongst others, Lord Ridley was appointed to chair his second committee set up to consider the system of rent control. The committee agreed that in the light of the shortages it would be necessary to extend rent control for a considerable period. An additional concern was expressed that, rather than tying rents to some historic level (1914 or 1939) and then allowing percentage increases to cover maintenance costs and inflation, a new system should be devised. The proposal was that rent tribunals should be established for determining 'fair rents' for unfurnished dwellings. In the event, the Landlord and Rent (Rent Control) Act of the same year retained the existing basis for rents in the unfurnished sector.

However, as in the period immediately following the First World War, the major impetus of the government's policy for

housing lay with the construction of as many new houses as
possible. Quite apart from housing, the building industry was
faced with the burden of providing other buildings such as
factories and schools: a problem compounded because building
materials were in short supply and prices generally had risen
over their 1939 level. The government chose to implement a
system of controls and licences in order to regulate the
allocation of scarce resources with the major responsibility
being placed on the shoulders of the local authorities.
Bevan's 1946 Housing Act made local authorities eligible for
large central government subsidies on each house built, and in
addition made finance available from the Public Works Loan
Board at low rates of interest. The immediate response was
tardy 'for the whole economy was out of gear, and industry was
not immediately able to supply the materials and components'
(Lewis 1965, p.239). But the combination of subsidies to
local authority development and restrictions on the private
sector did nothing to encourage the private landlord to reduce
the shortage.

Although by 1951 almost a million dwellings had been built
the census revealed that the number of households exceeded the
number of dwellings by rather more than one million. In these
circumstances any relaxation of rent control would have been
followed by large increases in rent. Nevertheless there was
mounting pressure for reform of rent legislation (Greve
1965). This arose not least because nothing had been done to
eradicate the injustices and inconsistencies in rent levels
which had been apparent a decade earlier so that tenants of
identical houses were still sometimes paying different rents.
But important too was the state of repair of the privately
rented stock. Post war inflation in prices generally, and in
costs of building, repairs and maintenance in particular, made
the fixed returns to landlords lower in real terms than in
earlier years. Even in these circumstances many landlords did
carry out repair work and consequently 'made a loss over the
year' (Greve 1965, p.16). But many did not carry out such
work nor had they done so over the previous decades. And by
the start of the 1950s the bulk of the privately rented
sector, which had after all been built before 1914, was old.
The age of the dwellings combined with years of neglect meant
that 'they needed a good deal of money spent on repairs if
they were not soon to be demolished' (Greve 1965, p.16).

The same reduction in real terms in the rents which
landlords could charge must also be seen against the
background of increasing prices in the owner occupied sector.
House prices, with vacant possession, had risen markedly and
the inducement to sell, rather than to continue to let, was
even higher than it had been in the 1930s (DOE 1977b). The
result was that sales to owner occupation over the period
1938-1960 amounted to some 1.5 million dwellings, almost one
quarter of the 1938 stock (Table 2.1). By 1951 the sector had
declined to 52 per cent of the nation's total housing stock
and by 1960 to only 31 per cent (Table 2.2).

31

Against this background of growing concern about the fortunes of the privately rented sector the output of the building industry had increased. The 1951 General Election had been won by a Conservative government pledged to an expanded housing programme of 300,000 new dwellings per year. Subsidies to local authorities were increased and the system of licencing used to allow more private sector involvement. Success was immediate with the 300,000 target being surpassed by 1953. That year, and the following, were the peak years for the construction of council housing, achieving figures which have never been approached since. Over the decade 1951-1961 the housing stock increased by over two and a half million houses, the net result being that 'in terms of national aggregates, the housing shortage was all but over' (Lewis 1965, p.251).

As early as 1953 attention had begun to focus on the issue of housing condition in terms of both state of repair and lack of basic amenities. The White Paper (MHLG 1953) identified two causes for the poor standards in the privately rented sector. First, licencing of building work and materials since the war had restricted the carrying out of all the necessary improvements. Second, rent control, by not giving sufficient returns to landlords, often meant that they could only undertake improvement work at their own expense.

The white paper also referred to the 'hopelessly illogical system of rents' (MHLG 1953, p.6) which had developed by this time. Some properties, often the worst in terms of standard, had been first controlled in 1920 or before and never decontrolled. Their 'old control' rents were generally the lowest. 'New control' properties which had been brought under control since 1939 included some new tenancies - those let for the first time after 1939 - and some whose rents had been reviewed by rent tribunals. The result was that:

'...tenants are paying very different rents for identical houses in the same street - it may be for adjoining houses: and also that while many rents of essentially sound houses are very low, too low for it to be possible for the landlord to execute repairs out of rent, others are higher than had generally been supposed' (MHLG 1953, p.6).

As on numerous previous occasions the government's dilemma was based on the difficulty of decontrolling rents in the presence of a 'severe housing shortage'. But neither was an across the board percentage increase in rents deemed desirable on the grounds that it 'would accentuate all the anomalies' (MHLG 1953, p.7).

Following the report of the Girdwood Committee which had been concerned with the problem of the poor state of repair in the sector, the 1954 House Repairs and Rents Act was passed. This permitted limited increases in the rents of properties which had been let before September 1939 and which had been maintained or put into a good state of repair. The intention was to renew the incentive to landlords to add to the stock of dwellings since any built or converted after 29 August 1954 were excluded from the rent restriction acts. All this had taken place in the context of a changing public attitude toward the housing problem. Berry (1974, p.53) wrote of the period:

> 'By the mid to late 'fifties public opinion was shifting. Housing was no longer undisputed king. There were great difficulties in the immediate post-war years but everyone was agreed on a fundamental policy which was to get as many houses built as possible and to see that they went to the people who needed them most. It had been an emergency situation, but one that by 1956 had been going on for ten years and one cannot go one for ever thinking in terms of emergency. Moreover, the view was gaining ground that the crude shortage of houses, at any rate, was virtually over and that a surplus ..... was just around the corner'.

There was also a continuing debate about the wider role of government in housing. There was general agreement that housing was 'to some extent a social service' (Barnett 1969, p.36). But there was a change in emphasis during the 1950s, with the Conservative government gradually placing less reliance on the public sector and more reliance on the private sector (Banting 1979).

## THE RETURN OF DECONTROL

New legislation in the form of the 1957 Rent Act took the privately rented sector further along the path of decontrol and higher rents. It introduced block decontrol of those houses with higher rateable values although there was to be a period of 15 months during which rent increases could only be made with the consent of the tenant. For other properties 'creeping' decontrol was possible if the landlord obtained vacant possession. Landlords of properties remaining under control could raise rents by certain amounts dependent on their responsibility for repairs and decorations.

Examination of the formulation of this policy and its course through Parliament indicates that those concerned did not base their conclusions on factual knowledge of the social and economic nature of the housing system, but on 'political symbolism in which myths about landlords and tenants defied rational discussion' (Barnett 1969, p.1). The debates themselves were characterised not by analysis of the failures and working of the market place, but by rhetoric, so much so that 'arguments presented by one side were incomprehensible to the other' (Barnett 1969, p.159). On the Conservative side decontrol was deemed to be feasible because any shortage had been all but eliminated. They appeared to have little understanding of the effect of decontrol on the many poor tenants, but equally the 'Labour opposition never confronted the genuine difficulties of the landlord' (Barnett 1969, p.159).

Enoch Powell, Parliamentary Secretary to the Ministry of Housing and Local Government, opening for the government on the second reading of the bill, echoed statements forty years earlier when he argued that rent control had been a 'product of the temporary derangement of the relationship between demand and supply which the war inevitably brought with it' (Hansard (560) 1760). The circumstances of the day however were, as he argued, that the house building achievements since 1945 had been of such an order that the gap between supply and demand was closing: 'I think we are now within sight of, and should in 12 months' time or so be level with, an equation of the overall supply and demand for homes' (Hansard (560) 1760).

Not only had the raison d'etre of rent control come to an end, or at least was shortly to do so, but it was 'becoming productive of greater and greater and widely recognized evils' (Hansard (560) 1761). Powell argued that there were five 'evils' which were a direct product of rent control and which could be easily righted by the return to a free market. Firstly, there was the waste of accommodation brought about because low rents provided an incentive for sitting tenants to stay put even when the household had shrunk in size. Many large dwellings, it was claimed, were thus occupied by small households. Neither was sub-letting encouraged by the rent acts since this could result in the creation of a protected tenant. Secondly, the level of rents gave every incentive to landlords, on obtaining vacant possession, to put the house up for sale rather than to relet at a controlled rent.

Thirdly, there was the problem of immobility amongst those in controlled tenancies, who often had to choose between staying where they were or moving to another place where they might have been unable to find suitable alternative accommodation but 'must seek furnished accommodation until they can get to the head of the council waiting list in the place to which they have gone' (Hansard (560) 1762). The fourth problem arising from rent control was that it was one of the main factors in the disrepair of property since controlled rents commonly failed to provide a sufficient return to enable the landlord to carry out even essential works. Powell's final 'evil' related to the 'injustice of the whole system':

'There is the injustice between tenant and tenant occupying identical property rented entirely differently for no reason whatever except the vagaries of rent control. There is the injustice arising from the fact that there is no relation between the size of the property and its rent. There is the injustice arising from landlords being called upon in many cases, by rent restriction, to subsidize the incomes of tenants who are better off than they are' (Hansard (560) 1763).

The solution to these 'evils' was seen in the phasing out of rent control, and thus 'the creation of a really free market in housing accommodation' (Hansard (560) 1820). An equality would be achieved between the tenures so that there would be 'no difference between the value of the house with vacant possession and the house with tenants' (Hansard (560) 1767). Without regulation the market itself would thus overcome the present difficulties. Market level rents were also considered to generate acceptable levels of profit.

It was expected that 4 million houses would remain controlled under the act and that their tenants would continue to enjoy security of tenure. However it was to be made possible for landlords, subject to their maintaining the house in an adequate state of repair, to increase rents to some multiple of the 1956 gross value. The basing of rents on gross value would, Powell argued, provide 'for the first time some means of bringing into uniformity the gross variations at present between controlled rents. It will eliminate the existing unfairness and anomalies since, for the first time, we have got a nationwide valuation of the 1939 rental of dwelling houses' (Hansard (560) 1771).

At first the 1957 Act made little impact, except on those landlords and tenants directly concerned with individual cases (Burke 1981). As far as it was monitored, the act did not appear to be achieving its objectives. It did not, as had been its stated intention, increase the supply of rented accommodation. On the one hand neither new construction nor conversion was significant in scale, whilst on the other hand sales to owner occupation and demolitions each accounted for about 150,000 dwellings between 1958 and 1964 (Barnett 1969). In many cases therefore landlords were using the freedom of the act not to raise rent returns but to extricate themselves from the industry before this was again prevented by a future Labour government. At the same time whatever rent rises resulted from the act either as a result of decontrol or of allowable increases for houses continuing in control, they did nothing to alter the unfavourable tax and subsidy position of the landlord.

Neither did the act 'redistribute the existing housing on a more rational basis' (Barnett 1969, p.245). In part this was because the continuing shortages encouraged many tenants to hold on to their tenancies rather than to attempt to find more suitable alternatives in a shrinking market. In addition households were splitting up into smaller sized units more rapidly than had been expected as a result in particular of 'demographic changes such as earlier marriage and greater independence in old age' (Banting 1979, p.18). The end of the housing shortage, far from being just around the corner as Powell had claimed, was receding faster than ever. There were some improvements in the general level of repairs but this was still inadequate given the extremely dilapidated condition of much of the stock (Beirne 1977). Those in the privately rented sector continued to be housed in conditions inferior to the average level in other tenures. Even the expectations regarding the direct effects of block decontrol proved to be inaccurate. It had been estimated that some three-quarters of a million dwellings would be immediately decontrolled but the figure was in fact less than 400,000. The rate of decontrol following vacant possession was, on the other hand, greatly underestimated, witnessing to the level of ignorance on which the legislation had been founded (Barnett 1969).

Despite the failure of the legislation to achieve its objectives there was still some expectation that private landlords could be encouraged to expand their operations, if not directly by freedom from rent control then by example. The funding of housing associations under legislation enacted in 1961 set the lead to be followed:

'As an experiment, the Government propose to make arrangements under which money will be advanced to approved non-profit making housing associations which are prepared to build houses to let at economic rents. They regard this as essentially a pump-priming operation and hope that it will serve to show the way to the investment of private capital once again in building houses to let' (MHLG 1961, p.10).

But the emphasis of the debate was soon to shift markedly. The impact of the decontrolling legislation became gradually more apparent particularly where housing stress was at its greatest in London and the South East. Studies by academics and debates in Parliament did much to highlight the nature of housing problems. Reinforcing this criticism of government policy was a public scandal which linked a Secretary of State indirectly to one of London's more notorious landlords, Perec Rachman. The accompanying furore, fuelled by the media 'fixed general exploitation in the image of the private rented sector' (Banting 1979, p.26).

The setting up of a committee in 1963, under the chairmanship of Sir Milner Holland:

'to survey the housing situation in Greater London with particular reference to the use, maintenance and management of rented accommodation, whether privately or publicly owned, and to the relations between the occupiers of rented accommodation and private landlords'

did much to provide a more objective picture of the operation of the sector. It also illuminated some of the financial problems facing the landlord. Although the private landlords were finding themselves 'more and more concerned with those who have an average or below average income' (Milner Holland 1965, p.41) the lack of tax subsidies from the state meant that 'we have the situation of the higher rents being charged in that market in which we find the people with the lower incomes' (Milner Holland 1965, p.41). In a series of calculations the committee demonstrated that even when landlords were making the 'minimum possible return' on their investment the resulting rents were considerably higher than in other tenures. Table 2.3 shows that for a house which could be supplied for a cost of £5500 a local authority at that time would have needed to charge a rent of £3-3s-8d. to cover costs, a housing association a rent of £7-14s-1d., and an owner occupier a net monthly repayment of £6-7s-6d. The private landlord, however, would have needed to have charged a rent of £10-1s-8d.

The reason for this divergence arose 'solely from the fiscal burdens imposed on the landlord, and the limited availability of capital to him' (Milner Holland 1965, p.43). What this meant was that in comparison with the privately rented sector, and as a result of a series of measures introduced at various times, other tenures received preferential treatment by central government. In a variety of ways they received subsidies which were not enjoyed by the private landlord or the private tenant. Thus local authorities were able to charge lower rents because of a combination of exchequer subsidies, their ability to pool debts on old and cheaper houses with new and more expensive houses, and transfers from the general rates. Housing associations and owner occupiers received other advantages.

In practice rent control frequently meant that landlords would not be able to charge the higher rent, but the calculations of Table 2.3 show that even if they were in a position to do so, that is that rent control were removed, potential tenants might prefer the lower costs of other tenures. The result as the committee indicated was that, unless some way could be found of placing landlords in a similar subsidy position to those in other tenures, their attention would be more and more diverted to other forms of investment. Indeed the committee reported that 'the supply of privately rented accommodation in Greater London was diminished and is still diminishing fast' (Milner Holland 1965, p.227).

The report went on to argue that given existing parameters the result was an 'insoluble problem'. Tenants on the one hand expected to be able to rent accommodation at least as cheaply as they could buy it, whereas those people who viewed landlordism as a source of income or profit would be concerned to achieve returns which were commensurate with those available elsewhere. The result, as the committee argued, was 'an atmosphere of tension between landlords and tenants' which 'makes the negotiation of "fair" or "reasonable" rents quite unnecessarily difficult' (Milner Holland 1965, p.44).

Table 2.3
Illustration of the weekly cost of accommodation under
various types of owner

| | Total cost of dwelling | | | | | |
|---|---|---|---|---|---|---|
| | £5,500 | | | £3,750 | | |
| | £ | s | d | £ | s | d |
| Local authority (a) | 3 - | 3 - | 8 | 2 - | 7 - | 0 |
| Housing association (b) | 7 - | 14 - | 1 | 5 - | 9 - | 0 |
| Private landlord (c) | 10 - | 1 - | 8 | 7 - | 1 - | 6 |
| Owner occupier (d) | | | | | | |
| Before tax relief | 8 - | 13 - | 1 | 5 - | 18 - | 4 |
| After tax relief | 6 - | 7 - | 6 | 4 - | 7 - | 0 |

(a) Local authority rent set by LA owning dwellings in the two
examples
(b) 60 year loan at 6 per cent with £30 a year allowed for
repairs and management
(c) 9 per cent gross return with no allowance for repairs
(d) 25 year loan at 6 per cent with no allowance for repairs

Source: Milner Holland (1965) Table 3.16

The committee also presented evidence of the extent of
hardship and abuse in the sector. The acute shortage of
rented housing in London was resulting in hardship for a
substantial number of households in the form of overcrowding,
multiple occupation and lack of facilities. Although the
evidence suggested to the committee that the 1957 Act had not
been followed by 'any general excessive increases in rents'
(Milner Holland 1965, p.47), there was 'much evidence to
suggest that some rents are being set at a very high level,
reflecting not only the overall shortage of accommodation, but
particularly the shortage of accommodation available to let to
poor families with young children. We have also obtained
evidence of exceedingly high rents being charged by landlords
letting to members of the minority groups, particularly
coloured immigrants' (Milner Holland 1965, p.47).

There was also evidence of cases of abuse, practised by
landlords on tenants, in such numbers that they could not be
'dismissed as isolated instances or in any way insignificant'
(Milner Holland 1965, p.176). The range of abuse was
extensive but generally related to the desire on the part of
the landlord to gain vacant possession (Table 2.4). The
increase in the capital values of residential properties,
fuelled in part by subsidies, was thus providing landlords
with incentives to mistreat tenants: the more unscrupulous,
though not necessarily the majority, appeared to do so.
Although the report was at pains to emphasize that the
incidence of excessive rents and abuses should not be
overstated in general terms it was significant because it
demonstrated that the 1957 Act had not removed injustice from

the relationship between landlord and tenant. Powell's stated objectives had not come to fruition and any hope that the sector would start moving in that direction was clearly not realistic.

## THE INTRODUCTION OF FAIR RENTS

By the time a Labour government came into office in 1964 rent policy was a political priority. The late Richard Crossman introduced a bill which in many senses was a compromise between the views traditionally held by the two sides of the House. Its starting point was that the market place did not need rigid control because the majority of landlords and tenants acted reasonably. What was needed was some mechanism whereby tenants could be protected from the worst excesses of the few unscrupulous landlords, and whereby landlords were granted small regular increases in rent. The bill did not therefore come down wholly on the side of either the tenant or the landlord. The tenant was to be promised security of tenure, for which the landlord was to receive a rate of return on his investment which at least contained an inflationary element. Not only was the bill a compromise but many of the mistakes of the 1957 Act were so evident that there had been an 'ideological convergence in rent policy' (Banting 1979, p.58). It was thus difficult, even if thought desirable, for the bulk of MPs from both main parties to oppose the bill. Reinforcing this was the fact that leading professional experts were unable to offer viable alternatives (Banting 1979).

The 1965 Rent Act extended the protection of rent acts in the inter war period, not by bringing more dwellings under control, but by creating a system of rent regulation. This applied to unfurnished dwellings with rateable values in 1963 of not more than £400 in Greater London and £200 elsewhere, and which were outside the rent control system as a result of decontrol under the 1954 and 1957 Acts. The act thus created a dual system of control and regulation. The essential difference between the new and the old systems has been outlined by Donnison (1967, p.266):

'Unlike rent control, which was designed to freeze a market thus eventually depriving its prices of any systematic or constructive meaning, rent regulation is designed to recreate a market in which the overall pattern of prices responds to changes in supply and demand, while the local impact of severe abnormal scarcities is kept within bounds.'

Table 2.4
Type of abuse

|  |  | % of total abuses reported |
|---|---|---|
| 1 | Tenants illegally turned out of or excluded from their homes | 4 |
| WITH THE OBJECT OF SECURING VACANT POSSESSION TENANTS SUBJECTED TO: | | |
| 2 | Assault | 4 |
| 3 | Interference with their accommodation or its services | 14 |
| 4 | Interference with the tenant's personal possessions | 5 |
| 5 | Deliberate introduction of unwelcome or undesirable tenants into other accommodation in building | 2 |
| 6 | Any other deliberate or persistent annoyance | 14 |
| 7 | Threat of 1 to 6 | 17 |
| 8 | Tenants tricked or misled into having controlled accommodation | 1 |
| 9 | Rents in excess of controlled rent obtained by threats or other improper means | 1 |
| 10 | Exorbitant rents demands as the alternative to eviction | 7 |
| 11 | Deliberate withholding of rent books or the information which should be shown in them | 18 |
| 12 | Any other form of abuse, persecution, ill-treatment or unfair practices to which tenants have been subjected | 13 |

Source: Milner Holland (1965) Table III.2

Rent regulation thus introduced a system of 'fair rents', which were quasi market rents subject to the amendment that landlords were restricted from taking 'unfair' advantage of the existence of shortages to achieve exorbitant profits. This was achieved by statutorily defining criteria for determining fair rents and by setting up machinery to make the determinations. The precise nature of these will be discussed later, and for the moment it is necessary to note only that those involved in the sector had the right to an independently arbitrated rent. Thus central to the 1965 Act was the principle that the onus was on the parties concerned to approach the rent officer service. It was believed, and indeed the Milner Holland Report which was published during the drafting of the legislation expressed the view, that most landlord tenant relationships and their agreed rents were satisfactory. It was only in those cases where one or other was particularly dissatisfied that the rent officer service would be called into operation. Following from this the legislation was based on the individual assessment of rent and not some national standard such as the 1939 rent plus some percentage increase.

Although the fair rent legislation had achieved a measure of protection to curb some of the worst excesses of the market there were those who argued that it was little more than a 'holding operation in a decaying sector of the housing market' (Banting 1979, p.65). Many of the poorest members of society were trapped in a sector which by 1966 had already declined to 24 per cent of the nation's housing stock. Whereas for the nation as a whole the future lay in owner occupation and council housing these alternatives were not open to everyone. In the meantime it was necessary to strengthen the legal protection of tenants. The act did not go as far as the stated objectives of the 1957 Act: it provided little incentive to build new houses, to improve existing ones or to get a better fit between stock and tenants (Banting 1979, p.65).

Since 1965 more and more of the privately rented sector has been brought into the fair rents system. The 1969 Housing Act provided for the transfer of a letting from a controlled tenancy if the dwelling was in a good condition and contained all the basic amenities. The 1972 Housing Finance Act extended the transfer from control to regulation by providing for the gradual conversion of the remaining controlled tenancies over a two year period on the basis of rateable value. It excluded from this process, however, houses which were unfit. This act also sought to extend the fair rents principle to public sector housing. In the White Paper which had preceeded it (DOE 1971) it was argued that the level of public sector rents varied 'unfairly'. The variation was attributed to the housing subsidy schemes operated by central government; the age structure of each authority's stock; and rent pooling. The act laid down procedures for determining local housing authority fair rents which were similar to those set for privately rented houses. Opposition to the legislation and the substantial rent increases which it would have meant for many tenants was considerable (Beirne 1977) and the legislation was largely repealed in the 1974 Rent Act. The introduction of rent rebates for local authority tenants and rent allowances for tenants of unfurnished privately rented accommodation whose incomes were below certain standards was retained, however.

In the meantime a committee had been appointed under the chairmanship of Mr. Hugh Francis, to review the operation of the system of rent regulation particularly in the large centres of population, and the relationship between the furnished and unfurnished lettings codes. The general tenor of the committee's conclusions was that the system was working fairly well. Its 36 recommendations were, in the main, minor amendments to the existing system rather than fundamental reforms.

Interestingly, in the light of the weight of empirical evidence that had emerged, the committee argued that 'lettings of newly erected dwellings be taken out of regulation

altogether' (Francis 1971, p.119) on the grounds that it would
encourage new investment. It is a reflection on the
persistency of this particular myth that the cogent arguments
contained in a minority report by Lyndal Evans did not sway
the committee.

Of particular concern to the committee was the assimilation
of the furnished and unfurnished codes. The Rent Acts of 1965
and 1968 had excluded furnished dwellings from the definition
of regulated tenancies as a result of which there had 'been a
significant "switch" on the part of landlords from letting
unfurnished to letting furnished' (Francis 1971, p.83). The
addition, sometimes of only a few sticks, of furniture meant
that landlords could generally obtain both a higher rate of
return and easier vacant possession. Analysis of newspaper
advertisements carried out for the committee demonstrated the
extent of the 'switch' (Table 2.5) with the ratio of
unfurnished to furnished flats and houses declining from 9:10
in 1963 to 1:20 in 1970.

Table 2.5
Lettings advertised in London Weekly Advertiser

|  | Furnished | | Unfurnished | | Unfurnished as % of furnished | |
|---|---|---|---|---|---|---|
| Lettings | 1963 | 1970 | 1963 | 1970 | 1963 % | 1970 % |
| Rooms | 1,114 | 867 | 39 | 12 | 4 | 1 |
| Flats and houses | 855 | 1,290 | 767 | 66 | 90 | 5 |

Source: Francis (1971)

This anomaly was remedied by the 1974 Rent Act which
extended regulation to the furnished sector. However it
created a new distinction between resident and non-resident
landlords by excluding those dwellings with a resident
landlord from the fair rent system. The rationale for this
distinction was related to the differences in the security of
tenure provided to tenants by the two systems. With the rent
tribunals which continued to have jurisdiction over resident
landlord dwellings it was possible for the landlord to obtain
possession relatively easily since the tribunals could not
confer general security of tenure. At their discretion they
could grant only temporary protection against a notice to
quit. The landlord of a regulated letting, in contrast, had
to overcome a number of legal hurdles before gaining
possession.

Although the 1974 Act extended the scope of the fair rent
service, it did not do, as its predecessors had not done,
anything to increase the size of the sector. Indeed faced
with the prospect of a reduced ability to obtain vacant
possession and of reduced rates of return, non resident
landlords often chose to extract themselves from the industry

as quickly as possible (Henney 1975). Even only a short time after the act had come on to the statute book the number of lettings in parts of London had been greatly diminished.

Since 1960 the decline of the sector had continued (Tables 2.1 and 2.2). In 1960 there had been some 4.6 million dwellings in England and Wales which had declined by over a third to 2.9 million in 1975. Almost a quarter of those dwellings existing in 1960 were sold to owner occupiers during the period and a further one sixth were demolished, generally as part of slum clearance programmes or changed use. On the positive side only 300,000 dwellings were added and these were not all the work of the traditional private landlord. It has been estimated that almost 100,000 were supplied by housing associations with a further 50,000 by local authorities for their own employees (DOE 1977b).

An indication of the growth of the different subsectors of private renting is provided by DOE estimates (Table 2.6). Within the context of a general decline over the period 1966-1976 the major reduction was in unfurnished lettings, which during the decade had almost halved. The furnished sector had increased, as has been seen earlier, often at the expense of the unfurnished lettings and as a direct result of differences during most of this period in the furnished and unfurnished codes.

By the mid 1970s there was again recognition by central government that the body of legislation dealing with the privately rented sector was unnecessarily complex and consolidation was a major concern of Labour's Rent Act Review. Cullingworth (1979, p.73), for example, noted that 'For the most part the stated objectives of the Rent Acts Review and the thirty six questions posed in the consultation paper are concerned with tidying up and rationalising the complex of controls.'

Table 2.6
Major subsectors of privately rented dwellings in
England and Wales

| Subsector | 1966 | | 1976 | | 1966-1976 |
|---|---|---|---|---|---|
| | Thousands | % | Thousands | % | % change |
| Housing associations | 130 | 3.5 | 250 | 9.0 | + 92.0 |
| Rented with job/ business and by virtue of employment | 800 | 21.5 | 700 | 25.1 | - 12.5 |
| Rented unfurnished | 2770 | 74.4 | 1490 | 53.4 | - 46.2 |
| Rented furnished | 25 | 0.7 | 350 | 12.5 | + 13.0 |
| Total | 3725 | 100.0 | 2790 | 100.0 | |

Source: DOE (1977) Table IX.1

43

Whereas the results of the review were never published the Government's Housing Policy Review (DOE 1977a) largely confirmed Cullingworth's view. It also indicated that the Labour government at that time had experienced an ideological shift over the privately rented sector which closed the gap between them and the Conservative opposition. Whilst reaffirming the government's commitment 'to the broad principle that private tenants of non-resident landlords should enjoy security of tenure, and that their rents should be restricted to reasonable levels' the review also considered measures for stimulating supply (DOE 1977a, p.72). Firstly it considered the possibility that guarantees of repossession might encourage some resident landlords and home owners temporarily absent from home to let property for short periods. Secondly, it was argued that assurances about rent increases over the long term 'might attract new investment with a publicly accountable letting agency' (DOE 1977a, p.74). Both these proposals, albeit modified, emerged in the 1980 Housing Act, but in the meantime the 1977 Rent Act indeed did little more than consolidate previous rent restriction acts. It made no major amendments to previous legislation and the dual system of rent control and rent regulation continued.

When a Conservative government was elected in 1979 a housing bill was soon drafted. Although when in 1980 it entered the statute books it was called a Housing Act, it might, because it contained important provisions affecting the privately rented sector, be more accurately described as a Housing and Rent Act (Arden 1980). The main thrust of the provisions relating to rented housing in some ways reflected the 1957 Act. There was a continued concern that the sector should not be allowed to slip further into oblivion. In the House, the Minister argued:

'The previous government regarded the private rented sector as being in a position of irreversible decline and they seemed happy that that should continue. We suggest that that is fearfully wasteful and a self-defeating policy... What is the sense of continuing to build additional rented housing in the public sector when at the same time, we are allowing private rented accommodation to disappear almost as fast' (Hansard (967) 350).

In addition to decontrolling all existing controlled tenancies and transferring them to regulated tenancies, the act introduced two new types of tenancy with the intention of increasing the size of the private rental sector. Assured tenancies were introduced to encourage investment by approved bodies in new residential dwellings to rent, the bait being the opportunity to charge market level rents. The intention of shorthold tenancies was to encourage people with empty property, who were discouraged from letting because of the security of tenure provisions of the fair rent service, to become landlords. The intention of these provisions is in effect to test 'whether some weakening of rent control and security of tenure... could stem the seemingly inexorable contraction of the sector' (Harloe 1980, p.30).

# 3 The fair rent system

As has been seen in the previous chapter, to the incoming Labour government in 1964 rent policy was a major priority. Decontrol under the 1957 Rent Act was widely viewed as disastrous and yet the limitations of control, or at least some of them, were also recognized. Banting's well researched analysis of the formulation of the 1965 Rent Act (Banting 1979) shows clearly that there was considerable agreement, stretching across both main political parties, about the nature of the problem. As with previous rent legislation this was identified by many as a specific, rather than a general, failing of market processes from which some tenants needed protection. Arising from this view of the problem the solution was seen as being located firmly within the private rental market as a mechanism regulating certain excesses of that market. To the extent that this was an internalisation of the solution within the confines of one tenure, like both control and decontrol before, it ignored the important linkages and relationships within the housing system as a whole. Equally it was consistent with a view that the tenure was irrevocably in decline, but that some mechanism was needed which would bring some order and regulation to the consequences of that decline.

Having perceived a parochial framework, however, the detailed solution was devised only slowly, with extensive deliberation and at times great doubt (Banting 1979). What was finally arrived at was vague and ambiguous. Perhaps because it was capable of different interpretations the bill passed through Parliament more quickly than it might otherwise have done. The ambiguity, however, has provided the means whereby anomalies or inconsistencies in rent level could be promulgated. In rejecting the use of some national standard in favour of individual assessment based on unspecified notions of the equitable treatment of individual landlords and tenants the service was not provided with clear and unambiguous directions. This extended not only to the formula for determining what a fair rent should be but also to the administrative procedures within which rent officers were to operate. The outcome has been that those working in the service have been given a system which by definition might be expected to produce consistent results but without the means to ensure it.

In this chapter these assertions will be substantiated by firstly examining the principles upon which the fair rent system is based and which contrast it with the earlier principles of rent control. This will be followed by a description of the administrative machinery and the rules which were set up by the 1965 Rent Act and subsequently modified and extended. The main emphasis is placed on the ambiguity inherent in the system with the intention of identifying the framework within which rent officers operate and within which fair rent determinations are to be understood. The objective therefore is to gain some understanding of how the system works, and to what extent and where it guides, and fails to guide, decisions about fair rents.

## FORMULATING THE PRINCIPLES

The task of formulating rent policy and guiding it through Parliament fell to the new Labour Minister of Housing, Richard Crossman. On coming to office he quickly sought the advice not only of his own civil servants but also of people outside the Ministry including Arnold Goodman and David Donnison. Although there was a good deal of agreement between the individuals concerned, at least on broad issues, this agreement needed to be translated into specific proposals. This took place over several months and the arguments set forward for different alternatives help to illuminate the nature of the formula which eventually emerged.

It quickly became clear that amongst those concerned with drafting the new legislation there was very little support for the reintroduction of rent control even if the freeze was to be followed by periodic rent increases. The general view being that this 'would have perpetuated and, over time, worsened a host of anomalies that had crept into the rent structure under progressive decontrol' (Banting 1979, p.46). An acceptable alternative was not immediately apparent. The introduction of a national standard or norm to which the fair rents could be tied was given serious consideration. In particular considerable thought was given to the use of rateable values as a basis upon which rents could be determined. The arguments against their use were strong. These values exhibited many of the deficiencies of rent control being expected to 'generate injustices and controversies' (Banting 1979, p.46). It was argued that there were always errors in the valuation list and that it was in any case too infrequently updated. The Valuation Office of the Inland Revenue which had the task of setting and updating the rateable values was also concerned that their use for rent purposes would lead to more numerous legal appeals (Banting 1979). Crossman was later to argue that any attempt to relate rents to rateable values was too broad brush an approach largely because their measurement 'makes such a gigantic number of assessments on the basis of evidence often incomplete and inconsistent' (Hansard (710) 42). His view was that any attempt to slavishly relate rents to such a base would only result in 'rigidity without justice' (Hansard (710) 42).

The alternative to some universal standard was individual assessment of individual properties. The advantage of this was that it was compatible with the dominant view that the market did not have to be rigidly controlled since most landlords and tenants reached reasonable and amicable agreements without external enforcement. What was required was that tenants would receive protection from eviction and against rents rising to exorbitant levels as a result of scarcities, whilst landlords could at least be assured of regular increases. The problem then was conceived as being how to provide protection from certain aspects of the market without destroying other aspects of the same market.

Having accepted this, attempts to produce a formula which was simple and straightforward and yet at the same time sensitive to the many differences between individual properties proved difficult (Banting 1979). It became apparent that any temptation to reduce fair rent determination to some mathematical calculation would not give sufficient consideration to the adjective 'fair'. What was needed, as it was later to be argued, was the application of common sense to a decision which involves the balancing of conflicting interests (Prophet 1976). The solution was the establishment of a principle that whereas a fair rent was to reflect the particular characteristics of a particular property it was to ignore any scarcity element. That is, that in determining a fair rent for a particular property it was to be assumed that the supply and demand for that type of property in that area were roughly in balance.

Thus fair rents were intended to resemble market rents in so far as they would reflect the value of the accommodation under consideration. As one of the members of the working party was later to write this meant that:

> 'If a purpose-built, centrally heated flat, standing in an attractive London neighbourhood, commands an annual rent of fifteen shillings per square foot, then a self-contained house, without central heating or bath, standing in a clean but unfashionable street, should command a lower rent, and two rooms opening off a landing in a house that stands in a sleazy quarter should command a yet lower rent' (Donnison 1967, p.266).

At the same time fair rents were intended to provide an alternative to rents fixed by the interaction of supply and demand. Indeed, if market processes were not to be superceded legislation would be pointless (Samuels 1973). Crossman emphasized the importance of this when he said in his introduction to the bill that: 'the whole purpose of rent regulation is to protect the tenant from the market. A formula which related the fair rent to current market values would make nonsense of the idea of regulating rents at all' (Hansard (710) 42). He went on to say that the legislation was 'specially designed to ensure that ... rents do not gravitate naturally upwards, in areas where scarcity inflates them, towards scarcity levels ... the tenants' guarantee that [it] will not operate unfairly against them' (Hansard (710)

44). This did mean however that the formula was, in one sense at least, a contradictory statement which both supported and opposed market rents.

One of the advantages of the type of rent control embodied in the earlier rent acts and of certain other national standards was that the process of determining or specifying the relevant rent was fairly straightforward. The problem of individual assessment was that potentially it involved the establishment of a huge bureaucracy faced with the task of arbitrating on each individual property. The solution was to propose a two-stage process. Firstly a rent officer, having considered representations from both landlord and tenant, would determine a fair rent. The emphasis was to be on informality and, whilst having regard to the nature of the property concerned, conciliation of opposing views. If, and only if, either party was dissatisfied with the rent officer's decision would they proceed to the second stage which was an appeal to be heard by a tribunal. The introduction of a rent officer would thus 'reduce the number of cases going to a full tribunal and the machinery could be smaller as a result' (Banting 1979, p.52). Indeed, because it was believed that most landlords and tenants already had reasonable and fair agreements, it was hoped that even application to rent officers would be limited.

The nature of the role to be performed by the rent officer led Crossman to believe that it was important for the right sort of person to be appointed. He referred frequently to the importance which he attached to personnel: 'we must get people of real quality and standing to do this important job' (Hansard (710) 48). Moreover, he argued that if the right sort of men and women were selected there would be no need 'to smother them in detailed legal and statutory instructions, but to define their job and then rely on their powers of judgement' (Hansard (710) 48).

Finally, there was also concern that the rent officer should be seen to be independent of political institutions. If landlords and tenants were to accept the rent officer's objectivity a minimum requirement was that neither local nor central government should be seen to influence either the general level of rents or the rent of a particular letting. At first Crossman wanted the service to be supervised and made responsible to local authorities since they were the only bodies which could quickly establish it. Eventually it was resolved that the 'local authority was to have no role in rent determination and the rent officer would not technically be a local authority employee' (Banting 1979, p.53).

## THE ADMINISTRATIVE PROCEDURES

The introduction of the principle of individual assessment of rents was accompanied by the establishment of new administrative structures and procedures. The administrative unit upon which the service is based is the registration area,

49

which, at the present time, is in turn based upon the local authority structure with each shire county, metropolitan county, London borough and the City of London constituting a registration area.

However although the local authority plays some part in setting up the service and providing some of the personnel, buildings and equipment which enable the work of the service to be carried out it is not a local authority service. It is not, for example, a local authority department such as the Housing or Planning Department, neither does it come under the jurisdiction of the elected representatives. A number of rent officers have been appointed to serve in each registration area, the number being jointly agreed by the Secretary of State for the Environment and the local authority concerned. They are employed subject to the same general conditions which apply to local authority staff and they are subject to the supervision of the clerk of the local authority.

The authority of the rent officer service extends only to certain parts of the privately rented sector. In 1965 this included unfurnished lettings below certain rateable values and which were not subject to rent control. The 1974 Rent Act extended protection to the furnished sector, whilst under statutes subsequent to 1965 more and more controlled lettings have gradually been brought into the system. Nevertheless many types of letting still remain outside the system; these include holiday lettings, agricultural premises, licensed premises, lettings with resident landlord, and lettings to students by specified institutions.

Either landlord or tenant (or both together) may apply to the rent service in the registration area in which the dwelling is located for the registration of a fair rent. The application is made on a prescribed form and must contain a statement of the rent which the applicant considers should be registered. This procedure puts the onus squarely on individual tenants and landlords to enlist the intervention of this aspect of the rent acts. This conforms with the view of the situation that most of the sector could be left to itself to reach reasonable agreements. It is additionally possible for the local authority to apply for registration of a rent: a course of action which it might pursue if, for example, it wished to avert any hostility by a landlord against one of his tenants who had applied.

Having received the application, the rent officer dealing with the particular case is required to decide whether or not the tenancy is a regulated one. Where the application has not been made jointly by the landlord and tenant the rent officer is required to inform the other party that an application has been made and offer an opportunity to make written representation.

If no written representation is made (which may occur because the application is joint) the rent officer can, if he so wishes, register a fair rent directly. In these circumstances neither landlord nor tenant has any right of appeal against the rent officer's decision. This is not always the case, however. Although not obliged to do so the rent officer will generally visit the premises and hold consultations with the two parties either at that time or at some other time and sometimes on neutral ground. At the consultation both the landlord and the tenant may be represented by anyone from a friend or relative to a solicitor or surveyor. The visit and the consultation may be used both to establish material facts, say about the nature of the accommodation, and to conciliate between the two parties.

Once these stages have been completed the rent officer is required to determine what the fair rent should be. He is guided in this by Section 70 of the 1977 Rent Act, the nub of which remains from the 1965 Rent Act amended to cater for the later incorporation of furnished properties and other, minor additions. Formally Section 70 states:

'(1) In determining, for the purposes of this Part of this Act, what rent is or would be a fair rent under a regulated tenancy of a dwelling-house, regard shall be had to all the circumstances (other than personal circumstances) and in particular to -

(a) the age, character, locality and state of repair of the dwelling-house, and

(b) if any furniture is provided for use under the tenancy the quantity, quality and condition of the furniture.

'(2) For the purposes of the determination it shall be assumed that the number of persons seeking to become tenants of similar dwelling houses in the locality on the terms (other than those relating to rent) of the regulated tenancy is not substantially greater than the number of such dwelling houses in the locality which are available for letting on such terms.

'(3) There shall be disregarded -

(a) any disrepair or other defect attributable to a failure by the tenant under the regulated tenancy or any predecessor in title of his to comply with any terms thereof;

(b) any improvement carried out, otherwise than in pursuance of the terms of the tenancy, by the tenant under the regulated tenancy or any predecessor in title of his;

(c) the provision in the locality after the material date of any new amenity or the

51

improvement after that date of any amenities already existing in the locality, where the amenity is provided or improved -

(i) at the cost of a person other than the landlord or a superior landlord or a predecessor in title of the landlord or a superior landlord or

(ii) by a body of public nature which is a superior landlord, in the exercise of functions of a public nature;

(d) any deterioration after the material date in the amenities of the locality (including the disappearance of any of them) other than a deterioration attributable to any act or omission of the landlord or a superior landlord or a predecessor in title of the landlord or a superior landlord; and

(e) if any furniture is provided for use under the regulated tenancy, any improvement to the furniture by the tenant under the regulated tenancy or any predecessor in title of his or, as the case may be, any deterioration in the condition of the furniture due to any ill-treatment by the tenant, any person residing or lodging with him, or any sub-tenant of his.

'(4) In this section 'improvement' includes the replacement of any fixture or fittings.

'(5) In subsection (3)(c) and (d) above 'the material date' means -

(a) where a rent is registered under this Part of this Act, the relevant date as defined in section 67(a) of this Act, and

(b) where no rent is registered under this Part 8th March 1971'.

On receiving notice of the fair rent which the rent officer has determined either landlord or tenant has the right of appeal to the Rent Assessment Committee (RAC). The committee is a tribunal whose members are drawn from a Rent Assessment Panel which consists of a number of people appointed by the Lord Chancellor or the Secretary of State for the Environment and operating in a Panel Area each of which covers a number of registration areas. For example, the London Panel Area embraces 33 registration areas, and the West Midlands Panel Area 11 registration areas. In all there are 16 panel areas responsible for England and Wales. Whenever an application for an appeal is made the President of the Panel appoints a committee which generally consists of a lawyer, as chairman, a valuer and a lay person.

The task of the committee is not to start with the rent determined by the rent officer and to decide whether his was the right or wrong determination. The committee and the parties concerned are supplied with documents relating to the case including the original application, written representations, and the rent officer's report to the committee. The committee has the right to ask for further information and the landlord and tenant to make further representations.

The committee may hold a hearing and it may inspect the premises, both being usual. If there is a hearing either party has the right to representation although, because the committee is a tribunal, and not a court of law, legal aid is not available. The committee is then faced with the same task as the rent officer, being required to apply Section 70 of the 1977 Rent Act to determine a fair rent. It may have more evidence in front of it and it may be able to take a wider perspective since it operates over a number of registration areas but its statutory guidance is the same. Once it has reached a decision however there is no further right of appeal except on a point of law.

Once a fair rent has been determined, either by the rent officer or the rent assessment committee, an entry is made in the rent register held in the relevant registration area. In addition to the registered rent the register will also contain details of the nature and character of the dwelling and certain particulars such as name and address of landlord, and liability for repairs. The amount of the registered rent is exclusive of rates whether the landlord or the tenant bears the cost, but is inclusive of the value placed on furniture and services if provided. The register will show separately the values attached to the latter.

The registration form fulfills functions in addition to that of formally recording the fair rent. Firstly it provides a document to which the public has full rights of access and on the basis of which the probable outcome of applying for a fair rent settlement can be decided. Secondly, the decisions themselves act as a 'list of comparables' to which rent officers can make reference in deciding subsequent cases. The register thus forms a continually updated benchmark against which each new fair rent can be tested. This has helped to ensure that within each area the basis of consistent output has been established.

Once a dwelling has been entered on the register the registration is usually operative for as long as the dwelling is let. This is irrespective of whether landlord or tenant changes. The registration is, therefore, related to the accommodation and not to the people involved. The level of fair rent can however be changed. Landlord, tenant or local authority can apply to have the fair rent redetermined.

Following the 1980 Housing Act no such application will normally be entertained within a two year period but it is possible either when landlord and tenant apply jointly, or when there has been some significant change in the material circumstances taken into account in determining fair rents such as the state of repair, the amount and quality of furniture. These rights to re-registration ensure that the landlord can charge rents which increase at regular intervals and that additionally he gains recognition, in the form of higher rents, for repairs and improvements which he carries out.

## VARIATION IN PRACTICE

The previous section has provided a description of administrative procedures laid down by statute and which give much of the appearance of being carried out uniformly and objectively. Indeed one common claim for the system is that it is exact and that rent officers have a simple and precise technical task to perform:

> 'Basically we are simply operating under the terms of the Act. There is not a great deal of flexibility' (Anon. 1978).

In fact there is considerable evidence of very wide variation in the way in which the system is operated, largely because the legislation leaves the details of many aspects to those working in the service. Although some common working policies have developed the level of discretion is such that many differences are apparent. Sir Sydney Littlewood, the first president of the London Rent Assessment Panel, indicated shortly after the introduction of the fair rents legislation that there were no statutory rules for committee procedure but that he, like other panel presidents, had 'laid down his own rules of procedure' (Littlewood 1967, p.3). In response to this it was at the time argued that these differences were regrettable when one had regard to the fact that 'this is a national system of rent regulation presenting enormous difficulties' (Scott 1967, p.58). It was a further cause for regret that although the panels were learning as they went along, 'the indications are that they are learning quite independently and contributing relatively little to each other's knowledge and experience' (Scott 1967, p.58).

Despite the passing of a decade or so of rent acts and DOE circulars there is still evidence of variation in practices and procedures throughout the country. In 1979 a working party, consisting of a number of practising rent officers and members of the DOE, was set up. Its terms of reference indicated that it was concerned with increasing productivity in the rent officer service. In the course of examining existing working procedures and methods, however, many variations were found between different areas (DOE 1980a).

The working party began its work by examining returns which

had been completed for each registration area in England and Wales, and which showed the proportion of the rent officers' time spent on various aspects of the work together with the cost per case. They found evidence of considerable variation:

'The overwhelming impression which we got from the information we gathered was one of variety: in almost every aspect of rent officers' work we found an enormous variation in practices and procedures across the country' (DOE 1980a, p.4).

The working party thus sought to identify the significant variations and to evaluate their effect on cost per case (which varied from £16 to £91), in order that recommendations to reduce the average cost per case might be made. There is nothing new about this variation in output: the Francis Report (1971) found that the average output in some areas was more than twice that in others. In the Birmingham/Warley/Solihull area of the West Midlands the average output per rent officer was about nine cases per week and in the East Midlands it was eleven. The average output in London and some other areas, however, was about five cases per week or even lower. In the course of evaluating the effects on cost the different practices were discussed.

Firstly, practice was found to vary on the method of allocation. In some registration areas senior rent officers allocate cases to rent officers whereas in others this is done by administrative officers. In some areas re-registration cases are allocated to the officer who dealt with them on the previous occasion, and in others this practice is deliberately avoided. Some registration areas are divided into geographical zones in each of which one rent officer operates.

Secondly, in many registration areas a rent officer visits each property to be assessed, and in some a referencer will also visit. Other areas, however, have different policies. Earlier the Francis Report had noted that in the panel areas of London and Devon & Cornwall the practice was to inspect premises after the hearing; in the rest of England inspections were carried out before.

Thirdly, the rent officer is statutorily obliged to arrange a consultation under certain circumstances:

'This statutory framework seems to allow for a variety of interpretations: we found that the percentage of cases on which consultations are held varies in different areas between 20 per cent and 100 per cent; and the percentage of the rent officer's time taken up by consultations varies from 10 per cent to 40 per cent' (DOE 1980a, p.5).

The returns also showed that no consistent picture emerged regarding the reasons given to explain why consultations were held. In one area it was said that 75 per cent of consultations were held because the rent officer considered that the rent applied for was not a fair rent, whereas in another area 80 per cent were held because one of the parties had made representations.

Fourthly, practice also varies considerably as regards the location of any consultation:

'In London in particular ..... a separate consultation is arranged at the rent office; in most other areas, particularly in rural areas, consultations are frequently held on the premises, usually at the same time as the inspection' (DOE 1980a, p.8).

These variations in practice epitomise the discretionary nature of the legislation. Whether or not they have given rise to anomalies and injustices in fair rents is not known. Nevertheless, in combination with the vagueness of the statutory formula they raise questions about this possibility and particular aspects of the administrative practices will be returned to later.

## VAGUENESS OF THE STATUTORY FORMULA

In addition to the variations evident in the administrative practices and procedures of different registration areas, the fair rents formula provides further licence for inconsistency of application. Section 70 of the 1977 Rent Act provides a fairly extensive statement of what would be a fair rent, but as Robson (1974,p.306) has pointed out 'all of this sounds pretty helpful but when they got down to it rent officers and rent assessment committees found that they were being asked to apply these special factors such as age, repair etc. in a vacuum'. Similarly the section has been criticized as providing a 'subjective test' (Samuels 1973, p.720) and of failing to give 'any concrete definition' (Morris 1970, p.947).

The problem arises because the entire act was based upon the word 'fair' which in turn was little more than a catchword encapsulating 'undefined views of equity' (Nevitt 1966, p.160). 'Fair' was a description which it was difficult not to endorse. It was not necessary for fair rent levels to be defined since by definition they were fair (Banting 1979). By retaining this ambiguity in that section of the bill which defined what a fair rent for a particular dwelling should be, however, the service was not provided with a basis for ensuring consistency.

Central to the definition of a fair rent is that (1) all circumstances, other than personal circumstances, must be considered, but that (2) it must be assumed that supply and demand are in balance. One way of interpreting these two subsections is that the first guides rent officers on the relative value of the fair rent: that is whether the fair rent for property x should be higher than, lower than or equal to the fair rents for properties y and z. The second subsection

56

may be interpreted as providing some guide to the absolute level of the fair rent: that is what the actual fair rent for property x should be. The first subsection then indicates that fair rents should be consistent with market rents in as far as they reflect the values of the dwellings under consideration, whereas the second instructs that the scarcity element should be discounted. The failure of the formula is, however, that beyond this commonsense interpretation its first subsection is of little help because it is excessively general, and its second is of little use because it is almost, if not entirely, meaningless.

Although the first clause refers the rent officers to 'all the circumstances', other than personal ones, the list of particular circumstances, viz. age, character, locality, state of repair and furniture if any, is short. It could have specifically included many others for which there were prima facie grounds for consideration such as size and facilities. However there is nothing in the legislation which would lead rent officers in general or in particular to concur with this. Neither is there anything in the legislation itself which would prevent rent officers from considering circumstances which other people might not think relevant.

The nub of this problem revolves around the words 'all the circumstances', unqualified except as to personal circumstances. This is clearly subject to the qualification that the circumstances must be relevant to the determination of a fair rent and the question must be asked : what circumstances are relevant? (Farrand 1978).

The question has been examined by Leach who argues that what circumstances are relevant depends on what has to be determined:
> 'Is it an amount at large to be paid as rent which, on an outside view, would be fair as between landlord and tenant in all the relevant circumstances (of which relevant in the hypothetical market postulated in [paragraph 2 of Section 70] would be one)' (Leach 1977, p.861).

If this view is correct then, Leach argues, the circumstances to be taken into account would be very wide ranging. In addition to those mentioned in Section 70, viz. age, character, locality, state of repair, furniture, and omitting personal circumstances, these would include:

> 'a market without rent control (since fixing a rent is the object of the exercise), the effect of inflation and economic conditions on a market virtually without scarcity, the cost to the landlord of repairs and services provided for the benefit of the tenant (this would affect any person as landlord and is not a personal circumstance, and in fairness the landlord should have the cost while the tenant receives the benefit), the extent to which other forms have been affected by economic conditions and governmental intervention (including tenants' incomes

generally but excluding rent allowances which are provided
to assist tenants, not to subsidise landlords), the effect
of domestic rents on the cost of living, the intrinsic
value of the property measured by current costs of
construction, the relative burdens of tenants and owner-
occupiers, and any other circumstances considered to have
any possible bearing on what the tenant ought to pay the
landlord for possession of the dwelling house in question'
(p.861).

He adds further that 'Except by the sheerest coincidence no
two people could be expected to arrive at the same answer in
any particular case, and such an unworkable formula cannot
have been intended' (p.861).

The second view of what has to be determined is 'the rent
which, having regard to the effect of all circumstances
relevant to the hypothetical market, the landlord could fairly
be expected to accept and the tenant fairly be expected to
offer' (Leach 1977, p.861). The different approach can be
illustrated by reference to the cost of repairs and services.
If a tenant expected a landlord to keep a dwelling house in a
decent state of repair and to continue to provide services he
should fairly be willing to meet the current cost of this as a
minimum rental offer. The landlord's position would be that
the rent which he could fairly expect would be determined by
the hypothetical market. Since the investment was his own
speculation he is not entitled to (although he may get) any
amount as a minimum simply as a matter of fairness.

Thus many of the circumstances relevant to the first view of
what is to be determined are irrelevant to the second view.
What should be followed on the second view is the ordinary
practice of estimating rental value, without consideration of
whether the rent was fair to landlord or tenant 'that being a
matter already appropriately taken into account in estimating
the rent fairly to be expected in the hypothetical market on
which the estimate is to be made' (Leach 1977, p.861).

Having arrived at this point there remains little guidance
in Section 70. The interpretation of equity has remained
undefined. The clause gives rent officers scope to adopt
subjective criteria rather than criteria determined by
legislation. In addition there is no indication regarding the
way in which the criteria are to be considered. That is, the
legislation itself does not specify whether locality and age,
for example, are to be considered of equal or unequal
importance; or whether an old house in a good locality is to
have a higher or lower rent than a new house in a poor
locality.

It is perhaps significant, however, that in drafting the
legislation the reliance on advice from people associated with
the property valuation profession is evident in that the
formula bears some resemblance to standard valuation criteria:

'....the two principal factors which influence the value of residential properties are (i) accommodation and (ii) situation. The prospective tenant or purchaser will consider the nature and extent of the accommodation offered, and will at the same time have regard to the situation of the property as it affects the general amenities of life, time of travel to work, proximity to schools and like matter' (Lawrance et al. 1971, p.173).

However as far as rented property is concerned this definition of value is not particularly helpful. This is because, whilst these factors are the important ones in practice, the most commonly recognised method of valuation is the comparative method by which properties are valued by reference to other similar properties (Turner 1977).

Leach (1977) has pointed to the parallels between the problems of defining fair rents and gross values, and to the fact that:

'The Valuation Office, with all the expertise at its disposal has admitted that valuation officers cannot perform the task of fixing gross values for residential hereditaments for the purpose of new valuation lists, since evidence of rents in a market free from rent restriction does not exist' (p.861).

Similarly, for most of the private rented sector there are no similar properties for which rent has been set in the market place - making fair rent determinations dependent on comparables. This assertion was contested in the evidence to the Francis Committee when it was claimed that it was possible to extrapolate from the market rents set for dwellings at the luxury end of the market. However because in many parts of the country outside London no significant luxury market exists such extrapolation may be difficult.

This lack of market comparables has an important consequence in providing a measure of consistency against which individual fair rent determinations can be judged. By resorting to the 'tone of the list' rent officers have been provided with a mechanism for ensuring that similar fair rents are determined for similar properties. Where the use of comparables is limited however is that reliance on them does not ensure that the fair rent is the correct one (Glynne Evans 1980). Indeed with many rents having been set by the rent officer system the comparables and subjective criteria are mutually supporting. There is no independent frame of reference for rent officer decisions. Once a 'wrong' assessment of a fair rent has been made and enters the list it will breed as many 'wrong' assessments as are based upon it (Beirne 1977). Thus any standard of consistency emanating from the list of comparables is not a standard with any foundation in fact or in theory.

In addition to the argument about correctness, the list of comparables is limited by its geographical boundaries. The administrative area for which comparables are sought, usually the registration area, will determine the area of consistency. If rent officers search for comparable properties only within their immediate area of employment then this device provides no means of ensuring consistency over a larger area. In practice this could mean that consistency is higher within registration areas than it is between them.

The second clause, commonly referred to as the 'scarcity' clause, was intended to prevent excessive profits occurring in conditions of extreme scarcity. Underlying this, therefore, was some notion that whereas it was perfectly reasonable for landlords to receive some profit from their investment, that beyond a certain point this might be at an unreasonably high level. Whatever the justice of this position a major difficulty is that of ascribing to it either theoretical or practical meaning. Firstly one might argue that in the absence of scarcity there should logically be zero rents (Brittan 1974). Scarcity is a prerequisite of the existence of a market: for any product to have a cash value it must, amongst other things, be limited in supply (Turner 1977). Secondly, if the clause is interpreted as postulating equal numbers of suppliers and demanders this can be consequent upon the rent levels charged. If rent officers set rents for luxury penthouse suites relatively low then one might expect more tenants to seek such accommodation than if the rents are set relatively high. Indeed the concept of the perfect market includes the characteristic that prices attain a level which just clears supply and which just satisfies consumers. If prices are too low then suppliers will not supply as much and if prices are too high consumers will demand less. Although there are well recorded imperfections in the housing market nevertheless this principle can broadly be expected to operate. The third difficulty, arising from these definitional problems, is that of actually measuring scarcity. It seems generally to have been the practice for rent officers to apply some standard discount, say 10 per cent or 20 per cent, on market rents as attributable to scarcity. Although these discounts were first adopted in 1966-67 their use continued despite 'abundant evidence of greatly increasing scarcity in recent years' (Samuels 1973, p.720).

Moreover, there are no real grounds for necessarily reading subsection (2) as saying that the market rent is a fair rent if there is no evidence of scarcity. The question is left entirely open and states no more and no less than that the effect of scarcity on rent levels is to be ignored (Scott 1967). Even if this were the case it is arguable whether or not there is a market for privately rented accommodation in any purposeful sense of the word: the numbers of privately rented dwellings have experienced so great a decline, have for so long been subject to rent restriction and are so diverse in nature. In these circumstances it is difficult to identify the 'normal' or market rents.

Other parts of the formula are similarly unenlightening. As

60

far as subsections (3) (c) and (d) are concerned, which state
that if amenities have changed locally for better or for worse
without the landlord's assistance since 1971 or the last
registered rent then such changes are to be disregarded, they
provide further illustration of the lack of precision with
which the rent officer is faced. 'These paragraphs ... do not
seem models of clarity' (Farrand 1978) and in particular fail
to give any meaning for either 'amenity' or 'locality'.

A consequence of the vagueness of the formula is that
perhaps the only all embracing definition is a tautological
one : that is that fair rent is determined in accordance with
Section 70 of the 1977 Rent Act. The failure to provide
specific guidelines then begs the questions of how they have
been translated into practice and whether the results are as
intended.

CONCLUSIONS

The establishment of a set of principles was founded on the
rejection of an extension of the rigidities of rent control
with its crude, across the board, increases in favour of the
flexibility of individual assessment. The corresponding
administrative and institutional arrangements were also
flexible and there is clear evidence of differences in
interpretation and implementation at the local level. Such
differences are not uncommon in housing legislation. Central
government has until recently given each local authority an
almost free hand to devise policies for its own area which are
sensitive to the particular needs and problems of that area as
well as its political leanings. This situation has sometimes
been defended on the grounds that local action is responsible,
through the ballot box, to local pressure (Merrett 1979) but
this is explicitly not the case with the fair rents system.
It thus operates with neither central nor local government
control over differences in implementation.

The flexibility of the fair rent formula itself appears to
be consequent upon the lack of a prior definition of what was
fair. Nevitt's criticism (Nevitt 1966) that the legislation
was based on ill-specified notions of equity has identified
what underlies debates about the circumstances relevant to the
fair rent determination. The failure to address these dilemmas
in a situation already containing contradictions may be a
source of some confusion and anger. If, as it does, the
system of housing subsidies discriminates against the
privately rented housing sector, for example, any
interpretation by landlords that fair to them means a rate of
return on their investments comparable with what they could
obtain elsewhere is doomed to failure. The fact is that, as
shown in Chapter 2, without subsidies tenants would be
expected to pay in rent sums which far exceeded net mortgage
repayments on the same property. If, on the other hand, what
was fair to landlords did not mean a guarantee of some minimum
return they may continue to leave the sector whenever the
opportunity to do so occurs. The frustration of landlords in

particular but also of tenants may thus be exacerbated by the failure to define fair not only in relation to privately rented housing but also in relation to other tenures.

The ambiguity of the system is also a consequence of the onus having being placed squarely upon individual tenants and landlords to explicitly enlist the intervention of the rent acts. This procedure follows from the view of the situation that most of the sector could be left to itself to reach reasonable agreements. But if tenants are ignorant of the rent acts or for some reason reluctant to call upon them they are exposed to the very exploitation which the rent acts were intended to avoid. Evidence that this does indeed occur, and on a large scale, will be presented later. It is sufficient at this point to restate that the rational rent structure which the legislation was intended to achieve is dependent upon legislation which embodies considerable levels of flexibility and discretion.

# 4 The rules and methods of fair rent determination

As soon as the fair rent system came into operation its
personnel were faced with applications from landlords and
tenants for the determination and registration of fair rents.
In 1966 almost 30,000 applications were made, and during the
period up to June 1970 they totalled almost 200,000. The
number of applications each year increased rapidly,
particularly as a result of widening the scope of the rent
acts, so that by the end of the 1970s about 300,000
applications were being dealt with each year. The service was
thus at once, and continually, faced with the problem of
giving some operational meaning to the guidance about the
determination of fair rents contained in the rent acts.

Given the discretion built into the fair rents formula and
other aspects of the system it is relevant to ask how this
discretion has been translated into practice. In other words,
what methods, rules and procedures have rent officers adopted
to enable them to make determinations. As important as how
the work was and is carried out is what the results of these
methods and procedures are. Do fair rents, as intended,
differ from controlled rents and from rents set in the market
place? Do they, at the same time, also reflect rents in the
market place in that they are related to the value of the
accommodation? Do bigger houses in good locations receive
higher determinations than smaller houses in poor locations,
and so on?

In fact there has been remarkably little evidence of the
methods and rules which have been adopted. As will be seen in
Chapter 6 the courts have continued to defend the rent
officer's right both to use whatever method or methods he
chooses and not to have to disclose what they are or what
information he uses. Rent officers themselves are often
reluctant to discuss their methods except in the most general
terms. What evidence there is however points strongly to the
significant position of the method of comparables which refers
to the practice of setting the rent of one property in
relation to the rents already set for other similar
properties.

## THE METHOD OF COMPARABLES

When the Francis Committee examined the work of the rent
officer service it found, not surprisingly, that operational
procedures had been devised. Moreover, subsection (1) of the

statutory formula instructing rent officers to have regard for all the circumstances other than personal ones appeared, because it resembled straightforward property valuation criteria, 'to present no difficulties in practice' (Francis 1971, p.57). The committee went on to state, however, that rather more difficulty had been experienced with the scarcity clause. The initial practice in many areas had been to assess scarcity as some percentage, say 10 per cent or 20 per cent of the market rent, and to deduct that to arrive at the fair rent. Over a period of a few years this method was gradually superceded by a threefold approach:

(1) Over time the rent officers built up a record of fair rents assessed for different dwellings in their area. Taking account of changing circumstances these comparables could be used as guidelines for dwellings currently under consideration.

(2) Market rents negotiated for properties in respect of which there was no scarcity were used as a guide to fair rents for other property. Commonly this meant examining the character and market rents of expensive property on the apparent assumption that since not many people wished to consume expensive property there was no scarcity. Subject to extrapolation these market rents could then be used as guidelines for less expensive property.

(3) Reasonable rents, based on various conventional valuation criteria such as return on capital, economic cost or gross value, were calculated.

The fair rent would then be determined as some amalgam or compromise between the results produced by these different methods. In reality, it is unclear how these methods actually differ from one another. The method of comparables depends on the setting of rents whose levels reflect precedents set by the other two methods. The differences between methods (2) and (3) are blurred because the market rents for very expensive property might be thought to reflect market rates of return on capital and economic cost (Beirne 1977).

Macey (1972) has provided an example of the way in which fair rent determinations are made. Also based on the method of comparables it is justified on the grounds that the valuation of domestic property is much like the valuation of any other commodity:

'Just as one can study the records of the selling price of second-hand cars and decide fairly closely the value of a particular car, so one can study rental values and decide within fairly close limits the value of a particular house' (Macey 1972, p.14).

According to Macey, therefore, a central feature of the rent officers' method is the practice of identifying a number of properties which are similar in most aspects, and then 'trading off' the advantages of one against the fair rent determined:

'The rent officer looked at rents already agreed ..... between other landlords and tenants for similar houses. Some were in slightly better neighbourhoods, others worse - in that they faced a factory wall instead of similar houses across the street. To help make a comparison, he expressed the values of each in terms of so much a foot of effective floor area, as Table 1, in which D is one of the houses in question, shows:

Table 1

| House | Variables | Pence |
|-------|-----------|-------|
| A | near shops, bigger garden | 45 |
| B | nearer shops, but not quite so attractive | 40 |
| C | near factory, outlook poorer | 35 |
| D | 'subject' house, arrived at by comparison with above and other houses | 38 |

This gave the rent officer a figure of £4.50 as a fair rent, and this he applied to all the eight houses in question, but then minor additions were made to two of them which had rear access for cars; others had none. In another case he decided a figure of £4.00 a week to reflect the fact that this house was in poorer repair than the remainder' (Macey 1972, p.15).

The importance of comparables is also evident from submissions made to rent assessment committees. Appendix A contains verbatim reports (with the exception that names and addresses have been changed) of two submissions made by landlords with respect to pre 1919 terraced houses in Birmingham. The second submission is accompanied by a copy of the committee's decision. The emphasis in each which is placed on comparables suggests that Macey's description has not become outmoded. In the first the property in question was a house which was 'unimproved and does not have a bathroom'. The landlord's case basically consisted of presenting six comparable properties, some improved and some unimproved, and extrapolating from their recently determined fair rents to find the proposed rent for the property in question. In the second submission, the landlord argued that the rent officer's selection of comparables had been poor. He put forward five alternative comparable properties all of which were in some way inferior to the property in question, for example they were slightly smaller, and then argued that the rent of the property in question should be at least as high as that determined for these inferior properties.

The comparative method is also important in valuing residential properties which are to be owner occupied. They are not income generating in the same sense as rented properties so that the method of comparables is the only 'practicable method' (Lawrance et al. 1971, p.173) making the job of the rent officer similar in many respects to that of those who value owner occupied housing. It also conforms in a broad sense to the valuations which prospective tenants and purchasers make of available dwellings:

'The prospective tenant or purchaser will consider the nature and extent of the accommodation offered, and will at the same time have regard to the situation of the property as it affects the general amenities of life, time to travel to work, proximity to schools and like matters.

'For example, a prospective occupier viewing an ordinary three-bedroomed, semi-detached, suburban house, will probably already have in his mind some idea of the number of rooms he requires and their approximate size. He will consider the arrangement of the rooms for convenience in use, the adequacy of the domestic offices - kitchen, scullery, bathroom, etc. - the presence of central heating and the type of fuel used, the aspects of the rooms, the presence of a garage or parking space, the size of the garden, the state of repair, and all the other details which make the property attractive to him or otherwise.

'It is true that in some cases all such proper considerations may be swamped by the urgent desire to secure a house of any kind. But, even allowing for this factor, it is not difficult to imagine two houses of the same type identical in construction, size, accommodation and state of repair, and yet so different in their situation that one may readily fetch £4,500 in the open market, while the other may only be worth £3,000' (Lawrance et al. 1971, p.173).

The adoption of the method of comparables not only resembles valuation in the owner occupied sector but, by providing a benchmark against which to gauge any one determination, provides the service with a means of achieving a measure of consistency. In other words, by referring to properties already registered rent officers appear to have a mechanism, in the midst of a system otherwise founded in flexibility, for achieving consistency.

Unless the method is applied only crudely, however, such that the differences between the accommodation in question and chosen comparables are treated only roughly equivalently, this does not allow rent officers to ignore other criteria. The difficulty arises because each dwelling is a unique entity, even if only by virtue of its location (Lean and Goodall

1966). There can be no such thing as an exact comparable, therefore. Rent officers can only select comparables which at the best approximate to the property in question, differing from it in at least one respect. In turn, this means that the method of comparables rests on the assumption that monetary values can be placed on the characteristics of houses which make one house different from other similar houses. Monetary value is thus the common unit against which one characteristic may be traded off against another.

To place monetary values in the process of determining fair rents requires, if this is to be done with any consistency, the rent officer to have a model of what is a fair value. Taking Macey's illustration, for example, by adding or subtracting monetary amounts on the basis of the absence or existence of certain characteristics such as 'bigger garden' or 'poorer outlook' the rent officer has applied some rules about values to give practical meaning to the statutory formula. But given the imprecision of the statutory formula it is by no means clear where these rules come from. Why should the difference in value per square foot between properties A and B in Macey's illustration be plus 4 pence or even minus 5 pence, rather than plus 5 pence?

The remainder of this chapter will be concerned with what the rules appear to be rather than why those particular rules have been adopted.

## A DECISION MAKING MODEL

One approach to identifying the factors which are important contributors to the value of residential property, whether this value is capital value with vacant possession or weekly rental value, is through the use of an hedonic price index. This approach which has been developed within the discipline of economics is based on an assumption that commodities consist of bundles of characteristics or components (Griliches 1961): that is that commodities contain varying amounts of a number of different components and in varying degrees of quality. This has been applied to house prices in a number of studies which have emphasized the complexity of housing, varying as it does in terms of size, location, quality and so on. They have additionally assumed that different combinations and amounts of these components render different levels of satisfaction and that these levels are reflected in the value which is placed on the house in the market place. 'Basically the argument is that if one house has more desirable attributes than another, this higher consumer valuation will be reflected in a higher market price' (Ball 1973, p.213).

These studies have proceeded to examine relationships between the prices of houses and their associated components. In the main these have been carried out using the technique of multiple regression in which the components are defined as the independent variables on which price or rent is assumed to depend.   In general the relationship is expressed:

$$P_i = f(x_{i1}, x_{i2}, \ldots, x_{im})$$

where $P_i$ = price of the ith house

   $x_{ij}$ = jth attribute (j = 1,...,m) of ith house.

Thus a simple model for new semi-detached houses in a town might be:

PRICE = 10000 + (2000 x BEDS) + (1000 x CENTHEAT)
            + (1500 x GARAGE) - (100 x DISTSHOPS)

which implies that the price or value increased over a basic £10,000 by £2,000 for each bedroom, £1,000 if it had central heating, £1,500 if it had a garage and decreased by £100 for each mile to the nearest shopping centre.

This model thus has a characteristic of particular importance in the present context because it incorporates the notion of trade off such that less of one characteristic can be offset in monetary terms by more of another.  This implies quite correctly that the price may be the same for properties which are very different, and different for properties which are fairly similar.

A large number of such studies have now been carried out and the majority have used information about recent transactions from sources such as building societies, estate agents and public records.   In his summary of eleven studies based on samples ranging from 29 to 2,000 properties Ball (1973) divided the independent variables into three categories: locational, house related and environmental.   Table 4.1 shows which variables in each of these categories had a significant effect in at least one of the studies in various cities in England and the US.   The nature of the housing and the nature of the housing markets of course vary considerably, but nevertheless give some empirical evidence of the main supply factors which contribute to the value of residential property.

The results of such studies have been used for a variety of purposes.   One has been to statistically explain relative house prices in a valuation sense:   that is to quantify the extent to which a  group of characteristics contributes towards an explanation of market values.   A second use has been to statistically determine the relative importance and contribution to the value of each of these characteristics: that is to answer such questions as whether house size more significantly affects price than do locational factors.

Whereas there are a number of technical and theoretical difficulties associated with this approach (Doling 1978; Maclennan 1977) it can be adapted to examine the evaluations made by rent officers.   The model posited is:

TABLE 4.1
Independent variables significant in at least one study

| Locational | House-related | Environmental |
|---|---|---|
| US state | + Age | *+ Zoning type + |
| Topographic type | + Years of lease | Neighbourhood |
| Distance CBD *+ | unexpired | quality index + |
| Travel time CBD | + House type | * Air pollution + |
| Rail travel time CBD* | Condition * | * Proximity green |
| Rail travel cost CBD* | Dwelling unit | belt * |
| Accessibility to | quality + | Non-residential |
| main highway + | Plot area + | usage + |
| Accessibility to | First floor | Social class * |
| employment * | area + | Socio-economic |
| Accessibility to | Floor area * | index *+ |
| schools * | No. floors * | Average income + |
| Opportunity index * | Storey height * | % non-white + |
| | No. rooms *+ | Population |
| | No. bedrooms | density *+ |
| | Bath * | Housing density + |
| | Indoor toilet * | % recently |
| | Central heating * | built homes + |
| | Garage * | % housing over |
| | | 20 years old + |
| | | % dilapidated |
| | | housing + |
| | | Housing density + |
| | | Building value + |
| | | Schools index * |
| | | School quality + |
| | | Median schooling + |

*   Significant in British Study
+   Significant in American Study
CBD = Central Business District
Source: Ball (1973)


$$R_i = f(x_{i1}, x_{i2}, \ldots, x_{ij}, \ldots, x_{im})$$

where $R_i$ = the fair rent determined for property i

$x_{ij}$ = the jth characteristic (j = 1, ..., m) of the ith
property.

As for owner occupied housing this model can be made more
explicit:

$$R_i = a_0 + a_1 x_{i1} + a_2 x_{i2} + \ldots + a_m x_{im}$$

where the coefficients, $a_1$ to $a_m$, represent the rent officer's
assessment of the contribution which each characteristic
makes toward the fair rent. That is, if $x_{i1}$, for example, was
given the value of 1 if the property had a garage and 0 if it

did not, then the coefficient $a_1$ might perhaps be 0.50 implying that the rent officer's assessment of the fair contribution of a garage toward the total rent was 50p. The values of these coefficients can be estimated by subjecting information concerning properties for which fair rents have been determined to the technique of ordinary least squares regression.

The particular advantage of this approach is that it overcomes the difficulties of directly questioning rent officers about the way in which they make their determinations and which characteristics of the properties they consider important. Responses to such questions tend to be vague. The determinations are 'intuitive'; 'in line with fair rents already determined for similar properties'; 'made with reference to the characteristics of the particular property'; or 'use the guidelines set down in Section 70'. Such statements give little indication of either whether rent officers in different areas are using different rules and if so how they differ, or what the rules are which are applied by rent officers in any one area. From such generalisations we can understand little about the way in which Section 70 and its references to locality, size, character, scarcity and so on are interpreted.

This type of analysis - often called multiple regression analysis-allows an indirect deduction about what these interpretations might be. Instead of posing questions to rent officers it asks questions of their determinations and seeks to discover how they relate, in a statistical sense in the first instance, to the characteristics of dwellings. The coefficient related to any individual variable or characteristic describes the weighting attached to it which is implicit in the rent officers' determinations. This is not to suggest that such a model necessarily describes the actual decision making process of any or every rent officer, although there is some evidence that it is not entirely misleading. The model assumes that certain characteristics of a property are important and that more of one, say size, may in rent terms be offset by less of another, say location. This is a central feature of Macey's description of the rent setting process described above.

Even without this correspondence the model is one way of organising information and of extracting from that information certain relationships. Even if it does not accurately describe the actual thought processes it does identify rules which are implicit in the behaviour of rent officers. The method replicates the outcome of whatever thought processes are used and the coefficient relating to each dwelling characteristic describes what those processes resemble. Rent officers thus behave as if they were following the rules identified by the analysis.

## INFORMATION ABOUT FAIR RENT PROPERTIES

In the West Midlands Metropolitan County the registration forms for each tenancy for which a fair rent has been determined are filed by its seven metropolitan districts. The information contained on the registration forms is extensive including a full description of the physical characteristics as well as details of the tenancy such as liability for repairs. As public records the information is readily accessible. The data used in this study were extracted from the forms relating to 1,086 tenancies, not including tenancies owned by housing associations, in four of the seven districts and which had been registered during the period January to April 1980. The sample quotients and numbers are given in Table 4.2.

Table 4.2
Sample sizes

| Metropolitan district | Sampling quotient | Number in sample |
|---|---|---|
| Birmingham | 1 in 3 | 405 |
| Sandwell | full | 361 |
| Walsall | full | 172 |
| Solihull | full | 148 |
| Total | | 1086 |

In addition to the registered fair rent, for each of these 1,086 properties in the sample the information contained in Table 4.3 was recorded.

## Table 4.3
## List of property characteristics included in the data set

Address of property
House type; detached/semidetached house/bungalow, terrace
    house, flat converted/purpose built, maisonette,
    bedsitter
Date of construction
Mixed use
Self contained
Number of rooms; living, bed and box
Hall; exclusive/shared/none
Kitchen; separate/shared/with dining room/no hot water
Bathroom; exclusive/shared/none
Balcony
WC; one/two, exclusive/shared, internal/external
Cellar
Attic
Sunlounge
Coal store
Central heating; full/partial/storage
Double glazing
Need for modernisation
Garage; number, supplied by landlord/tenant
Parking space
Garden; front/rear, exclusive/shared
Rateable value
General rate; borne by landlord/tenant
Other rate; borne by landlord/tenant
Repairs; external/internal, liability of landlord/tenant
Internal decorations; liability of landlord/tenant
Registration number(s); present, previous
Fair rent(s); present, previous, on appeal
Furniture charge; present, previous
Service charge; present, previous

Locational and environmental variables for each of the 1,086
properties were also assembled from a number of sources as
shown in Table 4.4.  The choice of these was guided by hedomic
price studies of owner occupied housing as well as by
reference to statements about the working methods of rent
officers.

Much of the information from the registration forms was
expressed by the value of 1, to indicate that the property
possessed a certain characteristic such as a hot water supply,
garden or central heating, or 0, to indicate that it did not.
All the variables for all 1,086 properties were contained in a
basic data file.

The four districts for which information was collected form
part of the same continous built up area.  Although the West
Midlands Metropolitan County comprises a number of towns these
have expanded into one another so that there is frequently
little physical change noticeable in passing from one to

72

another.    Commuting patterns are such  that residence in one
and employment in another is by no means unusual.  The type of
house  to  be  found  in  one  metropolitan  district  closely
resembles  the  type  of  house  in  another.  The  essential
characteristics  of  the  housing  market  -  type  of  person
represented by household types, incomes, ages and occupations;
type of housing including age, size and quality; and many of
the institutions - are similar.

The nature of registered properties in the four samples are
also  broadly  similar.  Tables  4.5,  4.6  and  4.7  show  the
correspondence in the type, age and size of the properties
sampled in each area.  The exception is Solihull.  Although it
is part of the same continuous built up area it has as a town
specialized in more expensive middle class housing.  But the
general conformity of the housing market subject to the same
legislation enforced under a single county rent officer might
be reasonably taken as a priori evidence that methods and
outputs would be the same in all four districts.  It will be
shown later to what extent these expectations are unfulfilled.

Table 4.4
Locational variables

| Variable | Source |
| --- | --- |
| Socio-economic index of enumeration district | 1971 census |
| % with New Commonwealth born parents in ward | 1976 WMCC Household Survey |
| % Unemployed in ward | 1976 WMCC Household Survey |
| % Households in ward with income under £2,000 | 1976 WMCC Household Survey |
| % Houses in ward built before 1914 | 1976 WMCC Household Survey |
| % Houses in ward built after 1960 | 1976 WMCC Household Survey |
| % Houses in ward owner occupied | 1976 WMCC Household Survey |
| % Houses in ward private rental | 1976 WMCC Household Survey |
| % Households in ward with exclusive use of all basic amenities | 1976 WMCC Household Survey |
| Distance to nearest public transport route | Public transport map |
| Distance to nearest shopping centre | West Midlands Structure Plan |

## THE IMPLICIT RULES

### Statistical tests

The information collected from the registration forms can be
utilised to provide an indication of the rules implicit in the
determinations made.  This involves the fitting of a
regression model as described earlier in the chapter which
provides a measure (represented by the $R^2$ value) of the
overall closeness of the relationship between the fair rent -

the dependent variable - on the one hand, and the property and locational characteristics - the independent variables - on the other. This can be described as the proportion of the variation in rents which is explained by property and locational characteristics. If there was a perfect match, that is if all the variation was explained, then the $R^2$ value would equal unity, whereas if there was no match at all, such that none of the variation in rents was explained by these characteristics, then the $R^2$ value would be zero. In practice, the value of the $R^2$ statistic generally lies between these two extremes. A value of $R^2 = 0.50$, for instance, would mean that 50 per cent of the variation in the resulting rents could be accounted for by the combination of characteristics included in the equation.

Under certain circumstances, the strength of the contribution of each individual variable or characteristic in explaining the variation in rents is measured by the value of its t statistic. Examination of this helps in the assessment of whether or not rent officers are using that variable consistently enough to justify the conclusion that an implicit rule is evident. Basically this involves considering whether or not each such t statistic exceeds a critical value. If it does not this can be taken to indicate one or more deductions:

(i)     Rent officers do not consider that a particular variable should contribute to the fair rent. For example, rent officers might or might not consider that proximity to a park or a bus route was a relevant circumstance.

(ii)    Rent officers mis-measure, in a random way, that particular variable. That means, for instance, that they sometimes under-record and sometimes over-record the state of repair or character of the locality to such an extent that although they might consider the characteristic a relevant one mis-measurement makes it appear not to be.

(iii)   Rent officers measure that particular variable consistently but evaluate its contribution to the fair rent inconsistently. That is that sometimes they consider the number of bedrooms to be important and at other times they do not.

Under certain circumstances, the existence of a t statistic exceeding a certain value indicates the reverse of all three situations, i.e. that rent officers measure the variable consistently, consider it a relevant circumstance and evaluate its contribution consistently. It thus allows us to surmise the rules implicit in rent officers' determinations.

This test of the significance of a particular variable appears fairly unproblematic but in practice is complicated by the fact that some of the independent variables considered will be highly correlated with other independent variables. In such cases of multicollinearity it is possible for the importance or significance of one variable to be subsumed by

74

one or more of the other variables. For example, rent
officers may consider that both the external condition of the
property and whether or not it is situated on a main road make
important contributions to the fair rent. However if all
those properties situated on main roads are the only ones with
poor external conditions the correlation between them will be
perfect. In practice such correlations are generally less
than perfect but the effect of including both in the
regression model is that the variation consequent upon one of
them is subsumed within that consequent upon the other, and
one of the t statistics will almost certainly appear to
indicate non significance. Either one, entered into the
equation in the absence of the other, would have a significant
t value.

Table 4.5
Type of dwelling

| Type | Birmingham No. | % | Walsall No. | % | Sandwell No. | % | Solihull No. | % | Total No. | % |
|------|------|------|------|------|------|------|------|------|------|------|
| Detached house | 3 | 0.7 | 5 | 2.9 | 4 | 1.1 | 2 | 1.4 | 14 | 1.3 |
| Semi-detached house | 98 | 24.2 | 42 | 24.4 | 163 | 45.2 | 78 | 52.7 | 381 | 35.1 |
| Detached bungalow | 1 | 0.2 | 2 | 1.2 | - | - | - | - | 3 | 0.3 |
| Semi-detached bungalow | - | - | - | - | 1 | 0.3 | - | - | 1 | 0.1 |
| Town house | - | - | - | - | 1 | 0.3 | - | - | 1 | 0.1 |
| Terrace house | 249 | 61.5 | 113 | 65.7 | 180 | 49.9 | 23 | 15.5 | 565 | 52.0 |
| Flat purpose built | 16 | 4.0 | 2 | 1.2 | 2 | 0.6 | 41 | 27.7 | 61 | 5.6 |
| Flat converted | 22 | 5.4 | 1 | 0.6 | 3 | 0.8 | 2 | 1.4 | 28 | 2.6 |
| Maisonette | 8 | 2.0 | 1 | 0.6 | 2 | 0.6 | 2 | 1.4 | 13 | 1.2 |
| Bedsitter | 8 | 2.0 | 6 | 3.5 | 5 | 1.4 | - | - | 19 | 1.7 |
| Total | 405 | | 172 | | 361 | | 148 | | 1086 | |

Table 4.6
Date of construction

| Date | Birmingham No. | % | Walsall No. | % | Sandwell No. | % | Solihull No. | % | Total No. | % |
|------|------|------|------|------|------|------|------|------|------|------|
| Pre 1919 | 255 | 62.9 | 110 | 64.0 | 165 | 45.7 | 12 | 8.1 | 542 | 49.9 |
| 1919-1945 | 105 | 26.0 | 58 | 33.7 | 180 | 49.9 | 91 | 61.5 | 434 | 40.0 |
| Post 1945 | 45 | 11.1 | 4 | 2.3 | 16 | 4.4 | 45 | 30.4 | 110 | 10.1 |
| Total | 405 | | 172 | | 361 | | 148 | | 1086 | |

Table 4.7
Number of bedrooms

| Number of bedrooms | Birmingham No. | % | Walsall No. | % | Sandwell No. | % | Solihull No. | % | Total No. | % |
|---|---|---|---|---|---|---|---|---|---|---|
| One | 25 | 6.2 | 6 | 3.5 | 8 | 2.2 | 38 | 25.7 | 77 | 7.1 |
| Two | 155 | 38.3 | 94 | 54.7 | 90 | 24.9 | 40 | 27.0 | 379 | 34.9 |
| Three | 219 | 54.1 | 70 | 40.7 | 262 | 72.6 | 69 | 46.6 | 620 | 57.1 |
| Four | 4 | 1.0 | 2 | 1.2 | 1 | 0.3 | 1 | 0.7 | 8 | 0.7 |
| Five | 1 | 0.2 | - | - | - | - | - | - | 1 | 0.1 |
| Six | 1 | 0.2 | - | - | - | - | - | - | 1 | 0.1 |
| Total | 405 | | 172 | | 361 | | 148 | | 1086 | |

In practice the existence of high correlations between
independent variables is often even more complex with several
independent variables sharing a large proportion of their
variation. Indeed it is possible to have a regression model
which, despite a large proportion of the variation in the
dependent variable being explained, contains no significant t
values. Each t statistic represents the effect of taking its
related variable out of the equation, and as such relates to
the variation explained by the remaining variables. In such a
situation it may be impossible to disentangle the effects of
individual variables and so where there is a high level of
multicollinearity it may be difficult to identify the implicit
rules of fair rent determination.

This is made even more complicated by two further aspects.
Firstly where multicollinearity does exist, it is not
necessarily the case that a particular variable will not
appear as a significant contributor to the fair rent. What
this, together with the above reasons, implies is that if a t
value is significantly different from zero then rent officers
measure the variable accurately, consider it to be important
and evaluate that importance consistently. Moreover, at least
part of the importance is not accounted for by variation
shared with other variables. If t values are not significant
then probably all that can be said is that at least one of
these conditions is not met but which one or ones is unknown.

Secondly, although a t value may indicate significance and
can be interpreted in the manner described above, it is
logically possible for a variable included in the equation to
be highly correlated with a variable which has not been
included, and in fact it is the latter characteristic which
influences the rent officer. In such a case the included
variable which appears to make a significant contribution to
the fair rent determination is acting statistically as a proxy
for the real or actual contributor. Thus we cannot state
categorically that the coefficient of a variable, say the
floor area, indicates one of the rules which rent officers
have adopted. It is possible that floor area is acting as a

76

proxy for building type and it is the latter variable which rent officers use although it has not been included in the analysis perhaps because of oversight or inability to collect that information. Having stated this, it is possible in this case to be rather more confident about the interpretation of these coefficients and their t values. This is because the analysis includes a large number of independent variables for which the evidence of property valuation generally, and inclusion on the registration forms, provide prima facie grounds for their importance and the non-importance of variables not in the analysis.

## Results

When all the dwelling and locational variables from Tables 4.3 and 4.4 are introduced into a regression equation the existence of multicollinearity makes it difficult to provide a literal description of the rules of fair rent determination. The common variation is at such a consistently high level that it is impossible to separate or disentangle the influence of each individual variable. This does not mean that the model as a whole does not statistically represent the rules which rent officers appear to follow, but that these rules cannot be sufficiently disentangled to allow them to be verbally described.

In the present context the problems of multicollinearity can be reduced in two ways. Firstly, much of it is due to the fact that the variables related to dwelling type are strongly correlated with some other variables. Purpose built flats do not have gardens, but houses do, for example. Fortunately, in all four districts sampled, except Solihull, pre 1919 terraced houses were by far the largest single dwelling type. Separate regression equations for this dwelling type alone allow a number of the variables to be discarded. This has the further advantage that it controls for the possibility that rent officers make different assumptions about scarcity levels for different property types.

Secondly, it was found that most of the variation in fair rents which can be explained by the full set of variables even for pre 1919 terraced houses, can also be explained by a much shorter list of variables in which the problem of multicollinearity is reduced. In the case of pre 1919 terraced houses in Birmingham, for example, the full set of variables or characteristics gives an $R^2$ statistic of 0.687, whereas an equation containing only 12 variables has an $R^2$ value of 0.606. (Definitions of these 12 variables are given in Appendix B ). Similar approximations are found using the same set of 12 variables for pre 1919 terraced houses in both Walsall and Sandwell. This implies that the short list of variables contains almost as much information about the variation in rents as the full list so that so complex a model is not required in order to begin to understand the implicit rules of fair rent determination.

Indeed if the so called short list (of 12 variable) models are examined it is found that even they contain more variables than are necessary to explain most of the variation which can be explained by the model containing the full list of independent variables. For each of the four registration areas much of the variation in results explained by the full list could be explained by about 6 or 7 variables. This is apparent in Table 4.8 which records the increase in the $R^2$ value when the regression equation is estimated first with one independent variable, then with the addition of a second, then with a third and so on. In the case of Birmingham, although the 12 variables together give an $R^2$ value of 0.606, the first 6 variables to be included give a value not much lower, i.e. 0.586. The corresponding figures for Walsall are 0.614 and 0.562, and for Sandwell 0.760 and 0.751. This suggests that however many variables rent officers record on the registration form or collect in their inspection of each property, the greater part of their rent determination depends on a relatively small selection. In other words, rent officers seem to work with relatively simple decision models in that they appear to consider only a few property and locational characteristics in order to identify comparables.

Examination of Tables 4.8 and 4.9 suggests that not only are the significant characteristics few in number but that a different combination of 6 or 7 key characteristics is relevant in each registration area. Table 4.9 lists the variables included in the 12 variable decision models. The estimates of the coefficients are given in the columns headed 'a', the t statistics in the columns headed 't' and the level of multicollinearity in the column headed '$h^2$'. A t statistic equal to or greater than 1.96 is statistically significant at the 5% level. When the value of the $h^2$ statistic is low there is little multicollineanity present.

In all three metropolitan districts the only common statistically significant characteristics of the property are whether or not it has been improved by the inclusion of a bathroom (BTHRM) and internal WCs (NUMWC). The relevance of both can be readily appreciated: originally most pre 1919 terraced dwellings had no bathroom and an external WC only, and the cost to the landlord of such improvements and the benefit to the tenant are considerable. It is not unreasonable therefore that these should be regarded as important distinctions between properties which are duly reflected in their fair rents. However, beyond these two considerations rent officers in the three areas appear to have adopted different rules. In other words, apart from the bathroom and WC variables, each has a different pattern of significant coefficients which cannot be accounted for in terms of multicollinearity. For example, the common variation between NUMBEDS (the number of bedrooms) and the other independent variables was relatively small in all cases and yet this variable had a positive, significant coefficient in the Birmingham analysis, and a negative, significant coefficient in that for Walsall.

78

Table 4.8
Increase in variation explained with the inclusion of
further variables
Pre 1919 terraced housing

| Step | Birmingham Variable | $R^2$ | Walsall Variable | $R^2$ | Sandwell Variable | $R^2$ |
|------|---------|-------|---------|-------|---------|-------|
| 1 | NUMWC | 0.325 | BTHRM | 0.208 | BTHRM | 0.591 |
| 2 | HALL | 0.422 | PCOCC | 0.333 | NUMWC | 0.655 |
| 3 | BTHRM | 0.470 | RATVAL | 0.434 | RATVAL | 0.741 |
| 4 | NUMBED | 0.528 | EXTST | 0.493 | GENRAT | 0.745 |
| 5 | DTRANS | 0.569 | PKING | 0.533 | GARAGE | 0.748 |
| 6 | GARAGE | 0.586 | NUMBED | 0.562 | PCOCC | 0.751 |
| 7 | NUMLIV | 0.594 | GENRAT | 0.580 | NUMBED | 0.755 |
| 8 | PKING | 0.600 | HALL | 0.596 | NUMLIV | 0.757 |
| 9 | EXTST | 0.603 | NUMWC | 0.603 | DTRANS | 0.757 |
| 10 | RATVAL | 0.604 | GARAGE | 0.607 | HALL | 0.758 |
| 11 | GENRAT | 0.606 | NUMLIV | 0.611 | EXTST | 0.760 |
| 12 | PCOCC | 0.606 | DTRANS | 0.614 | * | * |

* The twelfth variable was omitted by the computer program because its share of the total variation was already fully accounted for by the other eleven variables.

It is possible to speculate on the reasons why this and other differences have emerged but this would be to obscure their primary significance. This is that whereas there is apparently some common ground between rent officers in different areas, in making fair rent determinations on similar properties in similar locations each has apparently and additionally developed rules peculiar to himself. Each appears to have a simple set of rules within which the fact of modernisation figures prominently; beyond that, however, the contents of the sets of rules differ.

The implications of these findings for the work of rent officers, in so far as this relies upon the use of comparables, is of some concern. It was argued earlier that the use of comparables, because no property is exactly like any other, did not obviate the need for rent officers to be able to place monetary values on differences. In an ideal world one would expect that rent officers would all be able to identify, measure and evaluate those differences in a way which would enable an observer to identify similar decision making rules. The evidence of the analysis described here is that this is far from the reality. Rent officers appear to have a very simple or crude model of which physical and locational characteristics of housing should add to or detract from its fair rent. Moreover, this simple model appears to be different in different areas. In other words rent officers in one area appear to have a set of rules which differs from that of rent officers in other areas.

Table 4.9
Fair rent decision models

| Vari-able | Birmingham | | | Walsall | | | Sandwell | | |
|---|---|---|---|---|---|---|---|---|---|
| | a | t | $h^2$ | a | t | $h^2$ | a | t | $h^2$ |
| RATVAL | 0.001 | 0.910 | 0.128 | 0.013 | 2.339 | 0.675 | 0.011 | 3.631 | 0.551 |
| HALL | 0.403 | 3.012 | 0.219 | 0.524 | 2.217 | 0.474 | 0.038 | 0.411 | 0.498 |
| NUMLIV | 0.302 | 2.168 | 0.212 | 0.265 | 0.855 | 0.444 | 0.115 | 0.908 | 0.551 |
| NUMBED | 0.493 | 4.082 | 0.304 | -0.364 | 2.275 | 0.298 | 0.137 | 1.493 | 0.399 |
| EXTST | 0.120 | 0.884 | 0.130 | -0.442 | 2.670 | 0.295 | 0.037 | 0.346 | 0.435 |
| GARAGE | 0.650 | 2.481 | 0.065 | 0.877 | 1.168 | 0.163 | 0.333 | 1.356 | 0.197 |
| PKING | 0.343 | 1.257 | 0.136 | 2.075 | 4.215 | 0.338 | - | - | - |
| GENRAT | 0.168 | 0.783 | 0.169 | -0.710 | 2.211 | 0.304 | 0.143 | 1.678 | 0.179 |
| PCOCC | 0.044 | 0.441 | 0.101 | 0.328 | 4.668 | 0.176 | 0.082 | 1.612 | 0.243 |
| DTRANS | 0.325 | 4.713 | 0.260 | -0.176 | 0.839 | 0.204 | -0.074 | 0.715 | 0.123 |
| BTHRM | 1.333 | 5.450 | 0.553 | 1.347 | 4.930 | 0.234 | 0.465 | 2.826 | 0.791 |
| NUMWC | 0.801 | 4.366 | 0.541 | 0.311 | 1.382 | 0.274 | 1.110 | 7.886 | 0.791 |
| CONST | 3.039 | 5.851 | | 3.958 | 5.476 | | 4.121 | 10.036 | |
| $R^2$ | | 0.606 | | | 0.614 | | | 0.760 | |
| $\bar{R}^2$ | | 0.582 | | | 0.554 | | | 0.739 | |
| Mean square residual | | 0.723 | | | 0.465 | | | 0.217 | |
| Number in sample | | 210 | | | 97 | | | 152 | |

Whether the simplicity of the implicit decision making models arises from choice is not known. But it suggests that comparables may often be very crudely chosen and that the differences between them and the property in question, with the principal exception of bathroom and W.C. facilities, may be very crudely evaluated. It also seems to be the case that, since rent officers working in different areas have different implicit decision models, faced with the same property they might choose different comparables or even evaluate differences differently. A consequence of some concern would be that fair rents might be determined not only on the basis of the value of the accommodation offered, which one of the architects of the legislation has stated was the intention (Donnison 1967), but also would be dependent upon the particular model or set of rules which the rent officer in that area was using. The adjective 'fair' would then have varying interpretations in different registration areas.

## FAIR RENTS AND CAPITAL VALUES

The similarities between, on the one hand, the statutory formula and the working methods developed by rent officers and, on the other hand, the practices of valuation in the owner occupied sector suggest that there might be a correlation between the fair rents and the vacant possession capital values of properties. Indeed, the expectation that fair rents should reflect the value of the accommodation in question might suggest a priori expectations that rent officers tend to set higher fair rents for properties which would command higher prices in the owner occupied market.

Confirmation of such a relationship would indicate a further aspect of the rules which guide rent officers: namely that the effect of whatever rules rent officers have adopted is to replicate outcomes in the owner occupied sector. A difficulty involved in establishing the existence of such a relationship arises if the existence of scarcity, as defined in the rent acts, has the effect of inflating some vacant possession capital values. This can be eliminated by considering only one type of dwelling; for convenience this was taken to be the 210 pre 1919 terraced houses about which information was extracted from the registration records for Birmingham. The vacant possession capital values of these houses were estimated approximately by comparing details of a sample of similar properties advertised for sale in the local Birmingham paper for the period during which their fair rents were registered. Information about these owner occupied dwellings, together with the same locational and environmental variables which were evaluated for the rented property, enabled the fitting of a multiple regresion model relating house price to dwelling characteristics. For the sample of 74 advertised properties an $R^2$ value of 0.730 was obtained, demonstrating that the variables used explained about three quarters of the variation in capital values.

Having determined the value of the coefficients of each of the variables from the owner occupied sample, the same coefficients were applied to the data relating to the rented properties to provide estimates of their vacant possession capital values. Although both samples contained similar properties in similar areas there may nevertheless have been unrecorded differences between them, such as their state of repair which would have resulted in some over or under estimates of capital values. There are other limitations to the estimates such as the fact that they are based on asking prices and not prices at completion. Nevertheless, if rent officers make determinations of fair rent which reflect vacant possession capital values then one should expect to find a strong relationship between the two.

For the 210 rented properties in the Birmingham sample the correlation between fair rent and the estimated vacant possession capital value is marked ($r = 0.51$). This seems to indicate that whatever discounts have been made to reflect scarcity they have set fair rents the relative size of which broadly mirror the relative level of the capital values of individual properties. In other words as an exercise in valuation rent officers in Birmingham at least appear to rank properties in a way not totally inconsistent with market rankings: the most expensive houses have tended to receive the highest fair rents.

## CONCLUSIONS

Faced originally with an immediate and growing workload and with minimum statutory guidance, the rent officer service has developed methods which have enabled it to determine fair rents. The Francis Committee reported in 1971 that at that time a number of methods were being used. More recently, there is evidence from a number of sources that the method of comparables is now widely used. This relies firstly upon the identification of similar, although not identical, dwellings to the dwelling in question. This is followed by the placing of monetary values on the differences between the comparables and the dwelling in question so that additions to and subtractions from the formers' fair rents provide a measure of the fair rent in question.

These additions and subtractions, if carried out consistently, represent the rent officer's implicit set of rules which together constitute his decision model. Statistical analysis suggests that the sets of rules are only loosely formulated and applied. Rent officers appear to have decision models which are simple in the sense that they are based upon only a few of the large number of possible characteristics of residential property and which do not always include all those which might be considered basic. The a priori expectation that, for example, the number of bedrooms is a characteristic which rent officers might consider relevant to the fair rent was not borne out for all areas.

But not only are the decision models apparently simple: they appear to differ from area to area. With the exception of bathroom and interior WC facilities the rent officers in each area appear to have adopted different sets of rules. This lack of uniformity between areas is disturbing because it suggests that the legislation may be implemented differently in different areas. One implication may be that the determination of a fair rent may depend not only on the objective characteristics of a dwelling but on whether the determination is the responsibility of a rent officer from one area rather than the rent officer from another. In other words, the fair rent becomes partly a result of the particular set of rules developed in that area.

Notwithstanding this concern, analysis of the relationship between vacant possession capital values and fair rents indicates that determinations in Birmingham do very broadly reflect the value of the accommodation offered. In so far as hedonic price studies indicate that capital values are a surrogate for the desirability of the objective characteristics of dwellings, it is important not to overstress the divergence between fair rent and objective characteristics. Nevertheless, in this context the hope that the legislation would bring a level of rationality to the structure of fair rents which exceeded the imperfections of the market place, does not perhaps seem to have been entirely achieved.

# 5 Fairness and consistency

Recognition of the intention of achieving a rational rent structure, particularly in the light of the apparently simple decision models adopted by rent officers, leads to a concern about whether the fair rent determinations for individual dwellings are consistent. That is, are landlords of similar properties able to charge similar rents, and are tenants of similar properties obliged to pay similar rents. This concern with consistency has been widely debated in the technical press (see, for example, Glynne Evans 1980). Whereas there has been some concern that the pursuit of consistency has been at the expense of the correct balance between individual landlords and tenants (see, for example, Hollamby 1981) it is widely recognized that this ideal is central to the spirit of the legislation. Indeed, if the system is not to become suspect it is essential that each assessment bears 'scrutiny as compared with other similar properties in the same area' (Prophet 1976, p.128). Without this, neither landlords nor tenants can be satisfied that they are receiving the same level of fairness as other landlords or other tenants. There may be dissatisfaction that generally the balance is tipped too far in favour of either the landlord or the tenant, but consistency in the level of fair rents would at least ensure that the system is treating each group equally fairly or equally unfairly.

Consistency may also be important in order to enable landlords and tenants to judge for themselves whether their negotiated rent is in line with the rent which would be set by a rent officer. In setting up the system Crossman appreciated that this was necessary if the system was not to break down through the congestion caused by every landlord and tenant feeling it necessary to have his own rent assessed by a rent officer. This could occur if the list of comparables showed that apparently similar properties had very dissimilar fair rents.

In the absence of the achievement of a level of consistency such that similar tenancies are similarly treated, the fair rent system is promulgating a particular pattern of anomalies which it would be difficult to equate with notions of fairness, however defined. This pattern may be different from that prevailing, say, in 1950 when some properties had controlled rents tied to different bases whilst others were not controlled at all. Nevertheless there is clearly a possibility, given the statutory vagueness described earlier, that even amongst those properties which have been registered anomalies on a wide scale do exist. This is separate from, but additional to, any anomalies between registered, regulated but not registered, and non-regulated tenancies. In this chapter an attempt will be made to seek to establish the level of consistency characterising fair rent determinations.

## EVIDENCE OF INCONSISTENCY

There is evidence that the fair rent system has indeed resulted in anomalies. Statistical information collected by the DOE and distributed to the service (DOE 1980b) indicates that the re-registration of unfurnished properties in 1978 resulted in very different increases in rent in different administrative areas. In the West Midlands panel area the average of the changes in Hereford and Worcester was 95.3 per cent and in Warwickshire 37.9 per cent. In the South West the change in Cornwall was 80.5 per cent and in Devon 51.2 per cent. Since the properties excluded housing association properties but included only those with no material changes to either the terms of the tenancy or the condition of the dwelling which had been re-registered within 4 years of registration, it would be difficult to argue that the changes occurred for reasons other than actual differences in the practical operation of the statutory formula. This may be due to the adoption of different methods or of different weights and objectives, at present or previously.

Not only has variation appeared over time, however, but variations continue to be found both between different areas and between individual cases at one point in time. Indeed this situation was recognized by the Labour government's review of the rent acts in 1977:

'.... the very flexibility which has been the strength of the system may be producing diverging levels of rent in different areas .... Quite apart from the effect of general trends in rent levels, the system can produce anomalies in individual cases: sometimes the fair rent in one area may not enable the landlord even to cover his immediate costs whilst in another, large increases in registered rent may cause hardship for tenants of limited means who have been living in the same house for years' (DOE 1977c, p.7).

Earlier the Francis Committee reported that the criticism had been made to it that there was 'often a lack of consistency between Rent Officers operating in adjoining areas in assessing the fair rents for comparable properties' (Francis 1971, p.85). Although they did not fully investigate the particular cases they concluded that 'it seems very likely, however, that instances of such inconsistency have occurred' (Francis 1971, p.85).

Statistical analysis, following that in the previous chapter, indicates that this inconsistency may be more widespread than Francis had recognized. Within some areas there appears to be some proportion of the fair rent structure which cannot be accounted for by reference to property and locational characteristics. This inconsistency is even more marked in comparisons between areas. The absolute and relative levels of fair rents set by rent officers from one area figuratively assessing the dwellings in another area diverge greatly from the actual rents. As in the previous chapter this suggests not only a pseudo random element in the fair rent determinations but also that the fair rent depends in part on the different practices which have developed in each area.

## MEASURES OF CONSISTENCY

It is difficult to substantiate the existence or absence of consistency. Because they are multi-dimensional phenomena only rarely can houses more or less identical in all respects, including the date at which they were registered, be identified. Obvious cases such as adjacent properties owned by the same landlord are known but it is to be expected that the rent officer or officers dealing with them will generally be particularly conscious of the need for conformity between them. At the opposite extreme, differing fair rents for similar dwellings in different parts of the country can always be explained away by reference to unique locational factors such as the level of scarcity or of employment opportunities.

Between these two extremes are cases of similar properties within the same built up area - perhaps in the same or neighbouring registration areas. Apparent anomalies in fair rents may be less easy to explain but the uniqueness argument, particularly in relation to location, is still possible. Additionally, there may be so few close comparables that casual observation may not confirm whether differences are being evaluated consistently. Is, for example, the existence of a third bedroom in properties otherwise identical always reflected in the same monetary addition to the fair rent?

Fortunately these difficulties can be overcome, as in the previous chapter, because a multiple regression model relating fair rent to dwelling and locational characteristics can provide a means of making direct comparisons. By conceptualising houses as consisting of different combinations of quality and quantity of certain characteristics, such a model gives all such characteristics a common base, namely their monetary contribution to the fair rent. The issue of whether or not identical properties - that is identical combinations of characteristics by quality and quantity - can be found, then becomes superfluous. The common basis through the contribution of each characteristic to the fair rent makes every property comparable with every other property.

This comparability among all dwellings makes possible an examination of the consistency demonstrated by rent officers. In effect it allows an assessment to be made, through quantitative measures, of whether rent officers always use the body of information about dwelling and locational characteristics, fully and consistently, to define the fair rent. This assessment of consistency can be made by examining two measures, the $R^2$ and the mean square residual values.

The $R^2$ value describes the maximum proportion of the total variation in the determined fair rent which can be explained by applying the same coefficients to the values of dwelling and locational characteristics. It thus indicates the extent to which any person, having obtained the information about dwelling and locational characteristics which is available to the rent officer, and applying weights to each item of information, could predict the fair rents which the rent officer had determined. In effect, the technique produces the best linear rule for relating dwelling and locational characteristics to fair rents such that there is no other linear rule which will explain more of the variation in the fair rents. Similarly the $R^2$ value indicates the extent to which rent officers themselves use the information contained in the set of independent variables in the same (i.e. consistent) manner and to what extent additional information or a random factor is introduced. Thus if an $R^2$ value of unity were to be found it would demonstrate that rent officers use only that information contained in the set of dwelling and locational characteristics and that they are completely consistent in their application of each characteristic. Each time they encounter a particular characteristic, in no matter which dwelling, they measure and evaluate it in the same way.

Where $R^2$ values are below unity the rent officers have in some way been inconsistent. They have been inconsistent in their measurement or evaluation of the relative contribution of the characteristics, or in using characteristics which are not those normally used in property valuation, or by using some random factor. Thus if an $R^2$ value was close to zero there would be no, or very little, identifiable relationship between the dwelling and locational characteristics and the fair rent.

A characteristic of the $R^2$ statistic is that any addition to the set of independent variables, whether relevant to the fair rent determination or not, cannot result in a decrease in its value. However any addition may, because of chance variations common to it and the fair rent, increase the $R^2$ value. An alternative measure is the 'adjusted $R^2$', (or $\bar{R}^2$), which compensates for such chance common variation occurring as a result of adding further independent variables. It is thus possible for the $\bar{R}^2$ statistic to decrease in value with the addition of further variables. The present examination of both $R^2$ and $\bar{R}^2$, however, differs from the analysis in the previous chapter in that it is not concerned with the identification of whether property and locational characteristics are used in such a way that individually they constitute rules. Rather it is concerned with whether the characteristics collectively constitute a consistent rule.

The second measure of consistency is the mean square residual. This provides a more 'common-sense' measure of the

consistency with which the available information is used.
Under certain circumstances it can help to answer the
question: if an individual tenant or landlord had access to
the same information about properties as does the rent
officer, and knowing what fair rents had been set for them,
what would be the greatest accuracy which he could achieve in
estimating the level of fair rent which would be determined
for the next property? In other words given the information
about previous determinations contained in the list of
comparables the mean square residual can be used to describe
how closely the fair rent of another property, not yet on the
list of comparables, could be predicted.

## CONSISTENCY WITHIN AREAS

### The districts

In the previous chapter a regression model which related fair
rents determined in Birmingham to all the available dwelling
and locational characteristics was described. Interpretation
of its $R^2$ and $\bar{R}^2$ values suggests that Birmingham's rent
officers are not particularly consistent (Table 5.1). The $R^2$
values indicate that the information contained in the list of
independent variables explains only about three quarters of
the variation in the fair rents for all dwellings together.
It is possible that the remaining and unexplained 25 per cent
of the variation results from different allowances made for
scarcity in different types of dwelling. That is, if a
variable measuring the scarcity element applicable to each
dwelling could be added, both the $R^2$ and $\bar{R}^2$ could be much
closer to unity. However the dwelling and locational
characteristics explain only about two thirds of the variation
in the fair rents of the single dwelling type - pre 1919
terraced house - for which scarcity deductions might be
expected to be constant. Thus neither sample of properties
supports the conclusion that in Birmingham the available
information provides a particularly good prediction of the
rent officers' determinations.

Table 5.1
Birmingham fair rent determinations:
measures of consistency

|  | All dwellings | Pre 1919 terraced houses |
| --- | --- | --- |
| Mean rent | £ 8.93 | £ 7.77 |
| Variance | 4.537 | 1.742 |
| $R^2$ | 0.767 | 0.687 |
| $\bar{R}^2$ | 0.732 | 0.630 |
| Mean square residual | 1.259 | 0.642 |
| Number | 405 | 210 |

If the coefficients found by fitting a multiple regression equation to information about previous determinations were used to estimate the fair rent of another dwelling, at a level of say £8, then the mean square residual allows one to predict the probable range in which the actual fair rent would lie. Thus, for all dwelling types taken together, on the basis of the 405 sample determinations in this study, one can say that there is a 0.95 probability that the actual fair rent lies in the range £8-1.96 $\sqrt{(1.259(1+1/405))}$ and £8+1.96 $\sqrt{(1.259(1+1/405))}$ or from £5.80 to £10.20. That is that one can predict the actual fair rent in 95 cases out of 100 no more accurately than to say that it would lie somewhere in the range £5.80 to £10.20. In the remaining 5 cases the fair rent could be expected to fall outside even these broad limits. For pre 1919 terraced dwellings the range, again with an estimated rent of £8, would be smaller, from £6.43 to £9.57, but still proportionately large. Thus if a tenant or landlord attempted to use the knowledge contained in the registration records to estimate what a fair rent for a particular unregistered property might be, there would be a fairly high probability of considerable variation. In other words many apparently comparable dwellings are to be found in the registration forms, but their fair rents cover a wide range of values.

The level of consistency is considerably higher in the other three districts (Table 5.2) although there were insufficient pre 1919 terraced houses sampled in Solihull to allow the results to be reliably computed. The $R^2$ values (and with one exception the $\bar{R}^2$ values) in these districts are all higher than they are for Birmingham, and the mean square residuals are all lower. Indeed the fact that the $R^2$ values are close to unity perhaps supports the view that the low explanatory level of the regression model applied to the Birmingham rent officers' determinations does not arise because of the inappropriateness of the technique. Given that there may have been some measurement error by the rent officer service, and some recording, coding and punching error by the researchers it could probably not be reasonably expected to find $R^2$ values higher than those for Sandwell. Since the housing markets of the four districts - and particularly Walsall, Sandwell and Birmingham - are so similar, and the duties of their rent officers identical, it is difficult to ignore the conclusion that as a group Birmingham rent officers are less consistent than those of Sandwell and Walsall.

**The rent assessment committees**

The raison d'etre of the rent assessment committees (RACs) is, in part, the provision of guidance to the rent officers in the form of 'benchmark' determinations. In determining fair rents for tenancies which are problematic, in the sense that either landlord or tenant expresses dissatisfaction with the rent officer's determination, the RACs provide guidelines as well as, in theory, promoting consistency. Individual rent officers are subordinate to the RACs, as the appellant body, and they are bound to have regard to decisions made by them.

The Francis Committee reported that it had 'no reason to doubt that Rent Assessment Committees would correct such inconsistencies if appealed to' (Francis 1971, p.55).

Table 5.2
Fair rent determinations in other districts:
measures of consistency

|  | Sandwell | Walsall | Solihull |
|---|---|---|---|
| All dwellings | | | |
| $R^2$ | 0.925 | 0.867 | 0.935 |
| $\bar{R}^2$ | 0.914 | 0.826 | 0.915 |
| Mean square residual | 0.292 | 0.361 | 0.411 |
| Pre 1919 terraced houses | | | |
| $R^2$ | 0.802 | 0.733 | - |
| $\bar{R}^2$ | 0.755 | 0.617 | - |
| Mean square residual | 0.204 | 0.406 | - |

There were 69 determinations for properties in Birmingham made by the RAC during the survey period of which 33 were for pre 1919 terraced houses. A comparison of the rent officer and the RAC determinations for the same properties indicates that the RAC is not itself a model of consistency (Table 5.3). Indeed, overall the statistical measures indicate less consistency in the RAC determinations than in those of the rent officers. For all dwellings taken together the $R^2$ and $\bar{R}^2$ values achieved by the RACs were slightly greater than those achieved by the rent officers, but the mean square residual was also greater. For pre 1919 terraced houses however all three statistics indicated less consistency by the RACs. If Birmingham rent officers demonstrate inconsistency in the rents which they determine, on this evidence the RACs' performance is no better.

Table 5.3
Fair rent determinations by the rent assessment committees
and Birmingham rent officers

|  | Rent assessment committees | Rent officers |
|---|---|---|
| All dwellings | | |
| $R^2$ | 0.936 | 0.931 |
| $\bar{R}^2$ | 0.820 | 0.806 |
| Mean square residual | 1.036 | 0.822 |
| Pre 1919 terraced houses | | |
| $R^2$ | 0.854 | 0.884 |
| $\bar{R}^2$ | 0.483 | 0.588 |
| Mean square residual | 1.108 | 0.564 |

## THE REASONS FOR INCONSISTENCY WITHIN AREAS

There are a number of possible explanations for the apparent low level of consistency in the determinations made by rent officers in Birmingham and the RACs. One possibility is that rent officers use information additional to that provided in the list of property and locational characteristics used here. Notable omissions from this list are any items of information about the physical condition of the dwellings and about environmental conditions.

Since these omissions are concerned with dwelling characteristics, which are arguably relevant to the determination of fair rents, they point to a possible weakness of the methodology adopted in this study. A second possible explanation for the identified inconsistency, however, is that circumstances, which are strictly irrelevant, have come to influence the determinations. Thus, it is a feature of the fair rent system that neither rent officers nor the members of the rent assessment committees generally make desk decisions. Usually they visit each property and discuss the determination with both landlord and tenant. This personal interaction introduces an additional element into the rent setting process because different people - whether by virtue of their age, character, education, occupation, experience or whatever - have different abilities to communicate and present their case effectively. It can be argued therefore that over and above the technical and impersonal task of placing a valuation on a particular tenancy, the persons involved, namely the landlord, tenant and rent officer (or members of the rent assessment committee) may interact in ways which influence the eventual decisions.

In this section the significance of the additional variables relating to the physical and environmental condition of the dwelling, and the significance of interaction between the parties concerned will be examined in an attempt to seek explanations for the variation as yet unexplained.

### The significance of physical and environmental condition

As a consequence of the difficulty of the necessary visual inspection of each of the dwellings sampled, a small number of the pre 1919 terraced houses whose fair rents differed considerably from the fair rents estimated from the regression model were identified. These comprised 16 dwellings whose actual fair rents most greatly exceeded, and 15 whose actual fair rents were most greatly below the fair rent estimated by the model: these variations are referred to as the positive and negative residuals respectively.

Each of these properties was inspected externally and information about the local environment - road type, other land uses, architecture, streetscape - and about property condition - need for repainting or repointing, signs of rot or corrosion, missing tiles - were evaluated and recorded. Since the fair rents of these properties had been very different, either above or below, from the rent indicated by their dwelling and locational characteristics alone, it might be expected that if these extra variables did account for the unexplained variation their own characteristics would differ greatly between the two groups of dwellings.

When the data had been collected it was possible to determine statistically whether the positive group scored differently from the negative group. This is shown in Table 5.4 in which the proportion of each group possessing certain attributes, such as glazing problems or missing tiles, has been recorded. On the basis of this, a test of the significance - the z test - between the two percentages has been carried out.

These tests do not strongly support the case that these variables did in fact account for the unexplained variation in rents. There is no evidence to refute the null hypothesis that environment variables exhibit no difference between the two groups. The situation with respect to the external condition variables is not so clear. Broadly, the probability that a house in the negative group required attention to external woodwork - door, window frames and facia boards - including a major repaint was significantly higher than for the positive group. This was however the only such external condition variable which performed in this way: faults with the walls or roof did not. Moreover reference to the unaggregated data indicates that the frequency with which properties require attention is uneven. In 5 of the positive group the windows showed signs of rot or corrosion, as they did in 11 of the negative group. Bearing in mind that these groups are at opposite extremes rather more marked contrasts might have been expected.

What this suggests is that there is no evidence to support the view that the unexplained variation in this model is due to the absence in the fair rent determinations of environmental variables. There is a little more evidence, though this is not strong, that external condition variables are taken into account. However, they do not differ consistently enough to suggest that if the exercise were to be repeated for all properties it would significantly lessen the unexplained variation and accordingly it is difficult to accept that the omission of these variables accounts for the identified inconsistency.

Table 5.4
Proportion of dwellings amongst those with large positive
and negative residuals with specified characteristics

| | Positive residuals | Negative residuals | z-value |
|---|---|---|---|
| **External condition** | | | |
| Doors and frames | | | |
| Distorted/misaligned | 0.01 | 0.13 | 0.56 |
| Physically damaged | - | 0.25 | 2.08* |
| Faulty door fixings/furniture | 0.07 | 0.31 | 1.69* |
| Rot | - | 0.37 | 2.61* |
| Windows | | | |
| Rot or corrosion | 0.27 | 0.75 | 2.68* |
| Faulty hinges/pivots/slides | 0.20 | 0.69 | 2.74* |
| Glazing problems | 0.20 | 0.62 | 2.37* |
| Walls | | | |
| Cracks | - | - | - |
| Render/hanging tiles missing | 0.20 | 0.13 | 0.53 |
| Cladding defects | - | 0.19 | 1.79* |
| Roof and rainwater goods | | | |
| Ridge sagging/uneven | 0.13 | 0.31 | 1.20 |
| Tiles missing | 0.20 | 0.31 | 0.70 |
| Sight/facia board needing attention | 0.07 | 0.38 | 2.07* |
| Gutter/rwp needing attention | 0.07 | 0.56 | 2.92* |
| Other faults | - | 0.25 | 2.08* |
| Paint | | | |
| In good condition | 0.40 | 0.13 | 1.72* |
| Needing touching up | 0.47 | 0.25 | 1.28 |
| Needing major repaint | 0.13 | 0.62 | 2.80* |
| **General Environment** | | | |
| Traffic | | | |
| Road type (main) | 0.27 | 0.25 | 0.13 |
| "    "  (light) | 0.33 | 0.38 | 0.29 |
| "    "  (residential only) | 0.40 | 0.38 | 0.11 |
| Off-street parking | 0.07 | - | 1.11 |
| Land use | | | |
| Adj./opp. industrial premises | 0.13 | 0.19 | 0.46 |
| Derelict land/property visible | 0.07 | - | 1.11 |
| Amenity | | | |
| Open space visible | 0.27 | 0.19 | 0.53 |
| Trees/grass visible | 0.87 | 0.50 | 0.61 |
| Visual quality (average scores) | | | |
| Architecture | 2.33 | 2.56 | |
| Streetscape | 2.33 | 2.75 | |
| Landscape | 2.40 | 2.94 | |

* Exceeds the critical value of z for the one tailed test at 95 per cent confidence level (z crit = 1.64)

## Interaction

The significance of the interaction of, on the one hand, members of the public seeking favourable judgement on their claims and on the other hand rent officers with considerable discretion can be illustrated by comparison with similar situations. The numerous studies of so-called urban managers have shown how their discretion is frequently practised in such a way that certain categories of people receive more benefits than others. In particular those low on the social and economic scales are often more likely to be excluded from benefits than are others. The processes which lead to these outcomes may vary from one type of urban manager to another, but it might be taken as suggestive evidence of a similar process and outcomes in the rent officer service. For example, there are some similarities between the work of rent officers and that of local authority housing allocation officers. There is a wide degree of latitude open to housing allocation officers partly because the state gives local authorities themselves only minimal legislative guidance over who should receive council housing which 'in the widest sense is extremely broad and is encumbered by the minimum of legal regulation' (Lewis 1976, p.149). This level of discretion is moreover often increased still further when the procedures for making decisions about priorities are themselves loosely drawn up (Corina 1976).

The principle of housing need is generally accommodated within allocation rules by adopting criteria such as income levels, existing housing conditions and family circumstances. Applied objectively these criteria would ensure that those people were housed who were in greatest need as defined by those criteria. Close examination of the process of allocation and its outcome have frequently shown that this is not always the case. Berry (1974) has argued that whereas local authorities ostensibly give preference to those who are more in need, in practice allocations have been made to those a 'number of steps up the social ladder' (p.107). He also concluded that local authorities show a preference for tenants who 'will maintain at all times a proper and respectful attitude towards the housing manager and his staff and anyone else whom authority may see fit to supervise and control them' Berry (1974, p.107). Earlier, Burney (1967) had shown that many local authorities were concerned that the housekeeping standards of those offered homes were compatible with the sort of homes they were offered. Thus there was a tendency for those defined as having the lowest standards to be allocated to the oldest, most run down property.

Such biases have been found to be a widespread feature of council housing allocation. The Cullingworth Report (MHLG 1969) found that frequently applicants were graded according to some notion of just desert:

'Part of our concern here stems from the feeling that there is a danger that applicants are graded according to an interpretation of their desert. This even extends, on occasion, to a rejection of some from the council house sector. We were surprised to find some housing authorities who took up a moralistic attitude towards applicants: the underlying philosophy seemed to be that council tenancies were to be given only to those who "deserved" them and that the "most deserving" should get the best houses. Thus unmarried mothers, cohabitees, "dirty" families, and "transients" tended to be grouped together as "undesirable". Moral rectitude, social conformity, clean living and a "clean" rent book on occasion seemed to be essential qualifications for eligibility - at least for new houses. Some attitudes may reflect public opinion' (p.33).

The evidence of local authority allocation procedure is, therefore, that even when well trained, well intentioned people operate formal and objective systems, there is evidence of some bias in the output. It would not be inconceivable, therefore, if another group, namely rent officers, of equally well trained and well intentioned people operating without the benefit of formal and objective guidelines allowed some bias to appear in their results. Nevertheless, the case requires substantiation in the particular context of the bodies concerned.

Consultations. Some recognition that such interaction might influence the outcome, at least for bodies such as the rent assessment committees, had been set down in 1957 when the Franks report asserted that in deciding that certain issues should be resolved through the means of a tribunal Parliament had clearly intended that they should manifest three characteristics: openness, fairness and impartiality (Franks Committee 1957). Openness was felt to be important because if the procedures were secret then the basis of confidence and acceptability would be lost, and the publicity of proceedings and knowledge of the reasoning underlying decisions was required. Fairness required that all parties were aware of the procedures, knew what case they needed to answer and had full opportunity to state that case. Finally, impartiality was essential if all parties were to be satisfied that the decision reached had been reached by those with open minds, and in particular required that tribunals were free from the influence of any government department.

It has already been noted that the principle of openness does not entirely apply to either rent officer or rent assessment committee since they are not required to detail their reasonings. It will be argued later that the third principle of impartiality is also not fully met. The immediate concern here will be with the second principle : fairness. It will be argued that, although tenants and landlords alike may in theory have full opportunity to state their case, in practice they do not have equal ability to do so. The same arguments can also be extended to the practices of the rent officer which, it may be posited, are such that different people may be able to exert different degrees of influence on the outcome.

The consultations held by the rent officer are informal. As was seen in Chapter 3 the rent officer may visit the dwelling and discuss the accommodation and the rent with both tenant and landlord. The discussion may be amicable and a decision freely and fairly reached. There are, however, grounds for supposing that this may not always be the case. The arrival through the letter box of official letters written in language which is not always easy to understand may engender feelings of anxiety for certain sorts of people, for example, the elderly or immigrants. They may not understand for what the procedures - the inspection, consultation etc. - are intended. There may be great anxiety and suspicion. Because such procedures are outside the normal range of their experience they may have no great appreciation of how they might influence the outcome : what sorts of arguments and evidence to put to the rent officer, and perhaps as important, how those arguments should be put. Comments from a number of those interviewed in the survey of tenants indicated that even after the determinations had been made they did not realise that any improvements to the property which they had carried out themselves should not raise the fair rent. In these circumstances they may have failed to draw the rent officer's attention to their own improvements and he may unknowingly have attributed the improved standards to the landlord. Some tenants may be more skilled than others at presenting a case for restricting rent increases. Rent officers may feel some sympathy for those presenting a cool, logical detailing of relevant facts and antagonised by others who may be abusive and who may fail to restrict their comments to what is felt to be the matter at hand, namely the standard and character of the property in question. This is highly speculative but nevertheless it is difficult to ignore the proposition that in broad terms certain sorts of people, be they landlords or tenants, will be able to muster more effective arguments than others.

It may also be difficult not to believe that if such bias does exist then more frequently it favours the landlord. Many, though certainly not all, landlords are successful, in conventional terms, having acquired by one means or another considerable holdings of wealth in the form of property. Many are companies rather than private individuals. Many of them have previous experience of the service. Tenants, in contrast, are frequently those who have neither the money nor the good fortune to gain access to the generally more preferred housing tenures. Frequently they are poor and/or elderly. A survey of some of the tenants of registered properties in Birmingham indicated that about two thirds of them were over retirement age, and about half were or had been engaged in manual occupations. In addition many tenants had had only a single meeting with a rent officer or the rent assessment committees at any stage.

This lack of experience of similar situations may be particularly important with respect to the RACs. Much is made of the informality of such committees (e.g. Franks 1957, para. 64). Without this it would be difficult to uphold the claim that all people of whatever race, class or age, are able to participate on an equal and fair basis. In fact the claim of informality seems to be based on a comparison with courts of law and, indeed, in so far as the tenant and landlord are not under oath, are not required to stand until a judge has sat down and members of the public are not generally present, the proceedings are informal. However the relevance of the claim depends very much on its benchmark. Whereas the committee proceedings are very much less formal than a court of law it is not perhaps sufficient to claim that before it all people have equal opportunities. To many the committee may seem very formal, very intimidating and very alien.

The meetings of the rent assessment committee in Birmingham are held in a large room in an office block in the city centre. The three members of the committee sit behind desks raised on a platform. In front of them sits the clerk (as in a court of law) and facing them two desks; one for the landlord and one for the tenant. Behind landlord and tenant are seats for the general public and although there may only rarely be a public audience this may have the undesirable effect of being intimidating for certain people. In these circumstances it is not difficult to imagine that some tenants fare better than others: in very general terms, middle class tenants better than working class tenants. Because the assessment is based on subjective criteria the ability to present a good case, the ability to perceive what evidence is, influential and the ability to argue that evidence through may be of telling consequence.

Representation. The abilities of different sorts of tenants to present good cases, however, may be less significant than the contrast between landlord and tenant. Class or race differences apart, the landlord is helped because either side is free to be represented by anyone including lawyer, surveyor or lay person. This is more advantageous to the landlord because his costs are tax deductible as trade expenses whereas the tenant must pay for services out of taxed income. Samuels (1971, p.825) has argued that:

'These taxation privileges enable the companies to obtain the most highly skilled professional assistance - accountants, valuers, lawyers - in pressing their demands for increased rents. This has two results:

(1) lacking such huge resources, tenants are placed at a complete disadvantage in opposing those demands, or are deterred altogether from doing so;

(2) the companies include these high professional costs in their general expenditure on management, and thus are

able to peg their demands for rent increases still higher '.

In those cases where the landlord is a big property company, lawyers or surveyors may already be employed within the company so the marginal costs of representation are low. Even where this is not the case there are considerable incentives to hire professional representation because on the 'outcome of one tested case may depend the rents of perhaps 1,000 or more identical flats. It is (therefore) worth spending money on the most expensive advocates' (Allaun 1968, p.59).

For the year ending 30 September 1970, there were in fact 2,278 panel hearings in England, Scotland and Wales excluding London. In 1,141 of these the landlord was represented by a lawyer and in 212 the tenant was similarly represented. In 1,490 cases a surveyor or other similar professional represented the landlord and in 122 cases the tenant. The 'official' view is that representation is not necessary. The Francis Report claimed that in many cases the landlord sent his agent because the agent knew the facts. In any case there is little scope for advocacy at consultations. The rent officer is concerned with finding out the facts (Francis 1971). Moreover, whilst noting that the inarticulate tenant needed help, it was claimed that the sort of assistance he needs is not a professional advocate but a friend who is acquainted with the facts and is able to communicate (Francis 1971).

Attendance at hearings of the rent assessment committees indicates that whereas much of the proceedings is concerned with matters of fact - what repairs the landlord has carried out, for example - much, as Appendix A shows, relates to technical valuation issues to which many tenants would find it difficult to relate. In these circumstances it can be appreciated that although the average tenant may try to advocate his own point of view he can sometimes feel outnumbered, and is often confused by the procedure (Morris 1970). The Franks Report, discussing the arguments for allowing representation at tribunals, noted that many people were quite unable to present their own case coherently and that there was evidence that lack of representation was not in their best interests (Franks 1957, para. 85). Littlewood (1967), himself a panel president, in giving advice to solicitors instructed to appear for a landlord or tenant, recognises the influence that appearance can have on the result. As Elcock (1969, p.66) records, it is a well known saying amongst lawyers 'that he who fights his own case has a fool for a client' and notes further the argument that 'the citizen before court or tribunal has neither the legal knowledge nor, usually, the eloquence, to present his own case effectively'.

Empirical evidence. Evidence supporting these deliberations is far from conclusive. The possibility that the interaction between the persons involved may bring about biases in

individual determinations may be difficult to deny. Yet proof
that such biases actually occur and that they are sufficiently
large or widespread to account for the high level of
inconsistency found in determinations made by rent officers
and the rent assessment committees in Birmingham is not easily
substantiated. Nevertheless there are suggestions of
substantiation. It has been suggested to the authors by one
rent officer that in the registration area in which he worked
a landlord with a large number of properties had employed
representatives who had succeeded in influencing the rent
assessment committees to make fair rent determinations on his
property which were significantly higher than the rents which
other landlords had obtained. The result was a system of
'dual-prices' with one landlord receiving higher rents than
others.

Fenton and Collard (1977) used data collected for the
Francis Committee to examine whether there was any evidence
that coloured tenants, all other factors such as dwelling size
and standard held constant, paid higher fair rents than white
tenants. There may be some technical deficiencies in the
study relating to the statistical techniques used.
Nevertheless there was cautious support for the assertion that
coloured tenants seemed to be paying higher fair rents than
non coloured tenants in similar property.

The evidence of the present study is restricted to the
possible influence of the interaction between rent officer and
tenant on the determination. As argued earlier it is based on
the fact that a feature of the rent setting process is that
the rent officer does not make desk decisions based upon
information delivered to him: although this can happen in
certain cases, particularly where there is use of referencers.
(Referencers are people whose job it is to visit properties
and to record information about it to enable the rent officer
to make a determination without himself inspecting the
property internally. Even where this happens some of the same
reasoning can be extended to the interaction between
referencer, landlord and tenant). Generally, however, the
rent officer visits each property and collects this
information himself. At the same time he may discuss aspects
of the determination with the tenant and/or the landlord. The
tenant may point out to him that certain repairs carried out
by the landlord are superficial but that the poor workmanship
is apparent only at times e.g. in the case of, say, rising
damp which may not appear serious in the middle of a long dry
summer, but would do so during a long wet winter. A landlord
might indicate that the poor condition of the dwelling was due
primarily to the treatment it had received from the tenant
which was over and above fair wear and tear.

Putting the issue simplistically the concern is whether
there is, for whatever reason, and holding property type
constant, a correlation between the fair rent and the
characteristics of tenants such as personality, age, social
class, occupation and family size. Thus one of the questions

which this study sought to answer was whether the fair rent determination was affected at all by characteristics of the tenants and the influence which they exerted on the meeting with the rent officer. For example, did the fact that the tenant was retired or that the landlord was present when the property was inspected result in a higher or a lower rent than would otherwise have been determined?

Given the difficulty of observing such meetings except in cases where there is personal knowledge of a landlord or a tenant, an alternative approach used was a questionnaire survey of tenants to establish certain facts about them and about their meetings with the rent officer. The significance of this information can then be judged by comparing the amount of variation in fair rent explained by property and locational characteristics alone, with the level of variation explained when the questionnaire variables are added to the analysis.

Table 5.5
The influence of the tenant on the fair rent

|  |  | Property and locational variables only | All variables (including questionnaire) |
|---|---|---|---|
| All dwellings | $R^2$ | 0.896 | 0.919 |
|  | $\bar{R}^2$ | 0.842 | 0.846 |
|  | Mean square residual | 0.486 | 0.473 |
|  | No. of dwellings | 134 | 134 |
| Pre 1919 terraced housing | $R^2$ | 0.866 | 0.915 |
|  | $\bar{R}^2$ | 0.799 | 0.821 |
|  | Mean square residual | 0.445 | 0.394 |
|  | No. of dwellings | 85 | 85 |

The information collected from about one third of the 405 Birmingham tenants related to: sex, ethnic group, previous knowledge of landlord; people present when the rent officer visited; advice sought; employment status; occupation; age and household structure. When these variables are added to the list of property and locational characteristics they result in a slight but definite improvement in the $R^2$ and mean square residual values suggesting that they do indeed affect the fair rent determination (Table 5.5). For example, for the pre 1919 terraced housing the $R^2$ increased from 0.866 to 0.915 whilst the mean square residual decreased from 0.445 to 0.394.

These improvements represent the minimum amount of variation which can be explained by the questionnaire variables. The level of correlation between on the one hand the questionnaire variables and on the other the property and locational variables is such that it is not possible to disentangle the effects of each. The maximum amount of influence which the questionnaire variables could have exerted is represented by the $R^2$ value found by regressing them on their own, without the property and locational variables, with the fair rent. In the case of the pre 1919 terraced housing this was 0.387 which indicates that their contribution lies in the range of about 5 per cent to about 40 per cent of the variation in the fair rents.

The high level of multicollinearity in the complete set of independent variables also prevents adequate interpretation of the way in which individual characteristics of the tenants, such as age or ocupation, might affect the fair rent. As a result it is impossible to confirm the nature of the interaction between rent officer and the parties concerned and how this might influence the fair rent. The statistical analysis does suggest however that there is an interaction effect which accounts for at least 5 per cent of the variation in fair rents.

Table 5.6
List of questionnaire variables

---

Head of household; sex, ethnic origin, present status, present/previous employment, unemployed, OAP, socio-economic group
Number of persons in household; total,<16, >16, <30
Family size

Previous knowledge of landlord
Persons present at first/subsequent visit by rent officer; tenant, member of family, neighbour, landlord/ representative, friend, other
Other advice sought

---

## CONSISTENCY BETWEEN AREAS

Whereas the analysis has shown that there is some inconsistency within the one registration area of Birmingham, a further dimension to this analysis is the level of consistency between registration areas. The question is whether or not, as suggested by the earlier analysis of implicit rules, similar properties in similar localities but in different registration areas, have similar fair rents.

An attempt to answer this was made by taking the regression model which had been fitted to one area's rent determinations and applying its coefficients to the equivalent set of independent variables from another area. In so far as the coefficients represent the implicit rules which rent officers apply this is equivalent to presenting the rent officers of one area with the workload of another area, and instructing them to make fair rent determinations in accordance with their usual practice. Formally:

$$R_{ist} = a_{ot} + \sum_{j=1}^{j=k} a_{jt} \; x_{ijs}$$

where $R_{ist}$ = estimate of fair rent on property i in area s
by rent officer from area t

$a_{jt}$ = coefficient of variable j from sample of
properties from area t

$x_{ijs}$ = characteristic j of property i in area s

The estimates of fair rents, so derived, can be compared in
two ways with the actual fair rents. Firstly, does the rent
officer from one area set rents whose average level differs
from those set by the rent officer in another area? Tables
5.7 and 5.8 indicate that the results of paired t tests on the
differences between mean fair rents were in most cases
significant. That is, for the same set of properties, the
mean rents determined by rent officers from one registration
area were frequently significantly different from those set by
the rent officers from another registration area. For
example, Table 5.7(a) shows that for all dwellings in
Birmingham the average fair rent actually set was £8.93. When
hypothetically giving other rent officers the Birmingham
workload the averages determined were £8.60 by rent officers
from Walsall, £9.05 by those from Sandwell and £12.06 by those
from Solihull. The paired t statistics of Table 5.7(b)
indicate that although the difference between the Sandwell and
Birmingham averages was not significant, those between
Birmingham and Walsall and between Birmingham and Solihull
were. Indeed, considering all the comparisons of Tables 5.7
and 5.8 there appears to be a fairly consistent ranking of the
level of rents set by the rent officers from different areas.
For similar properties Solihull rent officers set the highest
fair rents, and Walsall rent officers the lowest with those
from Birmingham and Sandwell falling somewhere between. This
is further evidence that fair rents depend, at least in part,
on who is making the determination. This means that the
financial relationship between landlord and tenant takes on a
different aspect because one set of rent officers rather than
another is responsible for the determination.

The second set of comparisons which can be made are the
correlations between the fair rents actually set by one group
of rent officers and the fair rent estimated for the identical
properties by another group. This provides a measure of
whether two groups of rent officers agree on the relative fair
rent of each property, that is whether irrespective of the
absolute levels of rent, they both determine the highest fair
rent for the same property, the second highest fair rent for
the same property and so on.

Table 5.7
Between area consistency: all dwellings
(a)   Average fair rents and standard deviations

| Variables from | Coefficients from | | | |
|---|---|---|---|---|
| | Birmingham | Walsall | Sandwell | Solihull |
| Birmingham | 8.93 | 8.50 | 9.05 | 12.06 |
| | (2.12) | (1.97) | (2.28) | (8.38) |
| Walsall | 8.46 | 7.69 | 8.16 | 10.48 |
| | (1.76) | (1.43) | (1.41) | (5.56) |
| Sandwell | 8.87 | 8.39 | 8.82 | 11.82 |
| | (2.05) | (1.71) | (1.84) | (5.08) |
| Solihull | 10.22 | 10.17 | 10.68 | 10.44 |
| | (1.41) | (2.70) | (2.19) | (2.17) |

(b)   Paired t test for differences between actual and estimated averages

| | | | | |
|---|---|---|---|---|
| Birmingham | - | 3.086 | 1.189 | 7.318 |
| Walsall | 8.655 | - | 7.250 | 6.357 |
| Sandwell | 0.787 | 8.719 | - | 12.066 |
| Solihull | 1.670 | 1.186 | 1.043 | - |


Table 5.8
Between area consistency: pre 1919 terraced houses
(a)   Average fair rents and standard deviations

| Variables from | Coefficients from | | |
|---|---|---|---|
| | Birmingham | Walsall | Sandwell |
| Birmingham | 7.77 | 7.62 | 8.02 |
| | (1.31) | (1.37) | (1.32) |
| Walsall | 7.49 | 7.01 | 7.66 |
| | (0.88) | (1.02) | (0.61) |
| Sandwell | 7.25 | 6.84 | 7.23 |
| | (1.17) | (1.44) | (0.91) |

(b)   Paired t test for differences between actual and estimated averages

| | | | |
|---|---|---|---|
| Birmingham | - | 1.817 | 2.917 |
| Walsall | 5.138 | - | 7.174 |
| Sandwell | 0.402 | 4.709 | - |


Tables 5.9 and 5.10 show the correlations between actual and estimated fair rents for all properties and for pre 1919 terraced properties only.  In each case, the elements in the

main diagonal contain the explained variation ($R^2$) obtained
from fitting the original regression equations, the results of
which were given in Tables 5.1 and 5.2. They describe the
level of consistency within each registration area. The off-
diagonal cells contain the squares of the correlation
coefficients between actual fair rents and the fair rents for
the same properties estimated by rent officers from another
district.

Table 5.9
Correlations between actual and estimated fair rents:
all dwellings

| Variables from | Coefficients from | | | |
|---|---|---|---|---|
| | Birmingham | Walsall | Sandwell | Solihull |
| Birmingham | 0.767 | 0.276 | 0.269 | 0.024 |
| Walsall | 0.577 | 0.867 | 0.684 | 0.001 |
| Sandwell | 0.756 | 0.746 | 0.925 | 0.137 |
| Solihull | 0.396 | 0.096 | 0.112 | 0.935 |

Table 5.10
Correlations between actual and estimated fair rents:
pre 1919 terraced houses

| Variables from | Coefficients from | | |
|---|---|---|---|
| | Birmingham | Walsall | Sandwell |
| Birmingham | 0.687 | 0.333 | 0.314 |
| Walsall | 0.295 | 0.733 | 0.257 |
| Sandwell | 0.534 | 0.503 | 0.802 |

These tables demonstrate that rent officers, hypothetically
placed in areas other than their own, perform with varying
degrees of consistency in comparison with the rent officers
normally operating in those areas. However, in all cases the
consistency between different areas is lower than the
consistency within separate areas. Some are indeed very
different. Solihull rent officers over all dwellings in
Solihull achieved an $R^2$ value of 0.935 but the correlation
coefficient between their estimates and the actual
determinations in Birmingham was 0.024 and in Walsall 0.001.
This shows that there was virtually no statistical
correspondence whatsoever, implying that rent officers in
Walsall and rent officers in Solihull are applying totally
different sets of rules. Even in cases in which dwelling

types and housing markets were very similar, as in the case of pre 1919 terraced housing in Birmingham and Sandwell, the correlation coeficient was only 0.314. These results suggest that groups of rent officers have developed rules peculiar to their own districts. These rules are followed with varying levels of consistency, but overall they bear limited similarity to the rules and performances in other areas. This substantiates the earlier analysis.

## CONCLUSIONS

Extending the analysis in the previous chapter this suggests that the rent officer service has not everywhere succeeded in achieving a high level of consistency in its fair rent determinations. In Walsall, Sandwell and Solihull knowledge of the property and locational characteristics enabled a reasonably close prediction of the fair rent actually set. Rent officers in Birmingham and the rent assessment committee however demonstrated a weaker relationship between fair rents and objective characteristics. Moreover inter-area comparisons indicate that rent officers from different areas would make very different fair rent determinations for identical dwellings. The actual fair rent therefore appears to depend on which group of rent officers is making the determination. The implementation of operational procedures has resulted in variation which conflicts with the spirit of the legislation. There is considerable evidence that fair rents do not always 'bear scrutiny' with fair rents set elsewhere. Although it is important not to overstate the extent of this inconsistency, particularly within some areas, neither should it be entirely ignored.

# 6 The search for consistency

**ANOMALIES AND DISCRETION**

The evidence of the previous two chapters suggests that rent officers in the sampled areas have developed relatively simple decision models which differ in some respects from area to area and are sometimes inconsistently applied. Although the resulting fair rents appear broadly to reflect vacant possession capital values they nevertheless depend to some extent on the particular group of rent officers which has jurisdiction over a particular case. They also contain a random factor. The existence of widespread anomalies both within and between areas is not without precedent. In Chapter 2 it was argued that such anomalies have been a feature of the privately rented sector since the last century. Neither under free market conditions nor under control had the sector acquired a rational rent structure. However the fact that such anomalies have not been eliminated indicates that expectations that the fair rent system would do so have been unfulfilled.

The bases for these anomalies were anticipated in earlier discussions concerning the underlying principles of fair rent legislation. In particular, it was argued that the legislation does not provide rent officers with precise and unambiguous guidance for determining what a particular fair rent should be. The explicit rejection of the desirability of tying fair rents to a mathematical formula provided rent officers with only the broadest guidelines. Indeed, it was argued in Chapter 3 that Section 70 of the 1977 Rent Act is so loosely formulated that it is open to a variety of interpretations.

In this chapter the nature of subsequent attempts to impose greater consistency on fair rent determinations are examined. First, it focusses on the initiatives taken through the courts by landlords who have been principally concerned with achieving higher rents but who, had they succeeded, would have reduced the personal autonomy of rent officers. Secondly, some of the organisational arrangements and working practices within the service, which may have encouraged inconsistency, are identified. It shows that the search for consistency through restricting discretion has met with limited success.

## PERSONAL AUTONOMY

The ambiguity of the statutory guidelines for determining a fair rent are accompanied, in the cases of both individual rent officers and the rent assessment committees, by considerable personal autonomy. They are not required to justify any rent which they choose to determine for a particular dwelling. They are not required, for example, to provide detailed explanations of how the calculation was made, on what evidence it was based or why the fair rent was determined at one level rather than another. Indeed, rent officers enjoy a degree of independence and autonomy which is unparalleled in the other major land legislation affecting the public, namely Compulsory Purchase, Town Planning and Rating Valuation:

'The rent officer's role is autocratic. He is not required to attend an appeal to justify his calculations, he is not required to answer cross examination, and the successful appellant on appeal is not entitled to claim his costs, and has to foot the bill himself.

'The rent officer is accountable only to himself. His file is closed with his decision, except for a few written notes to the appellant and the panel in the event of an appeal to the Rent Assessment Committee' (Tanner 1980).

Some indication of the level of accountability and justification required of those in the rent officer service is provided in Appendix A which contains examples of evidence submitted by landlords to (Parts I and II), and decisions made by (Parts III and IV), rent assessment committees in the West Midlands. In the committee's decision contained in Part III the justification for the particular level of rent set is essentially that:

'Having considered the above and all other relevant matters, in particular the comparables put forward by the landlord, we are of the opinion that the Rent Officer's determination is on the low side'.

and in Part IV the justification is:

'Bearing the above in mind, what we noted during our inspection and exercising our own judgement, experience and knowledge, we have reached the conclusion that the figure determined by the Rent Officer is somewhat low'.

Whereas the level of explanation formally required of such statements is low there is no one inside the service, or elsewhere in central or local government who can overrule the determination made by a rent officer. In other words the rents determined by a rent officer are not subject to ratification by any other individual. If the fair rent for a particular property is anomalous, relative to other fair rents, there is no other person who can rectify the decision, unless either the particular landlord or the particular tenant chooses to appeal to the RAC.

On the few occasions that appeals are lodged with the RAC its determination is final. As with the rent officer there is no other individual or body within whose responsibility or power it is to confirm or alter its decision. There is no further right of appeal except on a point of law. In other words, landlord or tenant can appeal only on the grounds that in some way the RAC has acted in contravention of the legislation, but not that it has determined an incorrect fair rent.

## Appeals to the courts

Recourse to the courts has also been singularly unsuccessful in placing any restrictions on the autonomy of those operating the service, by continuing to affirm their right to use whatever method and information they alone choose. In fact most of the appeals to the courts have been made by landlords, often based on the argument that the courts should lay down an unambiguous method of determining fair rents which favours the landlord. It has been argued that these appeals can be located within a twin strategy of seeking judicial backing both for a clear method and for the limits of admissible evidence:

'The first aspect of the landlord's strategy has been to seek the limitation of the rent fixing services' discretion. This would be accomplished indirectly through judicial direction as to the correct method of determining fair rents. The second part of the strategy involves seeking to "judicialise" the procedures of rent fixers - primarily the Rent Assessment Committees - by limiting what evidence is admissible and relevant on determining a fair rent. Landlords have sometimes appeared to differ in which particular method they wish the judiciary to embrace largely, it would seem, because of the response from the Bench' (Robson and Watchman 1978, p.1210).

The method often proposed by landlords is the return on capital value method, which involves considering the leasehold as a form of investment by the landlord. The attraction to the landlord of this method is clear since it 'tends to throw up a much higher level of rent than other methods' (Prophet 1976, p.137). There has been some judicial backing for this method particularly through the Scottish Courts. In Learmouth Property Co. v. Aitken (1971 SLT 349), for example, the Court of Session emphasized that: 'it is surely a material factor in fixing the rent that the landlord should receive a fair return on the capital value of his property'.

Later, in Skilling v. Acari's Executrix (1973 SLT 139) in which the tenant had appealed on the grounds that the rent assessment committee had erred on a point in law by estimating a capital value with vacant possession rather than with a sitting tenant, Lord Clerk stated:

'The Committee were considering the determination of a fair rent for these premises which had a sitting tenant. If they were taking into account the capital value of these premises in order to make a computation, they should have proceeded on the market value of these premises in an outright sale. The market value of these premises in an outright sale would be affected by the fact that they were burdened by a sitting tenant, as it would be in any case where such a burden existed'.

This decision introduced a further measure of inconsistency into fair rent determination. It is clear that the selling price of a property is very different with and without vacant possession, and in the latter case very different where the sitting tenant is a young married couple with children as against an elderly widow. That the same property should command a different fair rent depending on the tenant was clearly incompatible with the concept of a fair rent because it produced differing determinations when a basic premise was that landlords in similar positions could be seen to be treated similarly, and tenants in similar positions could be seen to be treated similarly. It also introduced personal circumstances into the equation. This decision of the Court of Sessions could be seen to arise directly from the failure of the rent acts to provide rent officers and rent assessment committees with precise directions on which to base their determinations (Robson 1974). If capital value were to be the major criterion on which fair rents were to be based, and if capital values were to be dependent on the tenant, then so would fair rents. In these circumstances far from landlords being able to gain a general increase in fair rents in line with residential property price inflation it was conceivable that decreases could take place when the tenant changed.

Before long, however, the Scottish courts retreated from this position. Moreover the rulings in English courts have been even less forthright in promoting a particular method or methods. The concern has been to reiterate the discretion open to the rent assessment committees. In Guppys Properties Ltd. v. Knott, for example, Lord Widgery noted that the landlords had:

'contended as a broad principle, first of all, that as the difference between market rents and registered rents under the Rent Acts widens, it becomes more and more necessary, if fairness is to be done to the landlord, to fix fair rents by reference to capital values and not merely by reference to existing registered rents. Fixing rents by capital values of course (sometimes called the "contractors' approach") is a method whereby a market value is put upon the house as the sale of the freehold. Having ascertained its capital value, an appropriate rate of interest is applied to that capital value, and that

108

gives you a basic figure upon which the fair rent can be ascertained. It would not be disputed, I think, that this is a method which tends to favour landlords, and it is not therefore altogether surprising if the landlords in the present case supported it ..... This was a matter which came very much into evidence in the Sandoe case, and in the Sandoe case we directed first that there was no obligation on the rent assessment committee to use capital values, or registered rents, or current market values, or any particular approach, provided it did its best after consideration of all the relevant matters which had been put before it.

'Accordingly, the fact that there seems little attention paid to capital values in the instant case is not an error of law on the part of the assessment committee. The assessment committee is entitled to take any of these courses, and in some instances to take more than one, and mould them together. Assuming that it stays within its jurisdiction and has not acted unreasonably, its conclusions are conclusions which do not raise questions of law and therefore which are not capable of being litigated in this court' ((1977) 245 EG 1023).

The second part of the landlords' strategy has been to limit the evidence which is relevant to the determination. Clearly in situations where tenants are only rarely represented professionally, and in many cases do not themselves appear before rent assessment committees, it is in the interests of landlords to restrict admissible evidence to that which they (or their professional representatives) give. Landlords have thus attempted to draw a parallel with courts of law in which the limits of admissible evidence are closely defined, and at the most include only that evidence which is brought to their attention.

The English courts have consistently maintained that whereas the committee have a duty to consider carefully all the evidence put to them, they are also empowered to go out and seek their own facts, or to use their existing knowledge and experience. For example, in Crofton Investment Trust Ltd. v. Greater London Rent Assessment Committee ((1967) 8 WLR 256) Lord Parker declared:

'I am quite satisfied that this committee, that is to say, a committee of this kind under a procedure which is clearly intended to be informed and not to be carried through with the precision of a court of justice, is fully entitled to act, as it has been said, on their own impression and on their own knowledge. It is idle in any view to think of gentlemen manning this committee and sitting maybe day after day acquiring experience and knowledge of conditions in the locality and to say that they should shut their eyes to what they know of their own knowledge, and act only on such evidence as may or may not

109

be set before them, seems to me to reduce the matter to absurdity.'

Similarly, in Metropolitan Holdings Ltd. v. Lanfer ((1974) 29 P & CR 1972) Lord Widgery stated:

'It is well established, so much so that I shall not refer to any authority, that rent assessment committees when fixing a fair rent are entitled, indeed bound, to have regard to their own experience and knowledge. Initially they are not perhaps to be described as an expert tribunal, but they acquire a really remarkable knowledge of prevailing rents in their area from the simple experience that they gain from doing their job, and it has been, as I say, firmly established for many years that in considering what is a fair rent, the Committee can and should take into account its own experience and knowledge'.

Two important principles are raised by this ruling. The first impinges on the concept of natural justice, in so far as the committee which decides a case on the bases of its own expertise or knowledge known only to itself does not seem obliged to necessarily present both parties with an opportunity to challenge (Robson and Watchman 1978). The lack of accountability of rent assessment committees is thus further reinforced by the implied powers to rule without affording either party knowledge of the basis for that ruling or the chance to question it. In addition to the particular ruling this gives little direct guidance to landlords and tenants alike of what they can expect from future rulings.

The second principle is the attention which committees are required to pay to expert evidence. It follows from the above that whereas they are not entitled to decline to consider such evidence they are not necessarily required to use it in their rulings. The uncertainty raised by this minimal level of accountability is unlikely to be deemed in the interests of individual landlords and a recent variation on the admissible evidence strategy has been to argue that committees should show the calculations underlying their rulings. This has been similarly rejected by the courts:

'The second matter of principle which has been stressed greatly by the landlords in these cases is that when the rent assessment committee gives its decision it is required by statute to give reasons, and it is contended in one way or another that an assessment committee fails to perform that duty if it does not show what one might call its arithmetical working. What is argued is that it is not enough for the assessment committee to say, "we have considered all the evidence and, doing our best, we have come to the conclusion that £x is the fair rent". It is argued that that will not do and in some way the figure of £x has to be justified by reasons. In the absence of such reasons the committee has not performed its function

.... [On the contrary] in the very nature of things the
reasons, in the scientific sense, are not possible in such
an instance. It is worth remembering that valuation is
not a science: it is an art. There will be many, many
cases where all the assessment panel can do is to say
"Doing our best with the information provided, we think
the rent should be £x". If they do that, they disclose in
my judgement no error of law' (Guppys Properties Ltd. v.
Knott (1977), 245 EG 1023).

In this and similar rulings the courts have contradicted the
recommendations of the Franks Report which was set up to
examine the constitution and working of tribunals in general.
One of its conclusions was that the transmission to the
affected parties of the details of the reasoning underlying a
tribunal's decision was of considerable importance on two
grounds. Firstly that the decision itself is likely to be
more soundly considered if the tribunal is required to make
its reasoning explicit. Without this there is a danger that
the process of determining a fair rent amounts to 'little more
than a magical exercise in total discretion' (Robson and
Watchman 1978, p.1212). Secondly that either party will be
better able to assess whether there are any grounds for appeal
and how strong they are. The report states:

'Almost all witnesses have advocated the giving of
reasoned decisions by tribunals. We are convinced that if
tribunal proceedings are to be fair to the citizen reasons
should be given to the fullest practicable extent. A
decision is apt to be better if the reasons for it have to
be set out in writing because the reasons are then more
likely to have been properly thought out. Further, a
reasoned decision is essential in order that, where there
is a right of appeal, the applicant can assess whether he
has good grounds of appeal and know the case he will have
to meet if he decided to appeal' (Franks 1957, para.98).

The necessity for reasoned decisions to be given had in fact
earlier been supported by the Donoughmore Committee. But an
opposing view is that any requirement to limit evidence or to
give detailed reasons for decisions will tend to favour
landlords. Legal aid is not available, and in many cases it
is only the landlord who is represented. Indeed it can be
argued that the taking of a decision 'on the basis of evidence
presented to a tribunal is satisfactory and fair only so long
as the adversaries are fairly evenly matched: in many cases
before rent assessment committees the parties are manifestly
unequal in strength and the balance can only be redressed by
the committee making use of its own knowledge and experience'
(Young 1978, p.207).

Whereas it may be fortunate that the courts have fairly
consistently refused to judicialise the fair rents system on
the grounds that this would formally tip the balance in favour
of the landlord, the refusal has made neither the procedures
nor the formula any less susceptible to other influences.

## ORGANISATIONAL ARRANGEMENTS

The personal autonomy vested in the rent officer is reflected
in certain administrative arrangements and working practices
of the service. Until the 1980 Housing Act legislation had
made reference only to rent officers and their powers. The
implementation of the service included, as an administrative
rationale, the appointment of senior and county rent officers.
Their appointments were on higher salary scales than the rent
officers whom they were to manage, but they had no statutory
powers over the rent officers or the rents which they
determined. This in itself created some conflict within the
service and also hindered the achievement of uniformity
generally as the report on output in the rent officer service
indicated:

'If the output of the rent officer service as a whole is
to be increased, and particularly if the practices and
procedures which rent officers have used are to be
altered, it is important for there to be a uniform
administrative approach throughout the rent officer
service. Equally it is essential that individual rent
officers should remain responsible for individual rent
determinations on the statutory basis. We have considered
the suggestion that in order to ensure uniformity of
approach, and to enable county and senior rent officers to
achieve streamlining and consistency, the legislation
should contain statutory backing for such reasonable
management action. We agreed that without some statutory
backing, county and senior rent officers heading
registration areas could find it difficult, or even
impossible in some circumstances, to ensure consistency of
practice. Even though difficulties would be likely to
occur in only a very small minority of areas and in very
few cases indeed, the present position, in which the Rent
Act made no mention of the powers of the county and senior
rent officers, was unsatisfactory. We felt that some
change was needed which was not more draconian than was
required to provide the solution in that very limited
number of cases, and in particular which would be
compatible with the individual assessment of rents by rent
officers, but that was also likely to be effective in
enabling suitable management action to be taken. We
accordingly concluded that it ought to be made clear that
the rent officer heading each registration area was
responsible for the operation of the rent officer service
in that area' (DOE 1980a, p.11).

This lack of a statutorily based administrative hierarchy
may have made it difficult in some cases to impose greater
uniformity of practice. It may be compounded however by the
physical difficulty of assessing the overall pattern of the
fair rents set by individual rent officers which is important
in terms of bringing the general level of rents set by each
individual rent officer into line with those of his

112

colleagues. It may be particularly significant where a rent officer is setting rents relatively in favour of either tenants (i.e. lower than the general pattern) or landlords (i.e. higher than the general pattern). However as we have seen, rents for even one type of property (such as pre 1919 terraced housing) do vary considerably, and unless a particular rent officer is setting rents widely outside the general pattern it may be difficult to recognize variation. This is complicated by the fact that the county or senior rent officer may have a considerable workload to oversee which prevents close supervision. A county or senior rent officer may be able, physically, to check only a small proportion of determinations made in his area. Nor can his checks always be very thorough particularly where there may be over a hundred determinations per week in the area.

The question of inconsistency in Birmingham is compounded by its size and workload. It is one of the largest and busiest districts in the country which during the period under study had eleven rent officers who between them were making about 100 determinations per week. Even with the best of intentions on the part of all concerned comparability between such a large number of people is difficult. It may not be a coincidence therefore that greater inconsistencies were apparent in the fair rents set by the eleven Birmingham rent officers than in those set by the 2 Sandwell rent officers.

Administrative arrangements may also underlie the inconsistency found in the fair rents determined by the rent assessment committees. It has always been regarded as one of the functions of the rent assessment committees that they provide guidance and promote consistency. Since each panel area encompasses a number of registration areas this should, in theory, be particularly relevant to inter-area consistency. However it is widely argued within the service that consistent guidance is not given; a conclusion supported by the statistical evidence in the previous chapter. The stumbling block may be the fact that any RAC does not have such frequent exposure to either any one registration area or indeed all its registration areas. As part time appointees, panel members do not have frequent contact with the job of rent assessment and have fewer opportunities to discuss similar cases with colleagues. Moreover, although they are required to take a broader view it is possible that depth is sacrificed as a result. In other words their infrequent cooption onto a committee, and the geographical spread of their workload may mean that their guidance is in fact not very consistent. Their ability to provide guidance may also have been rendered difficult by the requirement of pre-dating their determination, often for a considerable period, to the date at which the rent officer had originally registered the property. It is suspected in some quarters that RACs sometimes have allowed current determinations to influence their evaluation of old determinations.

In contrast to these arrangements, the relationship between rent officers and the rent assessment committees may in one respect encourage consistency. This may arise to the extent that those in the service tend to have regard for criteria which reflect the work activity and professional standards of rent officers rather than the function which the service has been set up to fulfill. As Hill indicates, a characteristic of public services, which like the rent officer service have considerable levels of flexibility, is that 'policies may become unduly subservient to inward-looking concepts of professionalism, in which group protection for the professionals may be treated as more important than service to the public' (Hill 1976, p.101). This might be taken to suggest that rather than being overconcerned with either tenants or landlords, and the extent to which both groups are getting a fair deal from the service, rent officers as a group may have greater regard for providing the outside world - central government and pressure groups such as Shelter or the British Property Federation - with as little evidence as possible of the operation and possible inadequacies of the service. It is in their corporate interest to portray a service which is operated with efficiency and fairness. In this respect one criterion of efficiency and fairness is the number of cases which are taken on appeal to the rent assessment committees. A high proportion of appeals could be taken as prima facie evidence that the service is not doing its job properly, and a low proportion that it is.

Reinforcing the position of the profession is the position of rent officers as individual employees. Their performance may be judged in one respect by the number of cases on which they have made assessments which are subsequently subjected to appeal. In a work situation few people like to have their decisions questioned and, just as with the profession as a whole, high levels of appeal may be taken as evidence of an inability to make good decisions. Once cases have gone to appeal there is a further vested interest that the rent assessment committees support their assessments. When they do the rent officer can claim that his decisions have been endorsed and that the appeals were the result not of his bad judgement but of the appellants'.

However this situation may also lead to inconsistency because it places the rent officer's assessment in a contradictory position. In the first place the rent officer may be concerned with setting a rent the level of which does not precipitate an appeal. This may encourage him to fix the fair rent more in favour of the party which he considers more likely to appeal : the property company represented by a vociferous valuer rather than the quiet, subservient old age pensioner, for example. In addition to the level of assessment itself the rent officer may indicate to the parties concerned that his decision is an informed one, that he is an expert and that there is nothing to be gained by questioning it.

In the second place, arising in the event of an appeal, the individual rent officer will be concerned that his decision should not be overturned by the rent assessment committee. His concern then is that his assessment is proved to be right and that the basis for appeal was, therefore, in error. Fixing a fair rent at a level which satisfies his first concern that there shall be no appeal may be incompatible with his second concern of comparability with the committee.

## CONCLUSIONS

It might have been reasonably expected that since 1965 attempts would have been made to limit the discretion built into the fair rent system and that some of these attempts would have succeeded. In practice this has only marginally been the case and the warnings about the consequences of such failings, given long before the fair rent system was established, have been largely ignored:

'it is important .... that no Government shall give to .... tribunals matters to decide which they cannot adjudicate except by subjective considerations .... we should not give to any ... tribunals ... the power to decide matters on which there is no criterion by which any body of men can actually come to a practical decision' (James Griffiths quoted in Robson and Watchman 1978).

It is precisely the failure to take note of this message that may have allowed the assessment of rents in general, and in particular cases, to be influenced in certain directions. Because there are no objective statutory criteria the assessments can only be the result of subjective opinion on the part of the rent officer or the rent assessment committee. As Elcock (1969) points out: '.... their discretion is still very large .... Questions of what constitutes a fair rent ... are not decided by reference to rules; they are values which those hearing the case must to a large extent promulgate themselves. This can cause difficulties to the tribunals. They are exposed to attack for their decisions in a way that those tribunals which apply rules are not' (p.30).

The examination of the ways in which rents have in practice been determined in the absence of rules has concentrated mainly on statistical approaches. However, together with the discussion in Chapter 5 concerned with the importance of interaction, much of the present chapter also indicates another potentially fruitful line of enquiry which is largely unfulfilled here. In a situation of discretion which has been established by legislation and reinforced by the courts a valid question is: what does explain the particular patterns of decision making found? Adler and Asquith (1981, p.24) point to the 'working' or 'operational' ideologies which decision makers bring to their discretionary world as being of paramount concern, adding that many studies assert 'the theoretical primacy of the actors' construction of social reality with special reference to their professional activity, the possible (indeed probable) modification of the formal goals and practices of an institution or policy in the course of the day-to-day accomplishment of the professional task, and the importance of the individuals' tacit assumptions and knowledge for the exercise of discretionary powers granted to them under the auspices of their particular profession'. In a similar vein Young (1981, p.33) notes:

'The interpretation of formal rules, the creation of informal guidelines and the exercise of preferences within them comprise a set of subjective factors which enable discretionary decision-makers to make sense of and operate upon their everyday world'.

The substantiation of such assertions with respect to rent officers would require a very different approach from that adopted here, concentrating less on statistical analysis and more on 'infiltrating' the organisation and particularly the world of the profession. To that extent the preceeding chapters have laid a foundation stone but left much of importance still to be done.

# 7 Rent restriction and the decline of the privately rented sector

The preceeding three chapters have been concerned with the relative level of fair rents and the degree to which there was found to be consistency in relating dwelling characteristics to rents. As such they were concerned with a particular aspect of equity underlying the fair rents system, that landlords of similar properties received similar rents and tenants of similar properties paid similar rents. They thus sought to examine the notion of fairness amongst landlords as a group, and fairness amongst tenants as a group.

In the present chapter a second issue, which might also be viewed in part as an equity issue, is considered: whether the legislation has resulted in fairness between landlord and tenant. This takes the absolute levels of rent and asks whether these levels have provided landlords with sufficient incentive to remain in the industry. In the context of explaining the continued decline in the size of the privately rented tenure, the position facing tenants is also considered.

## THE ABSOLUTE LEVEL OF FAIR RENTS

In a situation of statutory rent restriction the overall level of rents partly determines how much profit is made by landlords in general and how much expenditure is incurred by tenants in general. However, although this is central to the rent setting decision, rent officers have received little specific guidance from the legislation. The discretion and personal autonomy which seem to underlie variations in relative fair rents apply also to the absolute levels. Notwithstanding this, at the national level at least, there appear to be certain broad empirical regularities: that fair rents have, on average, been set higher than controlled rents, but lower than many other indicators might suggest they should be.

The broad relationships between the average levels of registered rents and other measures appear to reflect in part the apparent intention of the fair rents legislation. The change in tenancies from controlled to regulated has on average resulted in rents some three and a half times greater (Table 7.1). Not only was the average controlled rent low, being about £2 per week in 1979, but in many cases this possibly represented a negative return, since the cost of insurance, repairs and maintenance and management expenses would frequently have exceeded this. In these circumstances it is of little surprise that landlords of controlled tenancies frequently neglected even essential repairs and maintenance work and that there should have been such a strong lobby in earlier years to repeal rent control. Whereas the increase, shown in Table 7.1, in the average rent determined by the rent officer may not always have been as great as landlords would have wished, it has, from their point of view, given them net returns which are more frequently positive. To that extent, the implementation of the legislation has achieved the objective of freeing some landlords from the inordinately low returns of rent controlled properties.

Table 7.1
First registrations of tenancies formerly rent controlled[a]
England and Wales

|  | Mean controlled rent £ p.a. | Mean registered rent £ p.a. | Ratio of mean registered rent/ mean controlled rent |
|---|---|---|---|
| 1973 | 63 | 202 | 3.2 |
| 1974 | 53 | 192 | 3.6 |
| 1975 | 59 | 213 | 3.6 |
| 1976 | 70 | 252 | 3.6 |
| 1977 | 82 | 284 | 3.5 |
| 1978 | 94 | 335 | 3.6 |
| 1979 | 109 | 379 | 3.5 |

(a) Dwellings decontrolled with a qualification certificate, which is a certificate of good repair, and the availability of a sink, a fixed bath or shower, a wash hand basin, a hot and cold water supply to all three, and a WC in or attached to the dwelling for the exclusive use of the tenant.

Source: Housing and Construction Statistics

In contrast changes over time in the average level of registered fair rents do not seem to correspond closely with changes in related indicators. In fact fair rents increased throughout the 1970s at a rate far slower than might have been expected by many landlords and tenants comparing their situations with other sectors of the housing market (Table 7.2). This is the case whether the average rents are considered over all unfurnished tenancies registered in each year, or only those that were re-registered not more than four years after the previous registration and with no changes in the terms of the tenancy. From the point of view of landlords housing repairs and maintenance costs increased at twice the rate that rents increased over the period 1970 to 1980, restricting their ability to carry out this work. Over the same period the very much larger increase in the purchase price of second hand owner occupied houses suggests that landlords' rates of return on vacant possession capital values also declined. From the tenants' point of view the comparisons with other indicators suggests a gradually more favourable position. Prices in other sectors have increased at a faster rate whilst the indices of average earnings and retail prices suggest that the tenants' burden has been reduced.

This conclusion may need modifying either for all tenants or certain tenants. Whatever the reduction in the ratio of average rent to average earnings some tenants may nevertheless have experienced an increase in this ratio. This may have occurred because wage levels in their particular employment sectors fell relative to other sectors, or because they moved from employment to unemployment or to retirement. Likewise if tenants differ from the population at large with respect to expenditure a more relevant index of retail prices might be chosen. Notwithstanding this, although there is little precise evidence of what market rent levels would be, the starting point and the diverging trends shown in Table 7.2 suggest that fair rents are well below them.

Table 7.2
Trends in fair rent and other indicators

| | Mean registered rents (Unfurnished lettings) | Mean rents at reregistration | Second hand dwellings bought with a mortgage | Local authority rents (unrebated) | Housing repairs & maintenance costs (inc.VAT) | Average earnings | Retail prices |
|---|---|---|---|---|---|---|---|
| | England & Wales | England & Wales | UK | UK | GB | UK | UK |
| 1970 | 100 | 100 | 100 | 100 | 100 | 100 | 100 |
| 1971 | 103 | 95 | 114 | 109 | 108 | 111 | 109 |
| 1972 | 110 | 97 | 152 | 127 | 116 | 126 | 117 |
| 1973 | 110 | 100 | 203 | 147 | 147 | 142 | 128 |
| 1974 | 126 | 110 | 221 | 161 | 179 | 168 | 148 |
| 1975 | 135 | 109 | 237 | 177 | 222 | 212 | 184 |
| 1976 | 150 | 118 | 253 | 203 | 261 | 245 | 215 |
| 1977 | 165 | 128 | 271 | 235 | 296 | 270 | 249 |
| 1978 | 189 | 150 | 309 | 249 | 327 | 309 | 270 |
| 1979 | 211 | 167 | 397 | 273 | 305 | 358 | 306 |
| 1980 | 246 | 196 | 461 | 341 | 490 | 424 | 361 |

Sources:  Housing and Construction Statistics; DOE 1981

## RENT LEVELS AND DECLINE

With the failure of attempts to limit the interpretation of the fair rent formula to specific criteria such as the rate of return, and with the evidence of Table 7.2 that rates of return apparently have fallen over the last decade, criticisms that the level of fair rents has led to the decline of the sector have continued unabated.  Housing economists, for example, whilst often acknowledging that decline might have been due to other causes have argued that rent control has perpetuated 'the housing shortage by discouraging new house-building' (Needleman 1965, p.164), 'progressively paralysed the supply of houses for rent and perpetuated shortage' (Stafford 1978, p.114) and has been the cause of the 'elimination of a small but important supply of rented housing, caused solely by the "fair rent" system' (Hallett 1977, p.50).

Professional institutions have also continued to echo the arguments for decontrol. The Royal Institute of Chartered Surveyors has argued for increases in the level of fair rents:

'clearly something must be done to make the yield from rents more attractive, if the decline in the private rental sector is to be arrested. We believe that the fair rent system should now be modified to make rental incomes more realistic in the light of inflationary trends' (RICS 1976, p.29).

Amongst the many institutions, private companies, pressure groups and individuals presenting evidence to the House of Commons Environment Committee there was a broad concensus with this view that if the sector was to be maintained at its present size rental incomes needed to be increased. As the committee itself summarized the evidence:

'there was general agreement that except for some small sub-sectors ... current rents were an inadequate incentive for the majority of landlords' (House of Commons 1982, p.xxiv).

In considering the possibility of expanding the sector, of encouraging existing owners to continue to let, and developers to invest in new building, the British Property Federation unequivocally supports the allocative outcome of the market place:

'One point is quite clear: none of these things will happen until there is confidence that there will be no Government interference in freely negotiated contracts. The only way to make use of the skills of the developers and to persuade the financial institutions and pension funds to invest in rented residential property is to legislate for all accommodation developed after a certain date to be let on terms negotiated in the open market without any fear by either party that the bargain which he makes with the other would subsequently be unilaterally altered by Parliament to his disfavour. Equally, this principle should be applied where a property becomes vacant and is relet' (British Property Federation 1975, p.6).

Similarly, the Conservative party have also decried the obscurring of the price mechanism:

'Rent controls made residential accommodation a poor
investment compared with the alternatives .... The quality
of these houses has declined with their numbers, again
mainly because rent controls have not made it worthwhile
either to keep existing investments in decent repair or to
build for letting' (Conservative Central Office 1976,
p.54).

Clearly the basis of such concerns rests in the belief that
rent restriction alone has reduced the profitability of
landlordism as an industry leading to a diversion of
investment towards other outlets. Whereas investment
diversion, as argued in Chapter 2, had been a feature of the
sector even before the rent acts, decontrol had not resulted
in reinvestment. It is therefore difficult to reconcile the
fact of rent control causing investment diversion and decline
with investment diversion occurring in the absence of rent
control. This leads to questions on the one hand of the
extent to which rent restriction has reduced rents below
market levels and how those restricted rents compare with
other investment opportunities, and on the other hand, if rent
restriction cannot fully or partly explain the decline of the
sector, then what can?

Analysis of the economics of landlordism indicates that the
criticisms reported above seriously misanalyse the position.
It can be argued that, notwithstanding rent restriction, the
rate of return accruing to landlords is in fact at a level
which compares favourably with many alternative investments.
Its major limitation is not the level of return but the way in
which that return can be realised. This will be discussed
later in this chapter where it will be argued that its
significance with respect to the decline of the sector is
partial. The major cause of decline will be identified as the
nature of subsidies to owner occupiers which has created a gap
between the capital values of dwellings with and without
sitting tenants. This possibility for a once-and-only profit
has encouraged landlords to extricate themselves from the
sector (Kemeny 1981). In other words the reasons for decline
lie not with the interference in the rented market but with
the intervention in the owner occupied market, and thus
decline may only be halted, if that is an objective, by
greater equality of treatment between tenures.


CAPITAL VALUES AND RATES OF RETURN

Landlords of residential property will often have some
estimate, perhaps only very approximate, of the rate of return
on vacant possession capital value which is implied by the
rent officer's determination. Although much of it has not
been publicly available, there has been an increasing amount
of evidence about such rates of return which gives some
general picture of the economics of landlordism.

Table 7.3, which presents some of this evidence, is based on a number of studies carried out by the DOE (DOE 1978; DOE 1981), a pressure group (British Property Federation 1975) and academic researchers (Allen and Joseph 1978; Doling and Davies 1981). Each involved estimates for different years or for different property types. Interpretation of the table depends in part on the way each study was carried out which varies because of the methodological difficulties involved. These difficulties arise basically because fair rents and vacant possession capital values are hypothetical quantities until a rent officer makes a determination or the dwelling is sold. Both quantities are also temporally specific. The result is that at any one time few dwellings will have both a relevant capital value and a relevant fair rent. Thus few dwellings sold to owner occupiers have had recently determined fair rents; and few dwellings with recently determined fair rents are sold with vacant possession. There are various approaches to tackling this problem each of which may result in some bias or inaccuracy in the calculation of the rate of return. (See Appendix C for details of the methodological procedures employed in each of these studies).

Notwithstanding the varying methods of calculation the evidence of these studies suggests that there are differences in gross rates of return between different years, different areas and different property types. The figures indicate that rates of return have generally been declining throughout the decade averaging 6 to 7 per cent at the start and 3 to 4 per cent at the end. The results from the Beacons exercise and the Birmingham study further emphasize the extent of differences in rates of return for individual properties and individual property types (Table 7.4). For example, for one property type - the mid-terraced houses built around 1870 - the rate of return ranged from 1.7 per cent in Hertfordshire to 10.1 per cent in Northumberland. Moreover there were also wide variations in the rates of return estimated for the different property types in any one registration area. In Tyne & Wear, for example, one property type obtained 9.2 per cent return, another 6.2 per cent and another 4.5 per cent. At the level of individual dwellings the Birmingham study also demonstrated a range of rates of return. The differences are such that although the accuracy of the estimates is debatable, the fact of variation is not.

Over the country as a whole the results of the Beacons Exercise show a clear pattern of differential rates of return (Doling and Davies 1982b). In the South West, South and South East of England the rates of return are mostly below 4 per cent; north of a line stretching roughly from the Bristol Channel to the Wash rates of return exceed 4 per cent. In Wales all except one registration area - Mid Glamorgan - have average rates of return in the 3 to 5 per cent range. This pattern indicates that tenants in certain parts of the country - principally the Midlands and Northern Britain - pay higher

Table 7.3
Annual gross rates of return on vacant possession capital values

| Dwelling type | DOE (1978) Capital values survey[a] England | | | British Property Federation (1975)[b] Britain | Allen & Joseph (1978)[b] Paddington | Doling & Davies (1981)[b] Birmingham | DOE (1981) Beacons Exercise[a] England & Wales |
|---|---|---|---|---|---|---|---|
| | 1970 | 1973 | 1976 | 1974 | 1978 | 1980 | 1981 |
| pre 1919 small artisan houses | 7.5 | 4.3 | 4.9 | - | - | 2.98 | 3.2[c] 3.7[d] |
| 1919-1939 speculative builders' houses | 5.7 | 3.3 | 3.8 | - | - | - | 3.3[e] |
| All properties | 6.9 | 3.7 | 4.4 | 3.1 | 3.95 | - | - |

(a) Averages given are medians
(b) Averages given are arithmetic means
(c) Dwelling type A (See Appendix C)
(d) Dwelling type C (See Appendix C)
(e) Dwelling type D (See Appendix C)

rents, in relation to capital values, for the properties which they occupy. Correspondingly, landlords in these areas will on average receive higher returns in relation to the values of their properties in the owner occupied market.

Notwithstanding these variations Tables 7.3 and 7.4 also suggest that gross rates of return are generally low, currently around 3 to 4 per cent. This conclusion, based on a number of separate surveys, has recently received further substantiation:

'A large body of evidence was presented to the Committee on the low rents and therefore the low rates of return available on regulated registered rent accommodation. A number of landlords gave examples of gross rents which gave returns of only 1-2 per cent on vacant possession capital values. More comprehensive material suggested that average gross returns were in the order of 2-5 per cent .... These averages mask significant differences between areas and dwelling types' (House of Commons 1982, p.xxii).

Landlords have a number of expenses and costs. These are the necessary costs of management, which may be in money or in kind, but which must be accounted for if landlordism is to be compared with other forms of investment. There are also the costs of insurance, repairs and maintenance. In addition residential property rent is a taxable item. Although the post tax return will depend on the tax position of the individual landlord, and even given the optional nature of some expenditure, at least in the short term, average net rates of return seem unlikely to be above 1 or 2 per cent: a range substantiated by the evidence to the Environment committee (House of Commons 1982).

Table 7.4
Variations in gross rates of return

| Gross rate of return % | Beacons exercise | | | Birmingham study |
| | Type A | Type C | Type D | Pre 1919 artisan dwelling |
| | % | % | % | % |
| 0 - 0.99 | - | - | - | - |
| 1.0 - 1.99 | 4.11 | 2.47 | 36.36 | 1.90 |
| 2.0 - 2.99 | 38.36 | 22.22 | 40.26 | 54.29 |
| 3.0 - 3.99 | 13.70 | 33.33 | 20.78 | 39.52 |
| 4.0 - 4.99 | 15.07 | 27.16 | 2.60 | 4.29 |
| 5.0 - 5.99 | 9.59 | 4.94 | - | - |
| 6.0 - 6.99 | 9.59 | 8.64 | - | - |
| 7.0 - 7.99 | 1.37 | - | - | - |
| 8.0 - 8.99 | 5.48 | 1.37 | - | - |
| 9.0 - 9.99 | 1.37 | - | - | - |
| 10.0 - 10.99 | 1.37 | - | - | - |

## ALTERNATIVE BASES FOR RATES OF RETURN

Taken at face value rents of this order might suggest that landlords are not receiving returns which compare well with those which could be achieved elsewhere and that it is hardly surprising that they have withdrawn from this form of investment. The reality of the situation is however somewhat different. Firstly it is arguable whether vacant possession capital value is the appropriate basis on which to calculate rates of return. Secondly even if it were it ignores the second source of profit which generally accrues to landlords, namely the rate of return arising from the increase in capital value over time. Once allowance is made for this, the evidence suggests that the landlord frequently enjoys a profit which compares reasonably with alternative investments. One is then obliged to look elsewhere, and particularly to the way in which these profits can be realised, to account for the decline of landlordism.

The relevance of questioning the appropriate basis for calculating the rate of return is that the opportunity cost of the investment is not generally its full vacant possession capital value. In fact this amount may be substantially reduced by the existence of a sitting tenant and the tax position of the individual landlord in which cases the computed rates of return will be correspondingly increased.

**The sitting tenant**

The significance of the existence of a sitting tenant figured in the earlier discussions about the attempts to persuade the courts to define a specific method of fair rent determination which backfired when it was proposed that rates of return should be based on capital value with a sitting tenant and not with vacant possession. The monetary implications of this are illuminating. Consider for example, a house with a vacant possession capital value of £20,000 for which a fair rent of £600 p.a. has recently been determined. This would represent a gross rate of return of 3 per cent which after deducting the costs of management, insurance, repairs and maintenance would give a pre tax income of, say, £400 or a 2 per cent return. An existing landlord who considered that such a percentage return was too small might seek to sell his investment and reinvest his capital elsewhere.

If the existing landlord were to obtain vacant possession he would be able to sell to an owner occupier for £20,000. If he cannot obtain vacant possession however the dwelling will not be sought by an owner occupier but possibly by another landlord whose estimate of its value will be influenced by the fact that its pre tax yield is £400 p.a. If such a prospective landlord wishes, perhaps on the basis of rates of return for other similar investments, to achieve a pre tax rate of 10 per cent then the maximum he will be willing to pay for the dwelling is £4,000. In so far as this landlord was typical of other prospective landlords then £4,000 and not £20,000 represents the capital value of the existing landlord's investment.

In these terms rent restriction does not limit the rate of return and therefore the profit accruing to landlords. Rather it constitutes a windfall loss to landlords at the time of introduction of the legislation. Once implemented the prices which landlords are willing to pay for additional investments in residential property will reflect the existence of restriction of rent at certain levels. This also implies that the general, absolute level of rents (as opposed to their relative levels) may in the long run be always 'fair', because landlords knowing of this general level will rationally pitch their bid for residential property accordingly. Similarly, in the long run there is not, as some writers imply, a subsidy from all landlords to all tenants. The tenant may be better off as a result of rent restriction but only at the expense of the landlord at the time rent restricting legislation was

125

introduced. In so far as the length of time since rent restriction was introduced in Britain is considerable many existing landlords have acquired their investments in a situation of rent restriction. If the price they paid reflected that situation then there is no subsidy. If it exceeded the price justified by the situation then they simply acted unwisely. However the error consisted in overpaying the previous owner not in subsidizing the present tenant. On similar grounds an argument can be constructed that a return to market rents would constitute a windfall gain to landlords at the expense of tenants.

Nevertheless within the context of the present discussion the opportunity cost of the investment to landlords with sitting tenants is an amount which reflects the existence of rent restriction. It may also reflect the nature of the sitting tenant. A dwelling with an old frail tenant with no one to whom the tenancy can be passed or a young, professional person saving to buy a house may, all other things being equal, have a higher capital value than one with a poor middle aged family which is never likely to be able to afford to purchase. This is because the latter has a higher probability of perpetuating the investment on the terms of the existing letting. On these grounds the appropriate basis for the rate of return is a variable amount depending not only on the nature of the accommodation and the nature of rent restriction but also on the nature of the tenant. The corresponding yields will never be lower than those based on vacant possession capital values, and generally somewhat higher.

Table 7.5
Annual appreciation in capital values 1970-1980

| Total appreciation 1970-1980 | Annual percentage appreciation Gross[a] |
|---|---|
| Three fold | 11.6 |
| Five fold | 17.5 |
| Seven fold | 21.5 |

(a)    If A is the capital value at the start and B is the capital value at the end of the decade, then the annual rate of increase r can be expressed as

$$r = 100 \ (\sqrt[10]{(B/A)} - 1)$$

**Capital Appreciation as a Source of Profit**

Even without a rental yield from the tenancy, landlords have a second source of profit from the dwelling which arises from the capital appreciation in residential property. Over the 1970-1980 decade in particular residential property has increased in value at a faster rate than many other indicators

126

such as average earnings and retail prices generally (Table
7.2). These increases have been sufficient to modify both the
distribution of wealth in the country as a whole as well as
the percentage of all wealth in the country which is held in
the form of dwellings. Thus in 1960 17 per cent of gross
personal wealth was held in the form of dwellings, but by 1975
this had about doubled to 37 per cent (Royal Commission on the
Distribution of Income and Wealth 1977). Landlords, like
owner occupiers, have shared in this gain.

Throughout the 1970s the average house prices recorded in a
number of published statistics have shown different but
clearly related increases (Fleming and Nellis 1981). Over the
country as a whole the increase was about fivefold, whereas
for pre 1919 terraced housing in Birmingham alone casual
observation suggests that the increase has mainly varied
between three and sevenfold. The annual rates of return
implied by these increases indicate that, in the long run,
landlords have enjoyed considerable capital increases.
Ignoring tax a fivefold increase over ten years is equivalent
to a 17.5 per cent annual rate of increase, and a sevenfold
increase 21.5 per cent (Table 7.5). These returns may be
somewhat reduced depending on the tax position of the landlord
although the 1982 Finance Act has reduced the burden, relative
to earlier years, for those subject to capital gains tax.
Notwithstanding this, Table 7.5 suggests that in the long run
landlords receive rates of return which compare favourably
with those from alternative investments. Indeed the total
rate of return on a landlord's initial investment can be
considerable particularly if the dwelling was acquired at a
price which reflected rent restriction. This suggests that
even with rent restriction some landlords could have achieved
a total rate of return, after taxes and expenses, of up to 20
per cent per annum. During this same period retail prices
increased 3.61 times (Table 7.2) corresponding to an annual
rate of increase of 13.7 per cent. Moreover comparison with
the rates of return for alternative investments given in Table
7.6 which are pre tax, indicates that a post tax return of
only 10 per cent per annum might be considered favourable.


## THE REALISATION OF GAINS

In the light of rates of return of the order of magnitude
suggested here it is difficult to concur with arguments that
landlordism as an industry is dying simply because its returns
are low. It should more correctly be argued that what makes
landlordism a 'poor' investment is not the low level of
returns but the fact that most of that return is not easily
realisable. The larger part of the income from rented
property is not from the money rent paid by the tenant but
from capital appreciation. But whereas it is the capital
appreciation which makes the total return appear to compare
favourably with alternative investments that same capital
appreciation cannot easily be realised in the form of a
regular flow of money income. It can only be realised by a

once-and-only sale of the property. Once that has been done
the landlord receives no more capital appreciation and rental
income as a landlord. In that sense investing in rented
property compares more closely with investing in long term
securities rather than with deposits which can be accessed
both in part and at short notice such as bank or building
society accounts. The capital increases and the compound
interest adds to that capital but neither the original capital
nor the interest can be realised separately or in part.
Having sold the property in order to realise the accumulated
capital appreciation there may be little financial argument
for reinvesting in the sector unless the landlord has some
relative advantage in the market. Having paid tax on the
capital appreciation, reinvesting in the sector would in many
cases do little more than make a free gift to the Inland
Revenue. The economic incentive is thus often to leave the
sector rather than to reenter it.

Table 7.6
Comparative interest rates

| Yr | Minimum lending rate | Local auth. 3-month deposit rate | Build. Soc. ord. shares (gross equiv.) | Financial Times index of ordinary shares | | | 2% Con. |
| | | | | Price index | Div. yield | Earn. yield | Net price |
|---|---|---|---|---|---|---|---|
| 70 | 7.00 | 7.25 | 8.51 | 361.0 | 4.75 | 6.54 | 27.3 |
| 71 | 5.00 | 4.56 | 8.16 | 386.2 | 4.76 | 6.21 | 27.6 |
| 72 | 9.00 | 8.75 | 8.57 | 503.8 | 3.26 | 4.98 | 27.5 |
| 73 | 13.00 | 16.00 | 10.71 | 435.6 | 4.12 | n.a. | 23.2 |
| 74 | 11.50 | 13.25 | 11.19 | 251.2 | 8.23 | 21.47 | 10.8 |
| 75 | 11.25 | 11.31 | 10.77 | 311.0 | 6.81 | 19.49 | 17.1 |
| 76 | 14.25 | 14.88 | 12.00 | 368.0 | 5.96 | 17.61 | 17.6 |
| 77 | 7.00 | 6.75 | 9.09 | 452.3 | 5.42 | 16.50 | 20.4 |
| 78 | 12.50 | 12.44 | 11.94 | 479.4 | 5.65 | 16.47 | 21.0 |
| 79 | 17.00 | 17.22 | 15.00 | 475.5 | 6.49 | 16.61 | 22.1 |
| 80 | 14.00 | 14.75 | 15.00 | 464.5 | 7.62 | 18.84 | 21.1 |

Source:  Bristol and West Building Society (1981)

Whereas the capital appreciation accumulated in a property
can only normally be realised by the sale of that property, a
fundamental precondition is that the sale is with vacant
possession. That is, unless the landlord is able to offer the
property on the market without a sitting tenant then the
capital appreciation will be depressed. In other words a
substantial part of the potential return to the landlord is a
return for obtaining vacant possession rather than a return
for holding rental property. Since many tenants have security
of tenure vested by the rent acts not only are the potential
profits from landlordism rarely realisable but the date at
which they will be realisable may be unknown. Thus many
landlords are faced with a situation in which their profits
are high but in practical terms they can only be realised at

some uncertain date in the future when vacant possession is obtained. Because certain tenancies can be handed on to the next generation the date may be in the distant future.

At most times, therefore, the landlord is faced only with the options of continuing to own the property and receiving a small financial income through the rent payable by the tenant, or of selling the property with a sitting tenant. This sale may be to the sitting tenant himself who is himself seeking to become an owner occupier or to another landlord who may eventually be seeking to sell the property (Hamnett and Randolph 1981). In either case the sale price is likely to be below the vacant possession capital value. There may only be a few occasions in the life of the landlord or of the property where vacant possession is achieved. In many cases unless the landlord seizes the opportunity to sell at that point he condemns himself to another period, of uncertain duration, during which his profits will be limited to rental income.

Whereas the high rate of capital appreciation in the past has not been responsible for the flight of landlords out of the sector, the difference between capital value with and without a sitting tenant has been particularly significant (Kemeny 1981). As Hamnett and Randolph (1981) have argued 'the fundamental reason for this decline has been the substantial and growing discrepancies between the tenanted investment value of residential property (i.e. the value of such property to a landlord as a long term source of income) and the vacant possession value' (p.31). This discrepancy or 'value gap' (Hamnett and Randolph 1981, p.33) may be considerable. It was shown earlier that a dwelling which with vacant possession might have a capital value of £20,000, with a sitting tenant might have a capital value of only £4,000. Similarly, Nevitt (1966) has stated that 'The difference between current investment price and vacant possession price is too large and the landlord is forced to take the best profit he can from the house and to wait with as much patience as possible for the day when he can stop being a landlord' (p.124). Indeed what has been seen over the last decade (Table 7.2) has been a high rate of increase in vacant possession capital values and a lower rate of increase in fair rents. Since, as has been shown, capital values with sitting tenants are tied to fair rents they have increasingly lagged behind. The value gap has become greater both in absolute and relative terms. Faced with rental income and capital gains tied to the whims of the fair rent system and with the latter not realisable at all until an unknown time has elapsed it is hardly surprising that many landlords have seized the earliest opportunity to gain the increasingly more profitable vacant possession capital value.

## HOUSING SUBSIDIES AND THE VALUE GAP

It might be argued that the value gap is explainable in terms of subsidies and taxation (Hamnett and Randolph 1981, p.31).

As seen in Chapter 2, successive governments have chosen to subsidize owner occupiers by relieving them of certain tax obligations, while not doing the same for the landlord or the private sector tenant. This is important to the present discussion because taxes and subsidies in the housing sector have in part become capitalised, so that the value of a dwelling is dependent in part on the relative treatment of its tenure (Robinson 1981).

The precise nature of the tax subsidy accruing to owner occupiers depends on the prior definition of tax neutrality (Hughes 1979). However, there are three particular taxation benefits which have been given to the owner occupier and withheld from the landlord. The house buyer who borrows money to finance the purchase receives a subsidy from the government in the form of a reduction in his tax liability. In effect this reduces the rate of interest which the purchaser pays on the loan. For example an actual rate of interest of 15 per cent would be reduced to 10.5 per cent for those with a marginal rate of tax at the standard level; at higher marginal tax rates the reductions are larger (Table 7.7). This mortgage interest tax relief also enables purchasers to pay higher prices for housing than they otherwise could afford: keeping the proportion of income spent on housing constant, the tax reduction enables purchasers to increase the price they are able to pay.

Mortgage interest tax relief is only allowed on a person's principal place of residence. It is not allowable on second homes, neither can it be claimed by a landlord purchasing a property to let to tenants. The landlord is thus in a position in which he must pay higher net repayments than an owner occupier for the same property. For example a dwelling with a vacant possession capital value of £30,000 bought with a 100 per cent mortgage over 25 years at 10 per cent mortgage interest would involve repayments for the landlord of £293.80 per calendar month. However, in the first year of repayment an owner occupier with a marginal rate of tax of 30 per cent would repay about £220 per calendar month or with a marginal rate of 60 per cent, £145 per calendar month. These repayments are about 75 per cent and 50 per cent respectively of the repayments which a landlord must make for the same property.

Table 7.7
Net rates of interest*

| Gross interest | Marginal rates of taxation | | | | |
| --- | --- | --- | --- | --- | --- |
| | 30% | 40% | 50% | 60% | 70% |
| 10 | 7 | 6 | 5 | 4 | 3 |
| 12.5 | 8.75 | 7.5 | 6.25 | 5 | 3.75 |
| 15 | 10.5 | 9 | 7.5 | 6 | 4.5 |

*These are approximations for the first year when repayments consist almost entirely of the interest element.

In addition to mortgage interest tax relief, owner occupiers also benefit from not being liable to tax on imputed rent or capital gains. The Housing Policy Review (DOE 1977a) argued that the former used to be extracted because it had always been extracted: 'application of tax under Schedule A to houses which were occupied by their owners was a by-product of the arrangements, rather than a policy' (DOE 1977a, p.62). Its abolition in 1963, however, meant that whereas a landlord continues to pay tax on the rental income which he derives from a residential property, an owner occupier is not liable to tax on the rental income he derives in kind. Finally, the owner occupier unlike the landlord or the investor in stocks and shares is not required to pay a capital gains tax on disposing of his property.

## BUYING VERSUS RENTING

The effect of these subsidies is felt not only directly by the landlord through the value gap. They also influence the demand for privately rented housing by altering the relative costs of buying and renting in favour of the former. In terms of the example above of a house purchased for £30,000, if a landlord is looking for an amount in rent which at least covers the cost of purchase it follows that he will expect a tenant to pay at least £293.80 for the privilege of renting such a dwelling, when for the smaller sum of £220 (if he pays tax at the standard rate) the same tenant could purchase the dwelling.

Although Table 7.8 does not take account of discounting consequent upon different relative payments in different years, it suggests that the equation is balanced in favour of the owner occupier even at much lower rents. In columns (b) and (c) the annual rental payments are recorded at five year intervals, for rents of 3 per cent and 7.5 per cent of capital value respectively. The former percentage reflects a gross rate of return, which was reported earlier as being about the national average, and the latter the rate of return which some landlords have argued would be desirable from their point of view. Following an article in Estates Gazette which had analysed the causes of decline of the privately rented housing sector correspondence indicated that this would be a generally acceptable return. For example, the managing director of the City of London Building Society asserted that discussions with 'one or two developers' indicated that 'they would be perfectly happy with a gross return of about 5 per cent or 6 per cent' (Trollope 1979). Likewise the chairman of the Residential Property Committee of the British Property Federation suggested as 6 per cent return net of outgoings. This he defined as 6 per cent of freehold vacant possession value after the landlord's reasonable provision, taken year by year, for what must be spent on such things as insurance, external repairs and maintenance and services (Evans 1979). This figure was further supported by the senior surveyor to a major pension fund on the basis of 'discussing the subject

Table 7.8
The cost in each year of buying and renting a dwelling
with capital value of £15,000

| Year<br>(a) | Rent at<br>3%<br>capital<br>value<br>(b) | Rent at<br>7.5%<br>capital<br>value<br>(c) | Net<br>mortgage<br>repayment<br>(d) | Insurance,<br>repairs and<br>maintenance<br>(e) |
|---|---|---|---|---|
| 0  | 450  | 1125  | 1240 | 198  |
| 5  | 724  | 1812  | 1278 | 318  |
| 10 | 1167 | 2918  | 1347 | 514  |
| 15 | 1180 | 4699  | 1473 | 827  |
| 20 | 3027 | 7568  | 0    | 1322 |
| 25 | 4876 | 12189 | 0    | 2145 |
| 30 | 7852 | 19631 | 0    | 3455 |

| Year<br>(a) | Cost of<br>loan<br>(f) | Gross<br>cost<br>d+e+f<br>(g) | Capital<br>appreciation<br>(h) | Net cost<br>(g)-(h)<br>(i) |
|---|---|---|---|---|
| 0  | 390 | 1828 | 1500  | 328    |
| 5  | 390 | 1986 | 2416  | -430   |
| 10 | 390 | 2251 | 3891  | -1640  |
| 15 | 390 | 2690 | 6266  | -3570  |
| 20 | 390 | 1712 | 10091 | -8379  |
| 25 | 390 | 2535 | 16252 | -13717 |
| 30 | 390 | 3845 | 16178 | -22333 |

| Year<br>(a) | Ratio Gross<br>cost to<br>3% rent<br>(g)/(b)<br>(j) | Ratio Gross<br>cost to<br>7.5% rent<br>(g)/(c)<br>(k) | Ratio Net<br>cost to<br>3% rent<br>(i)/(b)<br>(l) | Ratio Net<br>cost to<br>7.5% rent<br>(i)/(c)<br>(m) |
|---|---|---|---|---|
| 0  | 4.06 | 1.62 | 0.73  | 0.29  |
| 5  | 2.74 | 1.10 | -0.59 | -0.24 |
| 10 | 1.93 | 0.77 | -1.41 | -0.56 |
| 15 | 1.43 | 0.57 | -1.90 | -0.76 |
| 20 | 0.57 | 0.23 | -2.77 | -1.11 |
| 25 | 0.52 | 0.21 | -2.81 | -1.13 |
| 30 | 0.49 | 0.20 | -2.84 | -1.14 |

with colleagues on the institutional investment market' (Dunn 1979). This figure has been more recently confirmed as a lower estimate in evidence to the Environment Committee where 'many felt higher returns, ranging from 10 per cent to as much as 20 per cent would be necessary to maintain the supply' (House of Commons 1982, p. xxv).

Since vacant possession capital value is assumed to increase each year, as described in Appendix D, with constant rates of return the rental payment which will be expected from tenants will also rise. Thus a 7.5 per cent rate of return would indicate a rent of £1,125 in the first year but a rent of £19,631 in year 30. In this comparison lies one of the major differences between tenants and purchasers. Purchasers pay an annual amount related to the historic cost at the time of purchase: tenants may be charged rents which are periodically updated, to an extent which is related to the increasing capital value.

This contrast can be seen in column (d) which details the mortgage repayments on a loan of £12,000 net of mortgage interest tax relief assuming a marginal rate of tax of 30 per cent (Appendix D). Starting at year zero the net repayment increases each year as the interest element, and thus the amount of the tax relief, falls until the end of year 19 when the loan has been fully paid off. From that date there are no further repayments, the historic cost having been met.

These repayments must be added to the costs in columns (e) and (f) to provide the estimate of total gross costs in column (g). Column (e) has been calculated as the fixed percentage of the capital value which needs to be devoted to insurance, repairs and maintenance, column (f) as the interest payable on a £3,000 deposit, which is an expression of the opportunity cost.

Column (g) therefore represents the total monetary costs of purchase. Comparison with rental payments indicate that with a return which landlords would find acceptable, the tenant's outgoings would, within the time period of six or seven years, exceed those of the owner occupiers.

If capital appreciation at a conservative rate of 10 per cent is taken into account to produce a net cost of purchase, the owner occupier in effect pays a negative rate of interest. Column (i) shows that the net cost is negative at and beyond year 5 because the direct monetary costs are outweighed by capital appreciation. The tenant, in comparison, takes no share of the capital appreciation of the dwelling in which he lives. The result, as column (l) shows, is that even in the first year the tenant paying rent at the rate of only 3 per cent of capital value exceeds the net payments of the owner occupier. With financial incentives such as these it is little wonder that the demand for privately rented housing has diminished.

133

# CONCLUSIONS

Looking at the privately rented sector as a legally defined relationship between rational landlords and rational tenants seeking to maximize profit and minimize cost, there is little evidence to support the assertion that its decline is a direct result solely of rent restriction. Indeed the argument here demonstrates that the total returns accruing to landlords are not as low as generally supposed. Not only is vacant possession capital value not necessarily the most appropriate base on which to calculate rates of return but landlords have a second source of profit, beyond rental income, in the form of capital appreciation.

The major limitation of capital appreciation is that it is not directly realisable as a regular flow of money income accruing to the landlord, in the same way as rent. The capital value of a dwelling with a sitting tenant is lower than vacant possession capital value and in so far as it is a reflection of fair rents has increased less in absolute and relative terms. The difference is also a reflection of subsidies to the owner occupied sector which are not shared by landlords or tenants. The resulting value gap offers a large source of potential profit but it is one which can only be realised in full on the often rare occasions on which the tenant vacates the property. This means that rental dwellings as an investment might be likened more to investments which are for long and of uncertain duration. In this sense therefore it is the security of tenure provisions in the rent acts which have made landlordism unpopular rather than rent restriction although, as argued in Chapter 2, the one is a necessary adjunct of the other.

The rent restriction argument also loses its force as an explanation for decline once it is appreciated that capital values with sitting tenants reflect the determined fair rent. If landlords acted rationally they would purchase rented property only at capital values which would give them reasonable rates of return in the knowledge of the fair rent. Thus in so far as existing landlords were not the landlords at the date of initiation of rent restriction they are not, as sometimes claimed, subsidizing tenants but are receiving rents which by definition are fair to them.

The existence of subsidies to other tenures is also important. Those enjoyed by the owner occupier have helped to ensure that demand for owner occupation has grown at the expense of demand for private rental. Similar arguments could be constructed about the subsidy advantages of the local authority and housing association tenures. The relaxation of rent restriction does nothing to combat the relative advantage of the other subsidised tenures. Indeed in so far as it will increase the tenant's outlay it will increase demand for other tenures.

This chapter has also shown that the issue of fairness between landlord and tenant is one which, in the circumstances, is of partial relevance only. Landlords can be viewed as entrepreneurs who have made a free choice in investing in rental property and have done so with knowledge of prevailing market conditions, of which rent regulation is one and subsidies which differ by tenure another. Having entered the market of their own free will landlords have no more right to a certain return than does the entrepreneur who invests in stocks and shares. The existence of fiscal subsidies to the owner occupier also means that there can be no balance between landlord and tenant which on the one hand gives the landlord a sufficient return to encourage him to stay in the market and which on the other hand gives the tenant a low enough rent for many to afford or an incentive for many to remain as private tenants. With existing parameters the two sets of interests are incompatible, and the fairness of the fair rent system does not therefore have practical meaning in this particular respect.

# 8 The significance of rent restriction: past, present and future

## LIMITATIONS OF THE FAIR RENT LEGISLATION

The decontrol incorporated in the 1957 Rent Act did not solve the problems of the privately rented housing sector. Landlordism was showing little sign of developing into an efficient industry offering a product of satisfactory quality at a reasonable price. Higher rents had not automatically resulted in an adequate level of repairs and maintenance in a stock of housing whose condition was on average woefully deficient. Many landlord-tenant relationships continued on good terms but in many others the increased vulnerability of the tenant was exploited. In some areas, in particular, housing shortages forced tenants with no alternatives to pay exorbitant rents, whilst increased rents encouraged greater subdivision. At the same time some landlords harassed tenants with the intention of gaining vacant possession and the opportunity to extricate themselves from this form of investment. The very legislation which many claimed would bring order, efficiency and stability, therefore, had the effect of exacerbating many of the problems of the sector.

By the time that a new Labour government came into office in 1964 public attitudes combined with the views of large sections of the government, the opposition and senior civil servants to produce a widely based expectation that the sector should be recontrolled. But there was little agreement about what form that recontrol should take. Beyond a commitment to recontrol, the call for fair rents was in many ways little more than a slogan. The solutions were not 'dictated by party doctrine, electoral calculus or the clash of entrenched economic interests' (Banting 1979, p.62). The reliance on professional expertise in drafting the bill did not mean that the solution was based on a clear set of principles, however. The acceptance of the market place, curbed of its greatest excesses, as an adequate guideline to what constituted a fair rent obviated any clearer statement of what was meant by the adjective 'fair'. Once a working procedure had been proposed which was acceptable to those concerned with drafting the bill little progress was made in giving it a more detailed and specific definition. The level of discretion embodied in the formula meant that in some ways the implied definition of fairness was a relative one. To an extent what was fair was what individual landlords and individual tenants would accept as fair. Indeed, it was to be part of the rent officer's role to act as a conciliator between opposing sets of interest and to get them to accept his assessments. Whereas the proposals received widespread support from all parts of the political spectrum based in part on the lack of precision, that same lack of precision has been the foundation of the characteristics of fair rents identified in earlier chapters.

The legislation has met some of the objectives which were expected of it. It has, for example, allowed regular increases in rents whilst many excessive rental demands have been curbed, but in failing to relate the notion of fairness to any inter tenurial comparisons it provided no means by which landlords could be encouraged to remain in the industry. Subsidies to those in other tenures placed them in an advantageous position in comparison with the landlord and the tenant: a position which the landlord could achieve only by selling the property to an owner occupier, and the tenant by becoming a council tenant or owner occupier. There was nothing within the legislation to ensure that rent officers should be aware of, let alone concerned about, this. Indeed fair rents whilst continuing to be fair in the context of the legislation, have slipped further behind vacant possession capital value, increasing the financial motivation for landlords to move their investments elsewhere. At the same time the failure to relate fair rents to considerations of what would be necessary to encourage landlords to remain in the industry did nothing to create new housing either in the privately rented sector or elsewhere. With increasing pressure on public expenditure the demand for municipalisation of the sector has become less economically and politically viable. The fair rent formula meant that this form of housing could decline under control, protecting tenants from excessive rents and providing landlords with small but regular increases. But it did not address the problem of ensuring that the functions of privately rented housing continued to be met. Indeed by emphasising the 'fairness' of rents to landlords and tenants alike in response to legislation which appeared to have precipitated decline it may have discouraged thoughts of doing precisely that. In appearing to solve particular problems of the sector interpreted in terms of too little control of market mechanisms the legislation may have diverted attention away from the larger problems of housing shortage.

The failure to define more precisely what was meant by fair in this context also laid the foundation stone of further levels of inconsistency. The legislation was in part a response to the rent anomalies occurring in cases where landlords exploited shortage by charging 'excessive' rents. One solution to this would have been to supply sufficient housing to ensure that tenants were not placed in a position of great scarcity. But the legislation was directed at placing limitations on the housing stock which already existed rather than on expanding the supply of housing. In not being more explicit about those limitations, however, the system has promulgated another set of anomalies. It may or may not have curbed the ability of some landlords to obtain high rents for

137

what is often poor accommodation but it has certainly not been
sufficiently precise to ensure that the rational rent
structure intended would result:  namely that fair rents
should correlate with the value of the accommodation offered
so that better properties should have higher fair rents than
poorer properties. Crossman had argued for this in terms not
only of achieving consistency but also of ensuring that that
consistency was seen to be achieved:

> 'We need to ensure consistency so that the public at large
> and other rent assessment committees know of decisions
> that committees are making.  The decisions will set the
> tone for rent levels over wide areas and will help rent
> officers, landlords and tenants in subsequent cases'
> (Hansard (710) 48).

The evidence presented here has been that this consistency
has not been achieved.  Rents for similar properties in
similar localities are not necessarily similar, suggesting
that some landlords and some tenants are treated more 'fairly'
than others.  Moreover one of the explicit intentions of the
fair rent legislation was that consistency would be a central
feature.  In other words whereas it may be difficult to
specify what absolute level of rent would be fair, the
relative level should be less problematic.  It might be
reasonably argued that a rent would be fair if it was
proportional to the value of the accommodation offered.  But
in rejecting some more precise formula the means of achieving
this was limited.

The general level of rents which resulted from this
legislation is relevant in another way: the balance of
advantage between landlords and tenants. As argued in the
previous chapter, if landlords purchase property with the
objective of letting to private households and in the
knowledge of fair rent levels, then they can only reasonably
expect the rate of return which they calculated at the point
of purchase.  If, for example, the resulting rate of return is
lower than the landlord is satisfied with or lower than can be
obtained from alternative investments then this cannot be
taken as evidence that the balance is weighted too far in
favour of tenants.  There may be other grounds for arguing
that private sector tenants are not paying enough for their
housing, say in comparison with council housing tenants, but
not that this is inequitable to landlords.  Rather the
situation is that the landlord has acted unwisely.  Similarly
there may be grounds for arguing that landlords are receiving
returns which are too high if, for example, the investment is
more lucrative than investment in manufacturing industry.
Within the market context in which they operate however
landlords can perhaps only be congratulated for maximising
their investment.  Alternatively if the landlord has paid a
smaller amount such that the resulting rate of return exceeds
his expectations or what could be achieved elsewhere then the
previous owner may have acted unwisely.  In any of these cases
the question is not one of equity as between landlord and

tenant but whether, given the rules of the market in which he is operating, the landlord has acted wisely or unwisely.

The situation is different at the time when rent restrictions are introduced. Restriction then represents a windfall loss to the landlord, and a windfall gain to the tenant. Derestriction represents the opposite. Moreover the gain of one party is directly at the expense of the other, and neither has done anything to deserve this good or ill fortune: what is more than fair to one is less than fair to the other. However while there may be nothing fair in this neither is there anything necessarily fair in rents set in the market place. They are only fair, or not, in the context of the particular set of rules operating in the market.

Whereas the fair rent legislation has met some of the expectations held of it, therefore, it has not been a panacea. It has not resulted in consistent rent structures. Moreover, although the legislation itself has not been responsible for the continued decline of the sector, neither has it addressed that situation. Whatever concept of equity was intended and whether or not it has been fair to the individuals concerned the legislation has done little to keep landlords and tenants in the market.

In the remainder of this chapter the present significance of the legislation is considered. It argues that it now directly impinges on only a part of the sector largely because not all landlords and tenants are economic men and that the social nature of the landlord-tenant relationship in practice often precludes the use of the legislation by one or both. The significance of the legislation in terms of the number of lettings to which it applies in fact, rather than in theory, is thus reduced. In the context of the continued need for the functions which the sector fulfills, however, some of the possible policy options are considered.

**Landlords as economic men**

The significance of the general levels of fair rent and their relationship to rates of return has been discussed, both in this and in the previous chapter, in terms of the economic objectives of landlords. In so far as this has demonstrated the relevance, or lack of it, of frequently made criticisms that the decline of the sector has been a direct consequence of rent control and rent regulation, it argued on economic grounds. It started from the premise that landlords are rational economic men reacting to information about price and went on to argue that price levels are the consequence principally of subsidies to owner occupiers. It is arguable, however, whether it is appropriate in the present circumstances to construct a case solely around the existence of a single, uniform, set of landlord objectives. Although landlords may be economic decision makers in an industry in which, as in other types of industry, an objective may be to maximise profits it does not follow that all landlords pursue the same ends. The company which views the ownership of residential property as a means of obtaining a profit on an investment which should only be continued as long as alternative investments open to it are not yielding greater profits represents only one part of the spectrum. Between such profit conscious landlords and the charitable trust operating as landlord on a non profit making basis, or even subsidising tenants from other sources of income, are a number of landlord types and positions. The concept of economic man is not equally appropriate to all of them.

Nationally, there is a wide diversity of landlord types (Table 8.1) with only about one-seventh of landlords being property companies, although over half are individuals. Various studies over the last two decades also indicate that most landlords own only a small number of tenancies (Table 8.2). The precise percentages vary over time and space but the general picture is not of the large company landlord but of the individual owning one or just a few tenancies. In addition to influencing their objectives this may also have an important effect on the ability of landlords to carry out

Table 8.1
Type of landlord: privately rented housing in England, 1977

|  | % |
| --- | --- |
| Property company | 13.8 |
| Employment company | 13.0 |
| Employer individual | 6.8 |
| Relative | 5.5 |
| Other person | 52.9 |
| Other | 7.9 |

Source: National Dwelling and Household Survey

repairs and maintenance, since many small landlords have limited resources and little expertise to cope with these (Kemp 1979).The diversity of landlord type and ownership structure is further emphasized by the different ways in which landlords have come into the industry (Table 8.3). Thus although almost half the rented dwellings in Sheffield had been acquired in the last ten years, mostly with sitting tenants and for their investment potential, many had been inherited (Crook and Bryant 1982). Generally the large proportion of landlords who inherited property suggests that many of them have become landlords by accident rather than by design. There is other evidence that some people become landlords on a short term basis whilst they are abroad in order to cover fixed costs such as mortgage repayments and rates; others so that they can choose their neighbours.

Table 8.2
Number of tenancies owned (percentages)

| Size of holding | Lanc- aster(a) 1960 | Eng.(a) 1962 | Lond.(a) 1963 | Lond.(a) 1969 | Chelt- enham(b) 1975 | Dud- ley(c) 1978 |
|---|---|---|---|---|---|---|
| 1 | 61 | 41 | 60.4 | 34 | | 51 |
| 2-4 | 28 | } 54 | 25.1 | } 38 | } 81.2 | 30 |
| 5-9 | 8 | | 9.2 | | | 13 |
| 10-20 | } 2 | } 4 | } 4.5 | } 12 | 14.1 | 4 |
| 21-50 | | | | | 4.7 | |
| 51-99 | } 1 | | 0.5 | 3 | 0 | } 2 |
| 100-499 | | 1 | | 9 | 0 | |
| 500-999 | | | } 0.3 | } 2 | 0 | |
| 1000 + | | | | | 0 | |

Sources:  (a)  DOE (1977b)
          (b)  Forrest, R. and Murie, A. (1978)
          (c)  Housing Monitoring Team (1980)

Illustrating this one survey noted the diverse reasons for purchasing rental property:

'One property developer in the sample had bought a site for development which also included a number of rented houses. Whilst some individuals may choose to buy a' small terrace for purely investment reasons it is clear that in some cases an adjacent property had been purchased so that an appropriate neighbour could be chosen' (Housing Monitoring Team 1980, p.15).

Some are resident landlords who provide accommodation for friends or relatives as tenants whilst some consider themselves to be providing a social service. One survey showed that 92 per cent of lettings by resident landlords were viewed as a home or future home for the landlord or his/her family, and 10 per cent of lettings by companies were for some special use such as providing homes for the needy or employees. (Paley 1978).

Table 8.3
Method of property acquisition (percentages)

| | Lancaster 1960(a) | Cheltenham 1976(a) | Dudley 1980(a) | Sheffield 1980(b) |
|---|---|---|---|---|
| Inheritance | 71 | 13 | 42 | 24 |
| Bought/investment | 21 | 72 | 47 | 76 |
| Mixed inheritance and investment | 2 | 7 | 5 | - |
| Miscellaneous | 5 | 8 | 6 | - |

Sources: (a)  Housing Monitoring Team (1980)
         (b)  Crook, A.D.H. and Bryant, C.L. (1982)

141

Landlords cannot all be viewed as businessmen or women in the usual sense, therefore, even though they own resources which are actually or potentially income generating. For many rent is a secondary rather than primary source of income, and for some the asset may not be considered in terms of monetary resources. Paley's survey of rented properties found that, notwithstanding the existence of rent restricting legislation, almost 40 per cent of landlords nevertheless felt that the rent which they received from their lettings was adequate from their point of view. This proportion varied depending on whether the rent was controlled, registered or agreed privately, but even of those with registered rents over a quarter (28 per cent) felt that this was adequate. This same survey also indicated that not all landlords are primarily, or even at all, concerned about the rate of return which they receive on their investment. When landlords were asked what in their views an adequate rent for their lettings should cover, 8 per cent said that they did not let the property for financial reasons. Although this response was more frequent amongst landlords who were charities or public bodies, it applied to at least 5 per cent of all types of landlord (Table 8.4). Moreover far fewer landlords than many might suppose felt that an adequate rent should provide a return on either current market value or purchase price. Clearly many landlords' expectations of what financial benefits they should receive from tenants is confined to quite modest amounts which could probably be bettered elsewhere. This applied more to some types of landlord than others, but was by no means unknown even amongst non-resident individuals and companies (Paley 1978). Similarly amongst landlords in Dudley only 7 per cent considered rents to be their main source of income (Housing Monitoring Team 1980).

Ascribing the same objectives to all landlords is therefore to fail to appreciate the diversity of the sector. Although privately rented housing is frequently classified for statistical purposes as a single tenure form it is in fact an amalgamation of disparate relationships concerning people and dwellings. There are furnished dwellings and unfurnished dwellings; protected and unprotected tenancies; student lettings and holiday lettings; resident landlords and non-resident landlords; private landlords, institutional landlords and quasi-public landlords; rent and rent free lettings; permanent and fixed term lettings. The differences are numerous and perhaps the only common feature of all private tenancies is that they are residual: not being part of the two major tenures of owner occupation or council housing. A consequence of this diversity is that there is no uniformity of economic objectives among private landlords. As Elliott and McCrone (1975) suggest, there are a number of reasons for owning tenancies other than financial profit: as a means of social advancement or status confirmation; as a form of security; and to provide a service. The level of the rate of return, the possibilities of profits to be made elsewhere, and the value gap will thus have a different significance in different parts of the tenure.

Table 8.4

Lettings by type of landlord by items which the landlord felt an adequate rent should cover in densely rented areas of England and Wales 1976

| Items the landlord felt an adequate rent for the lettings in the address should cover | Type of landlord making the letting | | | | | | |
|---|---|---|---|---|---|---|---|
| | Resident individual | Non-resident individual | Company | Charity/ housing association | Non-charitable trust/ executors | Public body etc. | All types |
| | % | % | % | % | % | % | % |
| Nothing/address not let for financial reasons | 5 | 5 | 5 | 17 | 9 | 14 | 8 |
| Return on market value of property | 18 | 53 | 70 | 25 | 58 | 37 | 48 |
| Return on purchase price of property | 19 | 28 | 26 | 4 | 19 | 17 | 21 |
| Contribution to mortgage/loan repayments | 30 | 20 | 17 | 57 | 4 | 3 | 24 |
| Rates | 74 | 71 | 45 | 66 | 42 | 49 | 61 |
| Repairs/wear and tear | 67 | 85 | 82 | 79 | 85 | 68 | 80 |
| Management costs | 7 | 26 | 36 | 36 | 47 | 24 | 29 |
| Insurance | 1 | 17 | 18 | 9 | 21 | 1 | 13 |
| Heating/lighting/ water/telephone | 24 | 7 | 14 | 9 | 2 | 4 | 11 |
| Other outgoings | 14 | 12 | 12 | 3 | 9 | 23 | 11 |
| Improvements | - | 1 | 2 | 1 | 2 | 1 | 1 |

Source: Paley, B. (1978)

## The sub-sectors of the privately rented sector

The concerns, frequently voiced, about the nature of the fair rent system and the effects of rent restriction, further overlook the fact that these apply in practice to a minority of lettings in the sector. The evidence which will be presented in this section is that nationally the privately rented sector can be considered, from the point of view of rent restriction, as containing three sub-sectors. Firstly there are those lettings, about 25 per cent of the total, which are excluded by the legislation itself from the full protection of the rent acts. Secondly, there are those lettings, a further 45 per cent, which are subject to the fair rent legislation but for which no one has sought a fair rent determination. Thirdly, the remaining 30 per cent of lettings have registered fair rents. The effects of the fair rent arrangements are thus in practice limited to a relatively small proportion of the dwellings in this tenure. In this section the bases and significance of these three sub-sectors will be examined.

The 1977 Rent Act excludes a number of types of letting from the full protection of the rent acts. Excluded categories are: dwellings with rateable values above certain levels; dwellings where no rent, or only a low rent, is paid; dwellings let with land other than its own site; dwellings where the rent includes payments for board or attendance; where the tenancy confers the right to occupy the dwelling for a holiday; dwellings let by educational establishments to students; where the dwelling is an agricultural holding or licensed premise; and where the dwelling has a resident landlord. Whereas the 1980 Housing Act brought controlled tenancies into the fair rent code, it also created two new types of tenancy which were not to receive the full protection of the rent acts: assured and shorthold tenancies.

Estimates of the proportion of dwellings which fall into these excluded categories may not be precise because of the problems of carrying out surveys of privately rented housing (Doling and Davies 1983). Specifically the difficulties concern the construction of a sampling frame which includes all the various landlord-tenant relationships from the resident landlord who is letting a room to a friend and wishes not to disclose the fact to either his or her building society or the Inland Revenue, to the landlord letting his house whilst temporarily out of the country. Useful estimates are, however, available from a survey conducted by the Office of Population Censuses and Surveys in 1978 (Todd et al. 1982). At that time, of the estimated 2,364,000 privately rented dwellings in England about 7 per cent were controlled and 68 per cent regulated tenancies. The remaining 25 per cent of lettings contained some with resident landlords, but this broadly constituted the level of exclusions from the fair rent legislation. Rents for these lettings will have been established in a number of ways but in general will not have involved restrictions determined by the state.

There is now considerable evidence that landlords have proved very adept at using these exceptions or loopholes in order to circumvent the provisions of the rent acts. For example, following the introduction of the 1965 Rent Act which applied only to unfurnished tenancies many landlords sought to convert their unfurnished to furnished tenancies by the addition of a little furniture and consequently analysis of newspaper advertisements revealed that the number of new unfurnished lettings had diminished rapidly (Beirne 1977).

Attempts in the 1974 Rent Act to close that particular avenue of escape have met with renewed ingenuity by landlords: leading to the observation that 'the exceptions granted in the Rent Act 1974 towards certain kinds of tenancies and services have now become the new loopholes of today' (Stafford 1978). One strategy has been the conversion of lettings purportedly for holiday purposes even though they were located in such places as Brixton, Lambeth and East Ham and landlords required references from employers, parents and banks (Weir 1975). Another strategy has been pursued by many lodgings officers in universities and polytechnics who have established head tenancy schemes whereby they have taken over the management of dwellings owned by private landlords, let them to students at rents above the general level of fair rents in their areas but guaranteeing vacant possession to the owner (Finnis 1978). Similarly, some local authorities have negotiated schemes with private landlords whereby they sublet to their own tenants outside the protection of the rent acts (Pearce 1980). Some private landlords have sought to exploit the blurred distinction between a tenant who is normally taken to be a person occupying accommodation, paying rent and often protected by the rent acts and a licensee who is someone, such as a weekend guest, who has permission to remain in occupation but without security of tenure or fair rent rights. Having given tenants a document entitled 'Licence' the burden of proof rests with the tenant to establish otherwise, and since the courts have not established clear principles, but have taken each case on its merits, such licences have not been easily overthrown (Randall 1981).

The evidence presented to the House of Commons Environment Committee suggests that most new lettings are now being made outside the provisions of the rent acts. As one member of the committee observed:

> 'in some parts of London ... it is being said - and I think that the facts support it - that the regulated market, the Rent Act properties, are virtually at a standstill in number but in certain parts of central London and inner London the number of privately rented properties negotiated voluntarily outside the Rent Act is increasing' (House of Commons 1982, p.54).

This evidence does not necessarily mean that there is a widespread abuse of legal positions by landlords who are

flouting statutory provisions. The establishing of that
position centres on the issue of:

'whether the arrangements of landlords' affairs owes more
to appearance than reality: that is whether the
transaction is actually outside the Act, or is actually
inside the Act but disguised as another transaction
outside the Act' (Doling forthcoming).

The Environment Committee was unable on the basis of evidence
which it received to reach a conclusion on the extent to which
'disguised' transactions or evasions were occurring. Indeed
it seems likely that this issue could be empirically
established only by legally based evaluation of individual
contracts (House of Commons 1982). Nevertheless the existing
evidence does suggest that the 25 per cent of the sector which
lies outside the full protection of the rent acts may be
increasing and that landlords as a group are therefore slowly
achieving their own form of rent decontrol.

In the present context the significance of the rent
restricting legislation to which the remaining 75 per cent of
dwellings in the sector are subject, and which constitute the
second and third sub-sectors, is considerably reduced by the
relative dearth of applications for fair rents. The precise
numbers involved vary depending on the basis on which the
estimates are made, but a reasonable estimate would seem to be
that only about 30 per cent of the dwellings in the sector
have rents restricted by the rent acts. This figure is based
on two separate estimates. The first is from a survey carried
out by the Office of Population Censuses and Surveys
estimating that in England in 1978 22 per cent of all private
lettings had registered rents and 7 per cent had controlled
rents (Todd et al. 1982). Added to the small proportion of
the 6 per cent of resident landlord lettings which had
registered rents (Doling forthcoming) this suggests a figure
fractionally over 30 per cent. The second estimate is based
on an earlier survey of lettings (Paley 1978), which was
restricted to areas with large amounts of privately rented
property, and indicating that the figure may have been a
little higher. Amongst dwellings let by private landlords
(i.e. not voluntary or public institutions) 26 per cent had
rents registered by a rent officer or rent tribunal with a
further 15 per cent having controlled rents (Table 8.5). An
estimate by the authors, however, based on the number of
lettings registered between 1975 and 1978 suggested a somewhat
lower figure of about 28 per cent (Doling and Davies 1982a).

The existence of these three separate sub-sectors can for
present purposes more appropriately be reduced to two:
registered lettings which have rents determined by rent
officers and in a small proportion of cases by rent tribunals;
and non-registered lettings which do not. Expressed in this
way the direct impact of the fair rent legislation is felt by
under a third of all the lettings in the sector.

Table 8.5
Lettings by type of landlord by status of rent
densely rented areas of England and Wales 1976
(percentages)

| | Type of landlord making the letting | | | |
| | Resident individual | Non-resident individual | Company | All types |
|---|---|---|---|---|
| The rent for the letting was: | | | | |
| Controlled | 12 | 20 | 8 | 15 |
| Registered by rent officer or rent tribunal | 4 | 21 | 44 | 26 |
| Agreed privately | 84 | 59 | 48 | 59 |

Source:   Paley, B. (1978)


## The Registered and Non-Registered Sectors

One of the principles underlying the fair rent legislation,
was that because over the sector as a whole most landlord-
tenant relationships, including the rent relationship, were
unproblematic, there would be no need for all regulated
tenancies to have fair rents determined. This principle, if
sound, would suggest an hypothesis that rents in the
restricted and non restricted sectors were broadly equal.
This would follow because it would not be expected that rent
officers would determine fair rents at levels higher than
those agreed privately for similar properties. But if
privately agreed properties had higher rents than registered
rents for similar properties, those tenants able to do so
would seek to curb the excesses of landlords who were taking
advantage of scarcity to seek high rents (Doling forthcoming).

In fact the evidence, which is again incomplete, is that
rents in the non restricted sectors are on average
considerably higher. It has long been postulated that the
introduction of rent restriction has led to a 'two tier rent
structure of fair rents and market rents' (Stafford 1978,
p.103). Evidence of this was given by one member of the House
of Commons Environment Committee who had noted rents in London
'at the market level of something like double the registered
level' (House of Commons 1982, p.54). Other evidence
indicated the existence of an even wider divergence: in
Paddington market rents were claimed to be four times the fair
rent levels (House of Commons 1982, p.102).

A limitation of such estimates is that they are frequently
based on non random samples of private lettings and they fail
to take account of any differences in dwelling type between
the restricted and non-restricted sub-sectors. A set of
estimates for Birmingham which does not have these limitations
suggests that for pre 1919 terraced housing market rents were

probably about $1^1/2$ times fair rent levels, and for converted flats and rooms about twice (Doling and Davies 1982a).

The existence of this divergence between rent levels in the two sub-sectors, rather than equality, helps to establish further misconceptions about the underlying principles of the fair rent legislation. Specifically the legislation was based on a premise that landlord-tenant relationships were neutral, economic and legal relationships, in which both sides could act with full knowledge and without further repercussions. There is, however, an important 'social' aspect to the relationship which may have been overridden by this principle.

The significance of this is based on the predictable actions of landlords and tenants if the nature of their relationships were founded solely on neutral economic principles. Since rents are higher in the non-restricted sub sector it would be expected that landlords would wish to evade the provisions of the rent acts, and in particular would not seek fair rent determinations. Tenants, on the other hand, would seek to obtain fair rent determinations in order to reduce their rent burden.

Evidence from an examination of the rent register in Birmingham shows that neither expectation is borne out empirically. In a sample of 405 registrations in 1980, 98.5 per cent of the applications had been made by landlords alone: the corresponding proportion was 95.2 per cent for a sample of registrations in 1982. Explanation of this apparent paradox is revealing for as Doling (forthcoming) indicates:

'in many cases in Birmingham landlords rather than tenants have made these applications because that was the only legal method of securing an increase in the rent which they could charge tenants'.

This assertion is based on three empirical observations. Firstly, that in the sample of registrations made in 1980 over one half had been registered previously. Whether the landlord or the tenant had applied for the previous fair rent determination, since reregistration invariably results in an increase in the fair rent it is in the interests of the landlord, and not the tenants, to make re-applications. Secondly, of those properties in this sample which were being registered for the first time, their age, type and rateable value suggest that they were being transferred from the controlled to the regulated code. This also invariably means an increase in rents so that registration is again in the interests of the landlord. Thirdly, the tenants of many of the dwellings had been in occupation for some time so that 'even should they wish to do so landlords might find it a contentious step, in fact an illegal one, to either change the status of the tenancy by using one of the established loopholes or to increase the rent unilaterally' (Doling forthcoming).

This assessment may explain why some landlords apply for fair rents, but it does not explain why, in Birmingham, tenants have not. In particular this non-use of the fair rents provision seems significant:

'Since in Birmingham fair rents are on average only about half market levels there is an objective economic incentive for tenants to make applications to the rent officer service, although as we have seen these are extremely sparse in number. We might hypothesise that as with other benefits there may be elements of both ignorance and stigma which largely explain the low take up rate (Hill 1976). However in this case there are probably also special factors which are important. For example, Zander's survey indicated that the most commonly given reason for the non application to the rent service was lack of knowledge of its existence. Beyond this there were a number of reasons given: "satisfaction with the rent" was given as the reason 121 times (34.2 per cent) out of a total of 353 reasons given. Others included: "didn't want to offend or get on bad terms with the landlord" (43 or 12 per cent); "afraid of getting a notice to quit" (28 or 8 per cent, including six unfurnished tenants); "couldn't be bothered" (29 or 8 per cent); and "afraid of harassment by the landlord" (14 or 4 per cent, including four furnished tenants)" (Zander 1968)' (Doling forthcoming).

The nature and variety of these reasons suggest that many of the relationships between landlords and tenants are delicately balanced around non-economic principles. Consequently it is a misconception to view the relationships as no more than neutral financial arrangements made between individuals who operate in a social vacuum. The importance of this assertion can be seen in the non-utilization of the fair rent provisions by coloured tenants. In Birmingham special tabulations from the National Dwelling and Household survey indicate that at the end of the 1970s 9 per cent of all private tenants were coloured. In a random sample survey of 185 tenants with registered fair rents which was carried out by the authors, however, not one of the tenants was coloured (Doling and Davies, 1983). The probability that this observed absence of coloured tenants from the rent register was a result of sample selection, rather than an actual absence, is extremely small. The nature of the economic and legal relationship between landlord and tenant is of course not contingent upon ethnic origin. The absence of coloured tenants from the register would thus seem to be a result of social and ethnic factors:

'John's observations on blacks in Handsworth confirmed that fear of the landlord was a significant deterrent in applying to the rent officer or other official (John 1972). With a shortage of alternative oppotunities and with suspicion of legal machinery and officers, it is not difficult to appreciate the general relevance of this

amongst ethnic minorities, and particularly where landlord
and tenant are from different ethnic groups (Rex and
Tomlinson 1979). The shortage of alternative housing
opportunities also acts in a more subtle way: in a
situation of housing stress, many non-white tenants,
particularly if they are recent immigrants, have nowhere
else to go and feel that, even if the accommodation is
poor or the rent high, the landlord is doing them a
favour. In such circumstances, complaint to a rent
officer is not seen as an adequate repayment for the
landlord's kindness (Dhanjal 1978). The social pressure
to accept the conditions imposed by the landlord can be
expected to be even higher in cases where there is some
kin or village relationship between landlord and tenant'
(Doling and Davies 1983, p.491).

Whereas these speculations can only hint at fuller analysis
of the reasons for the utilisation of the fair rents system in
ways which point to certain paradoxes they do suggest the non-
neutral and non-economic aspects of many landlord-tenant
relationships.


## THE CONTINUING NEED FOR THE FUNCTIONS OF THE SECTOR

Throughout the last quarter of a century the numerical
significance of the privately rented sector has continued to
decline and today the fair rent system applies to only a small
proportion of the total housing stock. However, it has been
argued that the need for the functions of the sector continue
and should be protected: specifically, that the sector acts
as a compensating mechanism to meet fluctuations in demand,
and that it has a unique role as the supplier of easy access
housing.

The demand for housing in the privately rented sector has in
many areas more or less consistently exceeded supply. This
has been a direct consequence of, on the one hand, a general
shortage of dwellings relative to the number of households
and, on the other, the 'concentration of much of the effect of
that shortfall into the private rented sector' (DOE 1977b,
p.82).

This role, as a safety valve of housing provision, has been
important even at times when there has been a crude national
surplus of houses over households. Although local shortages,
in relation to the total housing stock, may be small, in
relation to the stock of privately rented housing they may be
much more significant (DOE 1977b). A consequence is that
there has been considerable pressure on the sector over a long
period of time often from people unable to obtain single
family housing and finding no alternative other than the often
cheap and shabby subdivisions of the private rented sector.

Whether or not this argument is valid it is important not to
be misled: the safety valve function is not a justification

150

for the continuation of housing shortage. Solutions to this, more fundamental, problem rest with, amongst other things, the provision of more decent housing to meet the needs placed on the housing stock. Moreover, it can be argued that the safety valve function of the sector is already anachronistic: that it has been in a state of decline for so long and reached such low numbers that any opportunities as general needs housing have disappeared. The validity of this must depend on the extent of its decline and the nature of demand and supply in different parts of the country, since housing markets are local rather than national. A surplus of cheap housing in the North East of England is of little value to those in the South West, for example.

The view of the House of Commons Environment Committee is that there are indeed specific functional and geographical needs for the sector:

'The sector is likely under most circumstances to continue to decline. However, traditional demands are also declining, so that the greatest problems arise in particular locations and for certain groups where the rate of change of supply is significantly greater than that of demand.

'It appears that given the continuation of current housing policies the need for the private rented sector will remain if there is to be reasonable access to housing for new households, for the mobile and for poorer non-family households of all ages; although increasingly local authorities and housing associations are adapting their allocation and management policies to meet some of their needs.

'Finally, although this cannot show up in detail in national statistics, it is clear that private landlords still play an important role particularly in certain inner city areas in providing accommodation for those who are unable to obtain it in the two major sectors where they would generally receive better accommodation, often at more reasonable prices' (House of Commons 1982, p.xxi).

These conclusions significantly point to the failure of other forms of housing provision in Britain today to meet the requirements of many households. These include the large proportion of tenants who are elderly and who require continued protection both from eviction and high market level rents by virtue of their often low incomes and reduced abilities to compete. In the future the greatest needs, in numerical terms, will probably come from those people who require housing which has easy access and does not require a large capital down payment. Those who are separated or divorced may fall into this category (Housing Monitoring Team 1980) as do the young single and young married households for whom privately rented housing offers an important gateway whereby they can leave the parental home to marry or to take up employment elsewhere. Significantly, 40 per cent of the 15,000 people on Birmingham's waiting list are single and without dependents (Gibson 1981). For many of these groups privately rented housing is prized as a temporary expedient and as a stepping stone to a tenure form which is seen as a more long term solution to their particular housing needs. This is important because they may not immediately have the financial resources to enable them to purchase a dwelling, nor sufficient need, as defined by local authorities, to make them eligible for council housing. The bureaucratic nature of local authorities and their statutory responsibility to provide for those in housing need in any case means that speed is not necessarily the essence of their allocation systems. In addition the age and residential qualifications imposed by many local authorities mean that the young, particularly young and single people, and those who have moved from another area cannot gain quick access to council housing. Indeed the pressure on local authority accommodation generally is becoming so acute in many places that only those in desperate need can be housed . Municipalisation for reasons in addition to public expenditure implications would not therefore seem to be able readily to fulfill the present functions of the private rental sector. It might have been expected that housing associations could have done so. In practice, however, it appears that they have rarely fulfilled this role although the evidence is very far from being conclusive. Comparisons by Niner (1979), for example, show that one local authority housed a larger proportion of young single people than did housing associations who, in general, concentrated particularly on the elderly single.

So buoyant has the demand been for easy access, short term housing that those parts of the sector, particularly furnished tenancies, which have sought to satisfy that demand have declined much less rapidly than the sector as a whole (Housing Monitoring Team 1980). Indeed where, as we have seen, landlords have ignored the fair rents legislation they have sometimes been able to charge their young, perhaps single and professional, tenants sufficiently large rents to encourage them to remain as landlords. Henney (1975) has indicated that nationally those in furnished lettings tend to be relatively young, well educated and well paid, which contrasts markedly with the elderly, poor tenants frequently found in unfurnished lettings. For many of those in furnished lettings the tenancy is often a short one, sometimes because the professional career ladders make them mobile or because the tenancy is no more than a stepping stone to owner occupation. It is not surprising that many landlords have sought to attract such tenants both because of their rent paying ability and the reasonable assurance of vacant possession sooner rather than later. Neither is it surprising that landlords of furnished property are more eager to consider reletting when they do get vacant possession than are other landlords (Whitehead 1978). The result is that rents in the furnished subsector have attained much higher levels than in the unfurnished subsector. The 1977 General Household Survey indicates that the average

annual rent per room in the furnished lettings was £161 and in
unfurnished lettings £49. The average gross annual income of
their heads of household was £2460 and £2080 respectively.

Nevertheless existing arrangements are far from
satisfactory. There is ample evidence that privately rented
properties account for some of the poorest housing in this
country. At the same time the issue over the rights of owners
and tenants is clearly fraught with difficulties, to the
extent that it arguably constitutes the greatest single cause
for concern by the individuals involved. Analysis of housing
advice enquiries in London, for example, has shown that 70 per
cent of those made by private tenants arose from concerns
about security of tenure (Housing Advice Switchboard 1982).
In the absence of additional investment in housing production
what is needed is not simply the continuation of the existing
relationships, but a continuation of some of the existing
functions.

**THE FUTURE OF RENT REGULATION**

Whatever the events may be in the housing sphere or
elsewhere over the next decade or so it seems inconceivable
that the private landlord will disappear. Although it is
likely that the sector will continue to decline in numerical
terms the variety of positions which privately rented property
can adopt will ensure that some forms of private renting
continue. This would be the case even were some radical (and
unlikely) political solutions sought, such as
municipalisation, since it would undoubtedly prove difficult
to eradicate many informal and sometimes hidden arrangements:
those involving some resident landlords for example.

Given its continued existence its existing problems will not
disappear of their own accord. The sector contains some of
the worst property with the fewest basic amenities and highest
levels of unfitness, whilst harassment, illegal eviction and
evasion of the provisions of the rent acts continue. Whereas
state intervention has relieved some of the problems and
helped to smooth over some of the results of decline, it has
not been entirely successful. Intervention in this particular
market is associated with results which many might not
consider as a priori grounds for successful policy: the
continued withdrawal of investment from the sector and the
inconsistent application of the fair rent provisions have been
noted. These concerns harbour the more fundamental issue of
what sort of place the nation wishes to give to private rental
housing. What should its role be, how should it relate to
other tenures, and what policies would best achieve these
things? Should the present fair rent system be kept as it is,
modified or swept away?

The House of Commons Environment Committee was in no doubt
that arrangements could not be left to continue as they were,
concluding that 'the current position of the sector is

unsatisfactory for both landlords and tenants' (House of Commons 1982, p.xliv). They added that 'as the sector is likely to continue to play a key role in housing provision, at least in the forseeable future, urgent attention must be given to the financial and economic basis of the private rented sector. The only way in which substantial improvements can be effected without placing unjustifiably heavy burdens on landlords or tenants is by significant changes in the distribution or the total of housing subsidies' (House of Commons 1982, p.xlv).

Notwithstanding this plea, strong reservations have been expressed about the desirability of using the private landlord to fulfill any housing function particularly where this was based on public funds. In its evidence to the Committee SHAC, for example, argued:

'If the government were to reverse its decisions on public expenditure and expand expenditure on housing it is questionable whether the most effective use of these additional funds would be to grant further subsidies to private landlords. The reason for this is that in many other respects - particularly security and maintenance -. private renting is inherently inferior to other tenures' (House of Commons 1982, p.93).

The political feasibility of such moves has also been questioned:

'A radical reversal of such policies, which have been welcomed by many investors as well as consumers of housing, could have a major impact on private rental, but is most unlikely to occur. Nor is it a high priority, at a time of economic stringency, to provide the scale of subsidies to private landlords which they would now require in order to carry out effectively and at a profit, what has become their major role - the housing of those at the bottom of the housing market' (Harloe 1980, p.34).

It has certainly been the case that central government itself has demonstrated no inclination to use public funds in the manner suggested. The Department of the Environment's response to the Environment Committee largely ignored the latter's recommendations without proposing serious alternatives (House of Commons 1983). There has been no hint of alterations to the pattern of subsidies to the privately rented sector. In fact central government, no matter what its real aspirations for the sector are, is in a catch 22 situation.

On the one hand given its overriding commitment to owner occupation it seems inconceivable that any of the existing subsidies could be diverted from it to the private rented sector. On the other hand the desire to limit the growth of public expenditure precludes the introduction of new, publicly

154

financed, subsidies. So whereas the Conservative government remains ideologically supportive of the private landlord other ideological positions supercede it.

Quite apart from questions of subsidy and revitalising the sector it is not inappropriate to question whether the existing forms of regulation should be maintained. Indeed an associated question is whether any form of regulation should be maintained or whether in some parts of the country the balance of supply and demand is such that regulation is no longer fulfilling a useful purpose. As Donnison has argued:

'I think that would be a pretty bold step to take in some cities and dangerous in London. There are other cities where it seems to me we could take that risk. I now find my own students in Glasgow can secure council housing coming into the city for the first time from other cities. That would have been unthinkable a few years ago, as you know better than I do. While that remains true, there are strong competitors to the private landlord who will exercise some restraint on the rents he is able to secure because there are other places people can go' (House of Commons 1982, p.233).

How widespread are conditions which would support de-control by area is unknown: but whereas nationally 30 per cent of private lettings have registered rents, the proportion varies greatly from area to area. Estimates of the proportion of unfurnished lettings with registered fair rents suggest that these are particularly low in many predominantly rural areas. In the Wiltshire registration area, for example, the proportion is about 5 per cent, in Lincolnshire and Shropshire, 6 per cent; and in Devonshire 7 per cent (Doling 1983a). These small proportions do little to suggest that the fair rent system is meeting an essential social objective. If this is the case then there could be a strong argument for gradual relaxation of the fair rent aspect of the rent acts. If nothing else it would remove an arm of the state which was no longer fulfilling a useful role of regulating a sector of the housing system in a situation of shortage. Before any such action was put into practice, however, very careful and detailed assessment of its consequencies should be carried out. In areas where great shortages continue, or are expected because of the removal of funding from local authorities and housing associations, any such de-control could have disastrous consequences.

In many parts of the country the system of fair rents continues to fulfill an important role in restricting the exploitation of tenants faced with no alternative access to housing. Here the dilemma is whether or not the rent acts should be strengthened both to deal with the problem of evasions and to achieve greater consistency in fair rent determinations. The latter in particular raises the issue of the extent to which rent officers, in common with other professional groups, 'should have their activities constrained by rules and to what extent they should be left with discretionary freedom' (Hill 1976, p.81).

Indeed since 1965 a number of attempts have been made to restrict discretion. For example, The Royal Institute of Chartered Surveyors, a body whose interests might be thought to lie more closely with landlords than with tenants, has proposed one such scheme. The basis of this was that landlords should receive some guarantee, albeit loose, of future increases in the earning potential of their investments:

> 'We recommend that the appropriate Minister should be empowered to make an order each year authorizing all regulated rents to be increased by a prescribed percentage related to (but less than) the increase in the Retail Price Index over the preceeding year' (RICS 1976, p.30).

This suggestion is primarily associated with the absolute level of rents and so tends to ignore the problem that the existing rents may not have consistent relative levels. Indeed in as far as there are existing anomalies in the rent structure this will exacerbate them by widening the gap between the under estimated and the over estimated rent.

In contrast, Professor Donnison, who had been involved in setting up the fair rents legislation in 1965, said in his evidence to the House of Commons Environment Committee's investigations into the private rented sector:

> 'I think the law about rent regulation and the principles developed by the panels and the rent officers are such a mess and so poorly applied that there is not a great deal to be hoped from multiplying law, procedures and principles of those kinds any further. We are only likely to confuse the issue further and discredit the system' (House of Commons 1982, p.237).

An associated point has been made, more generally, that it may be a mistaken analysis to view the narrowing of discretion by substituting more specific rules as essentially a technical process of tightening up existing arrangements. Rather the discretion may be there not simply because more specific rules are difficult to frame but because more specific rules would not allow the blurring of political views which has made the legislation possible in the first place. The case has been argued by Prosser (1981, p.169):

> 'the approach usually adopted has been to ask whether filling in the void with rules is feasible and whether it will assist in the performance of the overt legislative purpose, the assumption being that there is such a purpose embodying a concensus on aims. Thus the transition from discretion to rules is seen as primarily a technical

rather than a politial problem, as devising efficient and
fair administrative practices rather than choosing between
political values....this is to view the role of discretion
too simply: rather than existing because of a technical
inability to frame rules it may perform the distinct and
deliberate function of blurring political issues and
disguising the necessity of choosing between different
policies'.

In the case of the legislation which set up the fair rents
system and defined what a fair rent would be the very
discretion which has been identified as the foundation of
inconsistency may thus, in part, have been a necessary precondition of its passage onto the Statute Books and its
widening to other types of letting.  Certainly it would be a
mistake to consider that the existing discretion could be
substantially limited, at least in its central features,
without resolving some of the key political issues about the
role of the sector, the appropriateness of using private
landlords as an instrument of housing provision, the
appropriate rate of return which landlords could expect, the
proportion of income which tenants could be expected to pay in
rent and the relationship with other tenures.

# Appendix A
# The rent assessment committee: evidence and decisions

**PART I**

EVIDENCE TO BE SUBMITTED TO
THE WEST MIDLAND RENT ASSESSMENT COMMITTEE
IN RESPECT OF 54 HIGH STREET

This house is owned by Landlords Anonymous Limited. The tenant is Mrs. Smith who has always been a good tenant. We asked for a rent of £7.50 this was reduced to £6.75 hence the appeal.

This is another case where the property is unimproved and does not have a bathroom, we have not seen eye to eye with the rent officers for some time in respect of this type of house and have had a number of very recent appeals where every Panel has given us an increase over the rent officer's figure and I will send you examples of these in a moment. This house is a traditional six roomed villa with a hall entrance so that it is slightly bigger than the average villa which does not have a hall. On most of our houses of this type we have either fitted a bathroom in the rear bedroom or built one on as an extension at the rear. However the tenant of this house has always refused to let us carry out this work and the house, therefore, is in its original state. We have always kept it reasonably well maintained and the house was last painted in 1977.

If this house was fitted with a bathroom in the rear bedroom the rent would be assessed today at about £9.00 and I will send you an assessment paper and photograph of a typical case of a property which was registered about the same time in a similar district, 353 Elizabeth Road. You will see this was registered at £9.00. The Rent Officer has therefore reduced the rent on the appeal house by £2.25 or 33.33% because there is no bathroom. The bathroom at the Elizabeth Road house was fitted about 15 years ago, it cost about £200 to fit and half was given on grant so the total cost of fitting it was £100. For the Rent Officer to now reduce the rent by one third for a bathroom that would have cost £100 to put in is absurd, especially as we would have put the bathroom in years ago if the tenant had agreed. I would now like to show that where houses are being improved at the present time, and therefore to a higher standard than improvements carried out some years ago, much higher rents are being given.

14 Frances Road. This house already had a bathroom fitted
in the rear bedroom but we fully improved it with new porches,
rewiring, new sink unit, etc., the house had 2 bedrooms, you
will see the Panel gave a rent of £10.00 per week, the
effective date was April 1979 so it would be considerably
higher today.

Now what should the reduction be for the fact that a house
does not have a bathroom? The first thing I think we should
consider is this. If one fits a bathroom in the rear bedroom
of a property, a bedroom is lost, and this can be difficult
for a mixed family. Some of the advantage therefore of having
a bathroom must be lost by the fact that there is one bedroom
less. If one considers that if we had been allowed to put a
bathroom in this property when we wanted to, it would have
cost after taking the grant into account about £100 and if we
allow 15% on the outlay, the rent for the bathroom would have
been £15.00 per annum or 28 pence per week. I think the
better way of valuing it would be to allow equal amounts for
each room in the house and an equal amount for the garden. If
we assume that if the subject house had a bathroom the rent
would have been the same as the comparable I have mentioned at
Elizabeth Road at £9.00, if we divide that by 7 to give 7
equal proportions for each room and the garden, that would
value the bathroom at £1.28 per week, and on this basis the
rent we are asking for of £7.50 is very reasonable.

Now I would like to send the papers to you in respect of the
previous appeals we have had in connection with similar
properties.

6 Kathleen Road. This is a similar unimproved property,
rent assessed effective 22.10.79 at £7.25.

119 Angela Road. Rent similar, unimproved property rent
assessed effective 1.1.80 at £7.50.

87 Eileen Road. This is an interesting case and bears
directly on the bathroom issue. This is a similar house but
the tenant had installed the bathroom in the rear bedroom
himself at his own expense and this could not, therefore, be
taken into account when assessing the rent. The Panel
assessed the rent at £8.50, effective 1.1.80.

I would also like to mention one other case - 8 Patricia
Road. This is also a case where the tenant installed the
bathroom in the rear bedroom himself. The Rent Officer in
this case assessed the rent at £8.00 effective 14.1.80. If
you look at the papers I have sent you, you will see I have
included the previous rent assessment form. We applied for a
rent of £5.50 at the previous registration because we did not
realise at the time that the tenant had installed the
bathroom, and the asking rent was in line with other houses
being registered at that time. However the rent was reduced
to £4.75 by the Rent Officer because of the fact it was the
tenant's bathroom, this represented a reduction of 13.63%. As

159

I have shown a fair rent on this type of property today with a
bathroom would be about £9.00 if we reduced this by the 13.63%
reduction.  I have mentioned it would amount to £1.22 which
would give a fair rent of £7.78 which would be a lot more than
I am asking for in respect of the subject house.

**PART II**

EVIDENCE TO BE SUBMITTED TO THE
WEST MIDLAND RENT ASSESSMENT PANEL
IN CONNECTION WITH AN APPEAL IN RESPECT OF
25 WOOD ROAD, HANDSWORTH

As you are aware from his report, the Rent Officer did not call a consultation at this property relying on his referencer's survey and his own cursory external examination of the property. Just how cursory that examination was can be judged by the Rent Officer's choice of comparable. I refer to no. 35 Larch Road, Saltley. This really is a very poor little property in an even poorer locality. You will see the rateable value is only £111, it has no hall entrance, the subject property is half as big again having three large rooms on the ground floor as opposed to Larch Road's two and a scullery, there is almost twelve months difference in effective dates and it is impossible to understand by what justification the Rent Officer could call 35 Larch Road a fair comparable. With regard to the Rent Officer's comparable in Poplar Road, Handsworth, it has recently been established by a Rent Assessment Panel that Housing Associations do not necessarily request rents that are economic and indeed are known to accept rents which are definitely not economic so again they cannot be considered fair comparables.

For my evidence I prefer to offer properties which have recently been the subject of a Panel decision and firstly I would like to offer you 17 Birch Road, Handsworth. The Rent Officer here was again Mr. Smith and on the 26th February he awarded a rent of £8.80 in reply to our application of £10.25. As you will see on 18th May, 1981 the Panel awarded a rent of £10.00 per week and this for a property with a rateable value of £123 and effective floor area of 69.19 square metres with only two bedrooms and no hall entrance.

Another recent Panel decision 20 Oak Road, Sparkhill. A very similar property in a very similar area, not quite as large as Wood Road, having a rateable value of £148 and an effective floor area of 87.51 square metres. Here the Panel awarded a rent of £11.00 with effect from the 23rd April, 1981.

Not far from Wood Road is another property under our management 99 Firtree Road, Handsworth. Only 2 bedrooms to this property, rateable value £102 and as you can see from the photograph it is adjoining a small engineering workshop, the day to day running of which is quite clearly visible and audible from the kitchen of our client's property. Nevertheless the Rent Officer awarded it a rent of £9.50 with effect from the 9th March, 1981. By no stretch of imagination could this property be worth just 30 pence less than 25 Wood Road.

Another Handsworth property - 170 Plain Road, Handsworth. Rateable value £123, effective floor area 63.35 square metres, again only 2 bedroomed and the rent on this property was fixed at £9.75 as long ago as the 27th November 1980.

And a more recent rent decision in Plain Road - no. 265 rateable value here is £103, this property does have three bedrooms and on the 30th June, 1981 the Rent Officer awarded £10.80.

I have confined my comparables mainly to the Handsworth area in the hopes that this will make it easier to draw comparisons with the subject property. I contend that none of the comparables I have given are as good as the subject property yet in spite of the fact that they are smaller, do not possess such good facilities and in most cases the effective date is older, they enjoy rents almost as good as, or in most cases better, than the subject property. I trust therefore that the Panel will agree that the rent determined by the Rent Officer on 25 Wood Road is too low at £9.80. So low that I can only reiterate that the Rent Officer was obviusly misguided by his inexplicable choice of comparable namely 35 Larch Road, Saltley.

**PART III**

25 Wood Road, Handsworth, Birmingham 21.

DECISION OF COMMITTEE:

We inspected the property in the presence of the tenant Mr. G.H. Brown and Mrs. Brown. The landlord was not present or represented.

At the hearing the landlord was represented by Mr. Jones of Jones Estates Ltd but the tenant was not present or represented.

The subject property is an inner terraced house, built about 1905 in a fair residential area and is in a good state of repair both internally and externally.

Over the years the tenants have carried out a number of improvements but these of course we have ignored as we must do, when arriving at our decision.

At the hearing Mr.Jones said that he did not consider that No. 35 Larch Road, which had been put forward by the Rent Officer, was a relevant comparable and instead drew our attention to four similar properties in Handsworth and one in Sparkhill which had recently had rents registered ranging from £9.50 to £11.00. Two of these decisions were Panel decisions and three were Rent Officer's decisions.

We have carefully considered the representations made by Mr. Jones and we find it difficult to relate the rents of these comparables with that of £9.80 per week suggested by the Rent Officer for the subject property.

Having considered the above and all other relevant matters, in particular the comparables put forward by the landlord, we are of the opinion that the Rent Officer's determination is on the low side and we determine a fair rent of £11.50 per week exclusive of rates, on the basis of the landlord being responsible for all repairs and external decorations, tenant responsible for internal decorations. The date of the Committee's decision is 6 August 1981.

6 August 1981

**PART IV**

30 Victoria Road, Oldbury, West Midlands

DECISION OF COMMITTEE:

We inspected this house in the presence of the tenant and his wife. It is an inner terrace house built of brick and slate about 1900. The premises contain two living rooms, two bedrooms, a kitchen and a combined bathroom and W.C. Space heating is by gas fires, provided by the tenant. This house is in a good residential area and was in a good state of repair. The previous rent effective from the 22 May 1978 was £6.75 per week. The landlords proposed £11.50 and the Rent Officer determined £10.75 per week. The landlords and the tenant thought his report was fair and accurate.

At the hearing, on behalf of the landlords, Mr. Jones referred to a number of comparables - 31 Albert Road, Smethwick recently registered rent of £11.00 per week; 61 Edward Road, Kings Norton recently registered rent of £10.50 per week. He pointed out a number of ways in which each of these properties, in his view, were inferior to the house 30 Victoria Road, Oldbury.

He also referred to 184 George Road, Kings Heath where a Rent Assessment Committee had made a determination of £11.00 per week in May 1981 and suggested that the house was not as good as the house 30 Victoria Road.

The tenant did not appear.

This is a good terrace house in a good residential area; it has been well maintained. We have taken into account the "comparables" suggested by the Rent Officer and the landlord's representations.

Bearing the above in mind, what we noted during our inspection and exercising our own judgement, experience and knowledge, we have reached the conclusion that the figure determined by the Rent Officer is somewhat low. Accordingly we determine a fair rent of £11.50 per week excluding rates, the determination being on the basis of the landlord being responsible for all repairs and external decoration, tenant responsible for internal decoration. The date of the Committee's decision is 27 August 1981.

27 August 1981

# Appendix B
# The definition of variables

DEFINITION OF VARIABLES (Tables 4.8 and 4.9)

RATVAL      Actual rateable value
GENVAL      General rate borne by: 1 - tenant, 2 - landlord
NUMLIV      Number of living rooms
NUMBED      Number of bedrooms
HALL        Hall: 1 - exclusive, 0 - not exclusive
BTHRM       Bathroom: 1 - exclusive, 0 - not exclusive
NUMWC       Number of exclusive internal WCs
GARAGE      Garage: 1 - yes, 0 - no
PKING       Parking space: 1 - yes, 0 - no
EXTST       External coal store: 1 - yes, 0 - no
DTRANS      Distance in miles to nearest public transport
PCOCC       % of households in owner occupied property:
            1 - 0 to 24, 2 - 25 to 49, 3 - 50 to 74, 4 - 75+

# Appendix C
# Landlords' rates of return

Table 7.3 reports estimates of gross rates of return. The studies on which they are based differ methodologically because of the difficulties inherent in this type of study. Perhaps the most accurate way of estimating rates of return would be to take a sample of dwellings which in terms of the distribution of building types, location, number of bedrooms and other characteristics matches the dwellings currently registered. If properties in this sample have recently had fair rents determined for them then one or more professional valuers could place a vacant possession capital value on each of them: the average could be taken as the relevant value. Alternatively if the sampled properties had recently been sold with vacant possession one or more rent officers already working in the area in which each dwelling is located should be asked to make fair rent determinations. However, both courses of action imply considerable costs in terms of professional man hours. Each of the studies reported has used different ways of substituting an alternative and cheaper medium than groups of valuers or rent officers.

**Capital values survey (DOE 1978)**

The Capital Values Survey involved parallel studies during 1977 carried out by the Department of the Environment and the Welsh Office. Information about the way in which the survey was conducted is sparse. The survey and its results have not been made generally available to the public but some brief details are given in an informal 'Note for Rent Officers and Secretaries of Rent Assessment Panels'. A number of rent officers all over the country provided details of a sample of rent registrations for unfurnished lettings for each of the years 1970, 1973 and 1976. How this sample was selected is unknown. District valuers were then asked to estimate vacant possession capital values for the properties at the dates in question. The accuracy of such retrospective valuation is also unknown but it did allow computation of rates of return, summaries of which are included in the note referred to.

**Beacons Exercise (DOE 1981)**

In 1981 the Department of the Environment commenced what is intended to be a regular six monthly 'Beacons' exercise. This involves district valuers assessing the hypothetical vacant possession or capital values for four specified yet hypothetical dwellings. These four types are:

(1)   Beacon A.   Mid-terrace, brick house, built about
      1870.  The 70 square metres of floor area contain two
      living rooms joined by a narrow hall on the ground
      floor, and two bedrooms on the first floor.

(2)   Beacon B.   Mid-terrace, brick house, built about
      1880.  The 100 square metres of floor area contain
      two living rooms, kitchen and hall on the ground
      floor, and two double and one single bedrooms on the
      first floor.

(3)   Beacon C.   Mid-terrace, brick house, built about
      1880.  This is basically the same as Beacon B but
      improved to the so-called 10-point standard, which is
      a necessary requirement for an improvement grant.

(4)   Beacon D.   Semi-detached, brick house, built in the
      mid 1930s.  Its 95 square metres contain living room,
      dining room and kitchen on the ground floor, and
      three bedrooms and bathroom on the first floor.

In the cases of types A, C and D rent officers heading
registration areas have provided estimates of the fair rent
which might be fixed, and rates of return computed as with the
Capital Values Survey.  Although additional information is
given about each property type including floor plans, and
details of construction, basic amenities, heating, storage,
gardens and location, they are hypothetical. It is therefore
uncertain to what extent district valuers and rent officers
are assessing the 'same' dwelling and there may be over- or
under-estimation of capital values in some areas.  The DOE
also gives some warnings about their interpretation:

    'The Beacons results are not directly comparable with
    those of the Capital Values Survey because the property
    types differ.  They should be taken as illustrative rather
    than precise, because although the same town is always
    used for the fair rent and the capital value, there will
    inevitably be variations within each town of relationships
    between capital values and fair rents' (DOE 1981, p.3).

## Allen and Joseph (1978)

Allen and Joseph's method of comparison was to take a number
of property types for which fair rents had been determined and
then to match these with actual properties for sale with
vacant possession.   In doing this they warn that ...
'facilities may vary greatly between properties, especially in
the older inner areas of London; even some conversions to
fully self-contained flats are much better than others ... the
conditions of properties vary enormously' (Allen and Joseph
1978, p.297).

The present authors have taken Allen and Joseph's estimates, produced for three types of house and five types of flat, to compute an average rate of return. This average however takes no account of the particular mix of property types in the area. Thus all houses had an estimated rate of return higher than all flats so that the particular mix of houses or flats actually found in Paddington might be different from the estimate here.

## British Property Federation (1975)

The British Property Federation derived its estimates by carrying out a survey of landlords and agents asking them to furnish details of their properties. The present authors have no knowledge of the precise way in which this information was elicited although the resulting estimates are reported as covering a large number of properties whose total vacant possession capital value was reported as being £158.5 million in 1974.

## The Birmingham Study (Doling and Davies 1981)

Over the same period for which information about registered rents in Birmingham was collected information about houses advertised for sale in the local paper was extracted. In Chapter 4 it was explained how this information might be used to generate estimates of the vacant possession capital values of the sample of registered properties. These estimates were used as in the other studies to provide estimates about rates of return.

This involved using ordinary least squares regression analysis to explain variation in capital value in terms of dwelling and locational characteristics. The resulting coefficients were used, with the values of the dwelling and locational characteristics of each tenancy in the sample, to generate an estimate of its capital value. Because of the unavailability of certain variables there may have been some bias in these estimates. For example it might be assumed that owner occupied housing is generally in a better state of repair and without knowledge of this the model has probably over estimated capital values of the (poorer) rented sample.

# Appendix D
# Equations for calculating the costs of buying and renting

If the vacant possession capital value (P) is £15,000, increasing at the rate (i) of 10% per annum then the rent (e) at x% of capital value in year n, is:

$$R_n - Px \ (1+n/100)^n/100$$

For the same house, an owner occupier could put down a deposit (D) of £3,000 or 20% of the capital value, and take out a mortgage (L) of £12,000 at a rate of interest (I) of 13% and over a period (m) of 20 years. Paying tax at the rate of (T) in the £ the net repayments (N) in year n, are:

$$N_n = LI \ (T(1+I)^{n-m-1} + (1-T))/(1-(1+I)^{-n})$$

Insurance, repairs and maintenance (M) are assumed to be a constant proportion y% of capital value:

$$M_n = P(y/100) \ (1+i)^n$$

The Cost of the Loan (C) is assumed to be the cost of borrowing D at the rate of interest I, that is:

$$C = DI/100$$

Capital Appreciation (A) in year n is:

$$A_n = P(1+i)^n - P(1+i)^{n-1}$$

# Bibliography

Abbey, N.C., The Rents Acts 1920-1957, Eyre and Spottiswoode, London 1957.

Adler, M. and Asquith, S., Discretion and Power in Adler, M. and Asquith, S., (eds), Discretion and Welfare, Heinemann, London 1981.

Aldcroft, D.H. and Richardson, H.W., The British Economy 1870- 1939, Macmillan, London 1969.

Allaun, F., Heartbreak Housing, Zenith Books, London 1968.

Allen, J. and Joseph, M., 'Fair Rents: Two Viewpoints', Estates Gazette, vol.245, 22 April 1978, pp.297-300.

Anon., Letter to the Editor, Sunday Times, 1 October 1978.

Arden, A., 'A New Rent Act', Legal Action Group Bulletin, February 1980, pp.33-34.

Ball, M., 'Recent Empirical Work on the Determinants of Relative House Prices', Urban Studies, vol.10, 1973, pp.213-233.

Banting, K., Poverty, Politics and Policy, Macmillan, London 1979.

Bardach, E., The Implementation Game, M.I.T. Press, Cambridge Mass, 1977.

Barnett, M.J., The Politics of Legislation, Weidenfeld, London 1969.

Beirne, P., Fair Rents and Legal Fiction, Macmillan, London 1977.

Berry, F., Housing: The Great British Failure, Charles Knight, London 1974.

Board of Trade, Working Class Rents, Housing and Retail Prices, Cd.3864, London 1908.

Bowley, M., Housing and the State 1919-1944, Allen and Unwin, London 1945.

Bristol and West Building Society, Factual Background, Autumn 1981.

British Property Federation, 'Policy for Housing', London December 1975.

Brittan, S., Capitalism and the Permissive Society, Macmillan, London 1974.

Burke, G., Housing and Social Justice, Longmans, London 1981.

Burnett, J., Housing: A Social History 1815-1970, David and Charles, Newton Abbot 1978.

Burney, E., Housing on Trial, Oxford University Press, Oxford 1967.

Cairncross, A.K., Home and Foreign Investment 1870-1913, Cambridge University Press, Cambridge 1953.

Conservative Central Office, The Right Approach, Conservative

Central Office, London 1976.

Cooney, E.W., 'Capital Exports and Investment in Building in Britain and the U.S.A. 1856-1914', Economica, Vol.16, 1949, pp.347-354.

Corina, L., 'Housing Allocation Policy and its Effects', Papers on Community Studies No 7, University of York, 1976.

Crook, A.D.H. and Bryant, C.L., Local Authorities and Private Landlords, Centre for Environmental Research, Sheffield 1982.

Cullingworth, J.B., Essays on Housing Policy: the British Scene, Allen and Unwin, London 1979.

D.O.E., 'Fair Deal for Housing', Cmnd.4728, London 1971.

D.O.E., Housing Policy: A Consultative Document, Cmnd.6851, London 1977a.

D.O.E., Housing Policy, Technical Volume, Part III, HMSO, London 1977b.

D.O.E., The Review of the Rent Acts: A Consultation Paper, London 1977c.

D.O.E., 'Statistical Information of Use in the Assessment of Rent Levels', RO(S) 18, mimeo, DOE, 1978.

D.O.E., Report of the Working Party on Output in the Rent Officer Service, London 1980a.

D.O.E., Statistical Analysis of Rent Increases on Re-Registration, RO(S) 31, mimeo, DOE, 1980b.

D.O.E., 'Supplementary Memorandum to the House of Commons Select Committee on the Environment by the Department of the Environment', mimeo, DOE, 1981.

Daunton, M.J., 'House Ownership from Rate Books', Urban History Yearbook, 1976, pp.21-27.

Dhanjal, B., Asian Housing in Southall: Some Impressions, New Community, vol.VI, Winter 1977/78, pp.88-93.

Doling, J., 'The Use of Content Analysis in Identifying the Determinants of House Prices', Urban Studies, vol.15, 1978, pp.89-90.

Doling. J., Revitalising the private rented housing sector, Estates Gazette, vol.267, Sept. 1983a, p.1116.

Doling, J., 'British Housing Policy 1974-1983: A Review', Regional Studies, vol.17, 1983b.

Doling, J., 'How Much Protection do the Rent Acts Provide?', Journal of Planning and Environment Law, forthcoming.

Doling, J. and Davies, E.M., 'Fair Rents and Capital Values', Estates Gazette, vol.260, 14 November 1981, pp.677,680.

Doling, J. and Davies, E.M., 'The Two Privately Rented Housing Sectors',Housing Review, vol.31, 1982a, pp.192-194.

Doling, J. and Davies, E.M., 'Rates of Return, Scarcity and the Decline of Privately Rented Housing', Estates Gazette, vol.262, May 1982b, pp.415-417.

Doling, J. and Davies, E.M., 'Ethnic Minorities and the Protection of the Rent Acts', New Community, vol.X, 1983, pp.487-492.

Donnison, D., The Government of Housing, Penguin, Harmondsworth 1967.

Donnison, D and Ungerson, C., Housing Policy, Penguin,

Harmondsworth 1982.

Dunn, A.L., 'Letter to the Editor', Estates Gazette, vol.249, 31 March 1979, pp.1248-1249.

Dyos, H.J., 'The Slums of Victorian England', Victorian Studies, vol.XI, 1967, pp.5-40.

Dyos, H.J., 'The Speculative Builders and Developers of Victorian London, Victorian Studies, vol.XI, 1968, pp.641-690.

Dyos, H.J. and Reeder, D., 'Slums and Suburbs', in Dyos, H.J. and Woolf, M. (eds.), The Victorian City, Routledge and Kegan Paul, London 1973.

Elcock, H.J., Administrative Justice, Longman, London 1969.

Elliott, B. and McCrone, D., 'Landlords in Edinburgh: Some Preliminary Findings', Sociological Review, vol.23, 1975, pp.539-562.

Evans, M.D.T., 'In Defence of the Private Residential Landlord', Estates Gazette, vol.249, 3 February 1979, p.431.

Farrand, J.T., The Rent Act 1977, The Protection from Eviction Act 1977, Sweet and Maxwell, London 1978.

Fenton, M. and Collard, D., 'Do Coloured Tenants Pay More?' Working Papers on Ethnic Relations, Research Unit on Ethnic Relations, 1977.

Finnis, N., 'Students Wrinkle the Rent Act', Roof, March 1978, p.35.

Fleming, M.C. and Nellis, J.G., 'The Interpretation of House Price Statistics for the United Kingdom', Environment and Planning A, vol.13, 1981, pp.1109-1124.

Ford, J., 'The Role of the Building Society Manager in the Urban Stratification System: Autonomy versus Constraint', Urban Studies, vol.12, 1975, pp.295-302.

Forrest, R. and Murie, A., Landlords in Cheltenham, Working Paper 63, Centre for Urban and Regional Studies, Birmingham 1978.

Francis Committee, Report of the Committee on the Rent Acts, Cmnd.4609, London 1971.

Franks Committee, Report of the Committee on Administrative Tribunals and Enquiries, Cmnd.218, HMSO, London 1957.

Fuerst, J., Pubic Housing in Europe and America, Croom Helm, London 1974.

Gauldie, E., Cruel Habitations - Working Class Housing 1780-1918, Allen and Unwin, London 1974.

George, V. and Wilding, P., Ideology and Social Welfare, Routledge and Kegan Paul, London 1976.

Gibson, M. 'Single People at the Sharp End', Housing Review, vol.30, December 1981, pp.175-178.

Ginsburg, N., Class, Capital and Social Policy, Macmillan, London 1979.

Glynne Evans, R., 'Letter to the Editor', Estates Gazette, vol.253, 23 February 1980, p.770.

Gough, I., The Political Economy of the Welfare State, Macmillan, London 1979.

Green, G., 'Title Deeds: A Key to Local Housing Markets', Urban History Yearbook, 1980, pp.84-91.

Greve, J., Private Landlords in England, Occasional Papers in Social Administration No 16, G. Bell and Sons, London 1965.

Griliches, Z., 'Hedonic Price Indexes for Automobiles: An Econometric Analysis of Quality Changes', The Price Statistics of the Federal Government, National Bureau of Economic Research, 1961.

Habakkuk, H.J., 'Fluctuations in House Building in Britain and the United States in the Nineteenth Century', Journal of Economic History, vol.22, 1962, pp.198-230.

Hallett, G., Housing and Land Policies in West Germany and Britain, Macmillan, London 1977.

Hamnett, C. and Randolph, W., 'Flat Break-up and Decline of the Private Rented Sector', Estates Gazette, 3 October 1981, pp.31-35.

Harloe, M., 'Decline and Fall of Private Renting', CES Review 9, 1980, pp.30-34.

Henney, A., 'The Implications of the Rent Act 1974', Housing Review, vol.24, 1975, pp.37-41.

Hill, M., The State, Administration and the Individual, Fontana, London 1976.

Hill, M., Understanding Social Policy, Blackwell and Robertson, Oxford 1980.

Hollamby, J.P., 'Review of Rent Assessment Procedures', Estates Gazette, vol.258, 4 April 1981, p.7.

House of Commons, First Report from the Environment Committee Session 1981-82, The Private Rented Housing Sector, vols 1-3, HMSO, London 1982.

House of Commons, First Report from the Environment Committee Session 1982-83, The Private Rented Housing Sector - A Report on the Memorandum from the Department of the Environment in response to the Committee's First Report, Session 1981-82, HMSO, London 1983.

Housing Advice Switchboard, London's Neglected Homeless, London 1982.

Housing Monitoring Team, Landlords in Dudley, Research Memorandum 85, Centre for Urban and Regional Studies, Birmingham 1980.

Hughes, G.A., 'Housing Income and Subsidies' Fiscal Studies, vol.1, 1979, pp.20-38.

Jenkins, W.I., Policy Analysis: A Political and Organizational Perspective, Robertson, London 1978.

John, A., Race in the Inner City, Runnymede Trust Publications, London 1972.

Kemeny, J., The Myth of Home Ownership: Private Versus Public Policies in Housing Tenure, Routledge and Kegan Paul, London 1981.

Kemp, P., The Changing Ownership Structure of the Privately-Rented Sector, Discussion Paper No.17, Centre for Urban and Regional Research, University of Glasgow, 1979.

Kirkwood, J., 'The Decline of the Private Rented Sector', Estates Gazette, vol.249, 13 January 1979, pp.131-134.

Klein, R., Barnes, J., Buxton, M. and Craven, E., Social Policy and Public Expenditure, Centre for Studies in Social Policy, 1974.

Lawrance, D.M., Rees, W.H. and Britton, W., 'Modern Methods of Evaluation', Estates Gazette, London 1971.

Leach, W.A., 'Regulated Tenancies: Fair Rent', Estates Gazette, vol.242, 11 June 1977, pp.861,862,893.

Lean, W. and Goodall, B., 'Aspects of Land Economics', Estates Gazette, London 1966.

Lewis, N., 'Council Housing Allocation: Problems of Discretion and Control', Public Administration, vol.54, 1976, pp.147-160.

Lewis, P.J., Building Cycles and Britain's Growth, Macmillan, London 1965.

Littlewood, S., 'The Practice of the London Rent Assessment Panel', The Solicitors' Journal, vol.III, 1967, pp.3-5.

MHLG, 'Houses: The Next Step', Cmnd.8996, London 1953.

MHLG, 'Housing in England and Wales', Cmnd.1290, London 1961.

MHLG, Council Housing Purposes, Procedures and Priorities, HMSO, London 1969.

Macey, J., 'Making Rents Fair', New Society, vol.21, 6 July 1972, pp.14-15.

MacLennan, D., 'The Nature and Purpose of House Price Studies', Urban Studies, vol.14, 1977, pp.59-71.

Malpass, P. and Murie, A., Housing Policy and Practice, Macmillan, London 1982.

Megarry, R.E., The Rent Acts, 4th Ed., Stevens, London 1949.

Merrett, S., State Housing in Britain, Routledge and Kegan Paul, London 1979.

Milner-Holland Committee, Report of the Committee on Housing in Greater London, Cmnd.2604, London 1965.

Mishra, R., Society and Social Policy, Macmillan, London 1981.

Morris, M., 'How Fair are Fair Rents?', New Society, vol.16, 26 November 1970, pp.947-949.

Murie, A., Niner, P. and Watson, C., Housing Policy and the Housing System, Allen and Unwin, London 1976.

Musgrave, R.A. and Musgrave, P.B., Public Finance in Theory and Practice, 3rd Ed., McGraw Hill, Tokyo 1982.

Needleman, L., The Economics of Housing, Staples Press, London 1965.

Nevitt, A., Housing, Taxation and Subsidies, Nelson, London 1966.

Nevitt, A., 'The Nature of Rent Controlling Legislation in the U.K.', Environment and Planning, vol.2, 1970, pp.127-136.

Niner, P., 'Associations Match Council Selection', Roof, vol.4, July 1979, p.126.

Norman, P., 'Managerialism - A review of recent work' in Harloe, M. (ed.), Proceedings of the Conference on Urban Change and Conflict, Centre for Environmental Studies C.P.14, 1975.

Offer, A., 'Ricardo's Paradox and the Movement of Rents in England', Economic History Review, Vol.XXXIII, no.2, May 1980, pp.236-252.

Orbach, L.F., Homes for Heroes, Seeley Services, London 1977.

Pahl, R., Whose City? And Other Essays On Sociology and

<u>Planning</u>, Longman, London 1970.
Paley, B., <u>Attitudes to Letting in 1976</u>, HMSO, London 1978.
Pawley, M., <u>Home Ownership</u>, Architectural Press, London 1978.
Peacock, A. and Wiseman, J., <u>The Growth of Public Expenditure in the United Kingdom</u>, Allen and Unwin, London 1961.
Pearce, B.J., Prospects for Shorthold Tenure, <u>Housing Review</u>, vol.29, 1980, pp.23-25.
Pliatzky, L., <u>Getting and Spending: Public Expenditure, Employment and Inflation</u>, Blackwell, Oxford 1982.
Pressman, J.L. and Wildavsky, A., <u>Implementation</u>, University of California Press, Berkeley 1973.
Pritchard, R.M., <u>Housing and the Spatial Structure of the City</u>, Cambridge University Press, 1976.
Prophet, J., <u>Fair Rents</u>, Shaw, London 1976.
Prosser, T., 'The Policies of Discretion: Aspects of Discretionary Power in the Supplementary Benefits Scheme', in Adler, M. and Asquith, S. (eds.), <u>Discretion and Welfare</u>, Heinemann, London 1981.
Pugh, C., <u>Housing in Capitalist Societies</u>, Gower, Farnborough 1980.
R.I.C.S., <u>Housing: The Chartered Surveyors' Report</u>, Royal Institute of Chartered Surveyors, London 1976.
Randall, G., 'The Holes in the Rent Acts', <u>Housing Review</u>, vol.30, December 1981, pp.185-187.
Robinson, R., <u>Housing Economics and Public Policy</u>, Macmillan, London 1979.
Robinson, R., 'Housing Tax-Expenditures, Subsidies and the Distribution of Income', <u>Manchester School</u>, vol.49, 1981, pp.91-110.
Robson, P.W., 'Fair for Whom?', <u>The Solicitors' Journal</u>, vol.118, 10 May 1974, pp.306-307.
Robson, P. and Watchman, P., 'Determining Fair Rents', <u>New Law Journal</u>, 14 December 1978, pp.1209-1212.
Royal Commission on the Distribution of Income and Wealth, Third Report, Cmnd.6999, London 1977.
Samuels, H., 'Letter to the Editor', <u>The Spectator</u>, 4 December 1971.
Samuels, H., 'Fair Rents v Market Rents', <u>The Solicitors' Journal</u>, 5 October 1973, pp.720-721.
Saul, S.B., 'House Building in England 1890-1914', <u>Economic History Review</u>, vol.25, 1962, pp.119-137.
Saunders, P., <u>Urban Politics</u>, Hutchinson, London 1979.
Sayer, R.S., <u>A History of Economic Change in England 1880-1939</u>, Oxford University Press, 1967.
Scott, J.R., 'Rent Assessment', <u>The Solicitors' Journal</u>, 20 January 1967, p.58.
Singer, H.W., 'An Index of Urban Land Rents and House Rents in England and Wales 1845-1913', <u>Econometrica</u>, vol.19, 1941, pp.221-230.
Stafford, D.C., <u>The Economics of Housing Policy</u>, Croom Helm, London 1978.
Tanner, J.A.N., 'Letter to the Editor', <u>The Observer</u>, 2 November 1980.
Todd, J.E., Bone, M.R. and Noble, I., <u>the Privately Rented</u>

Sector in 1978, Office of Population Censuses and Surveys, Social Survey Division, HMSO, London 1982.

Trollope, A.G.C., 'Letter to the Editor', Estates Gazette, vol.249, 3 February 1979, pp.416-417.

Turner, D.M., An Approach to Land Values, Geographical Publications Ltd., Berkhamstead 1977.

Walker, A., (ed.), Public Expenditure and Social Policy, Heinemann, London 1982.

Weir, S., 'Landlords Exploit Rent Act Loopholes', Roof, October 1975, pp.11-14.

Whitehead, C., 'Private Landlords in London: Who Stays, Who Goes?', CES Review 4, Centre for Environmental Studies, 1978, pp.48-53.

Williams, P., 'Restructuring Urban Managerialism: Towards a Political Economy of Urban Allocation', Environment and Planning A, vol.14, 1982, pp.95-105.

Wohl, A.S., The Eternal Slum, Arnold, London 1977.

Young, E. and Watchman, P.Q., 'Fair Rents: Ignoring the Experts', The Scots Law Times, 25 August 1978, pp.201-208.

Young, K., 'Discretion as an Implementation Problem: a Framework for Interpretation', in Adler, M. and Asquith, S. (eds.), Discretion and Welfare, Heinemann, London 1981.